Development in Southeast Asia
Review and prospects

Edited by

RAYMOND K.H. CHAN
KWAN KWOK LEUNG
RAYMOND M.H. NGAN
Department of Applied Social Sciences
City University of Hong Kong

LONDON AND NEW YORK

First published 2002 by Ashgate Publishing

Reissued 2018 by Routledge
2 Park Square, Milton Park, Abingdon, Oxon OX14 4RN
711 Third Avenue, New York, NY 10017, USA

Routledge is an imprint of the Taylor & Francis Group, an informa business

Copyright © Raymond K.H. Chan, Kwan Kwok Leung and Raymond M.H. Ngan 2002

All rights reserved. No part of this book may be reprinted or reproduced or utilised in any form or by any electronic, mechanical, or other means, now known or hereafter invented, including photocopying and recording, or in any information storage or retrieval system, without permission in writing from the publishers.

Notice:
Product or corporate names may be trademarks or registered trademarks, and are used only for identification and explanation without intent to infringe.

Publisher's Note
The publisher has gone to great lengths to ensure the quality of this reprint but points out that some imperfections in the original copies may be apparent.

Disclaimer
The publisher has made every effort to trace copyright holders and welcomes correspondence from those they have been unable to contact.

A Library of Congress record exists under LC control number: 2002102835

ISBN 13: 978-1-138-73515-6 (hbk)
ISBN 13: 978-1-138-73514-9 (pbk)
ISBN 13: 978-1-315-18391-6 (ebk)

Contents

List of Tables	vii
Notes on the Contributors	xi
Preface	xvii

PART 1: SOCIETY AND POLITICS

1. Integrating ASEAN and Fragmenting ARF in a Subregional and Regional Context — 3
   Kwan Kwok Leung

2. Civil Society in Southeast Asia: Cases of Singapore and Malaysia — 17
   Ming Sing

3. Constructing the 'China Circle' in China and Southeast Asia: State Policy, the Presence of Chinese Overseas and Globalisation — 37
   Pak Nung Wong

4. Gender and Development in Post-Crisis Southeast Asia — 57
   Vivienne Wee

PART 2: ECONOMY AND LABOUR

5. Emergence of a Global Economy in Southeast Asia: 1990s and Beyond — 85
   Moha Asri Abdullah, Raymond K H Chan

6. Labour Standards in the Southeast Asian Region: Retreats and Advances — 107
   Duncan Campbell, Dorothea Schmidt

PART 3: SOCIAL POLICY

7   The Welfare System in Southeast Asia: 131
    Development and Challenges
    Raymond K H Chan

8   Social Security and Safety Net Development in Southeast Asia   163
    Amongst the Asian Financial Crisis
    Raymond M H Ngan

9   Educational Developments in Southeast Asia under the Global   193
    Impact of Marketisation
    David K K Chan

10 Full Equality and Inclusion for People with a Disability: 219
    Strategies for the New Millennium in Southeast Asian Countries
    Joseph K F Kwok

PART 4: REVIEW AND PROSPECT

11 Globalisation, Inequality and Governance   241
    Kevin Hewison

Index   257

List of Tables

Table 2.1	Average annual growth rates of GDP and population in the Asia-Pacific region (%)	19
Table 2.2	Unions membership, 1989-1999	21
Table 2.3	NTUC membership	23
Table 2.4	The five largest unions in terms of number of members in Singapore as of December 1993	23
Table 2.5	Union strength of Malaysia, 1957-2001	29
Table 3.1	Filipino reactions to Chinese-Filipino investment in China	45
Table 4.1	Lay-offs by sector and sex in Thailand, January 1997 - February 1998	58
Table 4.2	Women's percentage share in economic sectors in ASEAN	61
Table 4.3	Women's share of manufacturing employment and manufacturing's share of GDP in five ASEAN countries, 1970-1992	63
Table 4.4	Unpaid male and female family workers as a proportion of male and female labour force (%), 1990	71
Table 5.1	Average growth rate of GDP (%), 1950-2000	88
Table 5.2	Inflation and unemployment rates, 1991-2000	90
Table 5.3	Structural change in the GDP (%), 1970, 1980 and 1993	91
Table 5.4	Current account deficit of the Southeast Asia countries (% of GDP), 1992-1998	92
Table 5.5	Gross domestic saving rates (GDSR) and gross domestic investment rates (GDIR) (% of GDP), 1971-1995	93
Table 5.6	Regional interdependence by two-way trade (%), 1955-1990	94
Table 5.7	Foreign direct investment receipts, 1975-1997 (US$ M)	95

Table 5.8	Intra-ASEAN exports compared to country's total exports (%), 1985 and 1997	96
Table 5.9	Exports within ASEAN (US$ M), 1970-1999	97
Table 5.10	Basic indicators for Asian countries	100
Table 5.11	Export and foreign direct investment (FDI) (US$ M), 1996-2000	101
Table 6.1	2001 revisions in global output growth estimates	110
Table 6.2	Revision in official growth projections for 2001 (%)	111
Table 6.3	Evolution of unemployment since the crisis (%)	111
Table 6.4	Labour force participation of women, aged 15-64, before and after Asian financial crisis (%)	112
Table 6.5	Male and female real manufacturing wage index	113
Table 6.6	Female to male ratio of secondary school enrolment, 1997	114
Table 6.7	Changes in gender development index (GDI) relative to human development index (HDI) rankings	117
Table 6.8	Date of ratification of ILO fundamental conventions in the areas of freedom of association and freedom from discrimination	121
Table 6.9	Examples of improvements in climate of freedom of association	125
Table 7.1	Human development index (HDI), selected countries, 1975-1999	135
Table 7.2	Percentage of government spending on social policies, annual average	136
Table 7.3	Private enrolment as a percentage of total enrolment	138
Table 7.4	Public and private health expenditure	141
Table 7.5	Coverage of social security programme, 1992-1995	143
Table 7.6	Income inequality	145
Table 7.7	Social indicators	148
Table 7.8	Gender social indicators, 1999	149
Table 7.9	Economic change, inflation and unemployment in Southeast Asia	151
Table 7.10	Social trends (%)	154
Table 7.11	The Asian welfare system and its current threats	158
Table 8.1	Types of social security programmes, 1999	166
Table 8.2	Main types of social security programmes in Southeast Asia	168

Table 8.3	Share of government expenditure on social security, annual average (%)	169
Table 8.4	Coverage of all social security programmes (%), 1992-1995	169
Table 8.5	Incidence of poverty, Thailand, 1998-1999	171
Table 8.6	Employment situation in Thailand, 1995 and 1998	172
Table 8.7	Per-capita GDP during the crisis, Indonesia, 1997-1999	177
Table 8.8	Allocated government expenditure for the social safety net programmes, Indonesia, 1998	178
Table 8.9	Selected macroeconomic indicators, Malaysia, 1991-1999	181

Notes on the Contributors

Duncan CAMPBELL

Duncan Campbell is Chief of the *World Employment Report* Team in the Employment Strategy Department of the International Labour Organization. He has an A.B. from Bowdoin College, and holds a M.A., a M.B.A., and a Ph.D. in Applied Economics and Managerial Science from the University of Pennsylvania. He joined the ILO in 1990 from the Wharton School of the University of Pennsylvania where he had been a member of the Management Department faculty and Associate Director of the Center for Human Resources. At the ILO, he began his career with the International Institute for Labour Studies' programme on new industrial organization where his work concentrated on the effects of rising economic openness and the cross-border organisation of production and, later, on the economics of labour standards. In 1994, he joined the team preparing the ILO's first *World Employment Report 1995*. Thereafter, he was a member of the team preparing the *World Labour Report 1997-1998*. He spent three years with the ILO's East Asia Multidisciplinary Team in Bangkok, where he was Senior Industrial Relations Specialist, working with ILO constituents largely in Thailand, Cambodia, Vietnam, China, and Malaysia. He returned to headquarters in 2000 to co-ordinate the thematic section on decent work and the information society for *World Employment Report 2001*.

David K K CHAN

David Chan is currently the Programme Leader of the East and Southeast Asian Studies and Associate Professor at the Department of Applied Social Studies, City University of Hong Kong. He is also an active member of the Comparative Education Policy Research Unit at the Department of Public and Social Administration, City University of Hong Kong. He received his master degree from Stanford University and his Ph.D. from the University of Nottingham. His main research interests focus on comparative education policies and reforms in East and Southeast Asian countries, and has contributed many articles in both international and regional journals, such as *Comparative Education, Journal of Contemporary China, World Studies of Education, Asia Pacific Journal of Education, Chulalongkorn Educational Review, Educational Policy Forum*, among others.

Raymond K H CHAN

Raymond Chan is Assistant Professor of the Department of Applied Social Studies, City University of Hong Kong. He received his M.A. in Social Service Planning and Ph.D. at Essex University. His major research interests are in comparative social welfare and labour issues in Asia. He has published in the topics of welfare state, social policy and labour issues in *Social Development Issues, International Social Work, Indian Journal of Social Work, New Global Development, Asian Profile*, and *Journal of Contemporary Asia*. He is the author of *Welfare in Newly-Industrialised Society – the construction of the welfare state in Hong Kong* (Avebury, 1996), and co-author of *Foreign Labor in Asia* (Nova Science, 1999) and *Self-Help Organizations of People with Disabilities in Asia* (Auburn House, 2002).

Kevin HEWISON

Professor Kevin Hewison completed his Ph.D. at Murdoch University in 1984. He is now with the City University of Hong Kong, where he is the Director of the Southeast Asia Research Centre. Professor Hewison has held positions at the University of New England, Murdoch University, the Australian National University, the University of Papua New Guinea and Mahidol University in Thailand. He is the author of more than 150 publications on Southeast Asia, Thailand, democratisation and globalisation.

Joseph K F KWOK

Joseph Kwok is Associate Professor of the Department of Applied Social Studies, City University of Hong Kong, and Co-Chief Editor of the *Asia and Pacific Journal on Disability*. He has many years of professional involvement in the field of disability in both Hong Kong and the Asia and the Pacific Region. In Hong Kong he has served in the government's central committee on rehabilitation, and the Equal Opportunities Commission. He is the founding Chair of the Rehabilitation Action

Network for Asia and the Pacific, and also a founding member of the Regional NGO Network for the Asian and Pacific Decade of Disabled Persons, 1993-2002. He has a close working relationship in the field of disability with UN Economic and Social Commission for Asia and the Pacific, the International Labour Organization and the World Bank.

Kwan Kwok LEUNG

Kwan Kwok Leung is the Associate Professor and Associate Head of the Department of Applied Social Studies and Director of the Quality Evaluation Centre, City University of Hong Kong and Guest Associate Professor at the Peking University. He is also the President of the Foundation of China Studies, Director of the Centre of China Studies, and Co-Chief Editor of *China Studies*.

MOHA ASRI Abdullah

Moha Asri Abdullah received his B.A. from the University of Malaya, M.A. from the Essex University and Ph.D. from the University of London. He is an Associate Professor at the School of Humanities, University Science Malaysia, Penang and has been a Visiting Research Scholar at the Economic Research Centre, School of Economics, Nagoya University. He teaches small business management, and his interest and research focus is mainly on development economics, specifically the development of small and medium enterprises. He has published more than 30 books and papers, and presented a number of papers in the international conferences/forums. His recent books include, *Asian Small and Medium Enterprises: Challenges in the 21st Century* (editor) and *Small and Medium Enterprises in the Information Age: Asian Perspectives* (editor), *Small and Medium Enterprises in Asian Pacific Countries* (main editor), *Foreign Workers in Malaysia* (co-author), *Foreign Labor in Asia* (co-author), *Small and Medium Enterprises in Malaysia, Management of Small Enterprises*.

Raymond M H NGAN

Dr. Raymond Ngan is the Associate Professor at the Department of Applied Social Studies, City University of Hong Kong. He is also the Vice-President of the Hong Kong Association of Gerontology, and a former Chairman of the Committee on Social Security, Hong Kong Council of

Social Services, and formerly, the Chief-Editor of the *Hong Kong Journal of Social Work*. His research interest covers the East Asian welfare model, ageing and work, long term care, social security and programme evaluation. At present he is involved in a comparative study of quality care policies for elderly people in Hong Kong, Singapore and the United Kingdom, an evaluation of the goal attainment and excellence in Day Care Centre services for elderly people in Hong Kong, and social security reforms in China into the twenty-first century. He published extensively in international journals: *International Social Work*, *International Journal of Social Welfare*, *Hallym International Journal of Aging*, *Journal of Aging and Social Policy*, *Journal of Gerontological Social Work*, *Social Work in Health Care*, *Social Security (China)*, and the *Asia and Pacific Journal on Disability*.

Dorothea SCHMIDT

Dorothea Schmidt obtained a B.A. in political sciences and economics in 1990 and a M.A. in economics in 1994 from the Albert-Ludwigs University of Freiburg, Germany. In 2000 she obtained her Ph.D. in economics from the same university. It is hoped that her thesis on 'Family Economics, Theory and Reality' will be published in the future. During her professional life she worked as research and teaching assistant, first at the Institute for Research on Economic Development (1995 – 1997), then at the Institute for General Economic Research, Department of Mathematical Economics, both at the Albert-Ludwigs University of Freiburg, Germany (1997 – 2001). Since September 2001 she has been working as economist with the ILO's World Employment Report Team. Between 1999 and 2000 she published a quarterly newsletter on the economic situation in Germany and world wide. Her main research interests include Family Economics, Economics of the Labour Market, Econometrics, Business Cycle and Growth Theory.

Ming SING

Sing Ming is Associate Professor of the Department of Public and Social Administration at the City University of Hong Kong. He studied sociology and political science at Oxford and Yale University and received his D.Phil. from Oxford. His research interests include comparative democratisation, social movements, comparative political culture, comparative political participation and political institutions. He has published articles in journals such as *Democratisation*, *China Information*,

East Asia, Journal of Contemporary Asia, Chinese Law and Government, and the *International Journal of Public Administration*. He is now finalising the editing of a book on Hong Kong Government and Politics.

Vivienne WEE

Vivienne Wee is currently Programme Coordinator of the Southeast Asia Research Centre and Associate Professor in the Department of Applied Social Studies in the City University of Hong Kong. She received her Bachelor's degree at the University of Minnesota, her Master's degree at the University of Singapore and her Ph.D. at the Australian National University. Prior to joining the City University of Hong Kong in September 2000, she held academic positions at The Chinese University of Hong Kong, National University of Singapore, University of Singapore, Institute of Southeast Asian Studies (Singapore), Australian National University (ANU) and the University of Minnesota (USA). She was also Executive Director of the Centre for Environment, Gender and Development (ENGENDER). An anthropologist by training, she has done extensive research in Indonesia and is internationally known for her ground-breaking work on Riau, Indonesia, which relates religion and ethno-history to the politics of separatism. She has also done field research in most of the other countries of Southeast Asia and is recognised for her multi-faceted expertise on the region. She has wide-ranging research interests, including ethnicity, ethno-history, religion, gender, development, labour migration and globalisation. She has gained numerous consultancies and research grants from the United Nations, as well as organisations in Canada, the US, the Netherlands, Norway, Japan and Singapore. She is an Advisory Board Member of the World Bank Institute and serves on the Editorial Board of its journal *Development Outreach*. She is Series Editor of the Routledge - City University of Hong Kong Series on Southeast Asia.

Pak Nung WONG

Pak Nung Wong is firstly trained as a social worker in City University of Hong Kong, and studied sociology at London School of Economics and Political Science. He is currently a postgraduate student in anthropology at St.Antony's College, Oxford University. He had taught sociology at Hong Kong Shue Yan College. His research interests include processes of globalisation, ethnicity and identity, ethnography, social theory, global political economy and elite social movement.

Preface

Southeast Asia is one of the fastest growing regions in the world in late 20th Century. The 'miracle' is characterised by a high rate of economic growth, and rapid 'modernisation' of the nations in various aspects. The region has attained development, though to a different extent, in the construction of a modern-type of government, social infrastructure, and social development. The nations in the region also achieved a regional level of integration through the establishment of a political organisation, the Association of Southeast Asian Nations (ASEAN), and the recent establishment of the ASEAN Free Trade Area (AFTA). The nations also achieved steady progress in social development as revealed in the Human Development Index (HDI), compiled by the United Nations Development Programme.

However, the nations in the region also exhibits diversity, among all their similarities in their colonial history, legacy, and economic development plan. There are different races, religions, cultures, levels of economic development in terms of GDP / GNP and per capita income, poverty and inequality. These contribute to a variety of social, economic and political structures in different nations in the region. Nations in Southeast Asia have been seeking every effort to develop their nations, to strive for a stronger presence in the regional as well as international arena, and at the same time, to maintain their own unique identity as contrast to the 'West'. This may probably explain partially that nations in this region have been considered as under-developed in democratisation and freedom, low respect for individual human rights, lack of protection on labour and other socially marginalised groups such as women and disabled, inadequate social provisions of services and welfare.

Amidst the optimism that nations in the region can attain a prosperous economic future which can be continued into the 21st Century, the financial crisis in 1997 has brought an abrupt stop. The crisis has brought unprecedented challenges to the nations as well as the regional economy. It has led to various social crisis, such as massive unemployment, declining income, growing poverty and inequality. The crisis has also hit the governing parties in different countries, through massive political movement, such as in Indonesia, the Philippines, Thailand and Malaysia.

The chapters in this book aim to describe the development in different aspects, including political, economic and social, in the region and selected nations in recent decades. They will also provide evaluation of the development in these aspects, with particular reference to the Asian financial crisis. It is hoped that this book will provide an updated discussion and enrich the literature on development in Southeast Asia through the inclusion of material on these diverse aspects of development and be useful to those interested in the subject.

The formation of ASEAN is a milestone of political development and regional cooperation in Southeast Asia. Leung's chapter (Chapter 1) on ASEAN and ASEAN Regional Forum (ARF) will examine their opportunities and challenges in a regional and subregional context. The chapter will also evaluate the contributions of these two mechanisms to the integration or fragmentation of the Southeast Asian region, and their responses to the Great Powers in Asia. China and Chinese presence in Southeast Asia has a long history. The recent 're-emergence' of China and Chinese in Southeast Asia has received more and more attention. Wong's chapter (Chapter 3) on the 'China Circle' in China and Southeast Asia will describe the dynamic economic relationship between overseas Chinese and the Chinese in the mainland, particularly Fujian province. Wong argues that such economic relationship has been transformed and engendered a new identity of overseas Chinese entrepreneurs as a powerful player in an age of globalisation, which transcends political boundaries. Internally, the development of civil society has been a core concern of many academic researches.

Sing's chapter (Chapter 2) will use the trade unions in Malaysia and Singapore as case studies, to examine the development of civil society, and the responses from the state. Sing suggests that governments in both countries attempt to 'nip the buds in their early phase' by various legal and political strategies. However, this has been put into severe test in recent years. Wee's chapter (Chapter 4) on gender and development outlines the changing status of women in the region, particularly the impacts of the crisis, and examines implications for future development.

Globalisation of economy has been a central concern of individual countries and the region as a whole in recent decades. Moha Asri and Chan's chapter (Chapter 5) accounts for the historical development of a global economy in the region. Economies in the region are increasingly linked up with each other, and with other regional economies as well. Though globalisation of economies can be one factor explaining the outbreak of financial crisis, the trend of globalisation was not halted or reversed. Campbell and Schmidt's chapter (Chapter 6) on labour standards, i.e. freedom from discrimination and freedom of association, offers a comprehensive and critical review of the topic. They argue that there are economic costs resulting from the absence or underdevelopment of basic rights at work and in society. The chapter also shows that women are adversely affected by the recent crisis.

While economic development in Southeast Asia has received recognition, social development cannot receive the same attention from their governments. Chan's chapter (Chapter 7) presents a framework of the Asian welfare system. The system is different from the West in the sense that it relies heavily on informal transfer within families and kinship, community support and work-based benefit. However, it has been faced with serious challenges in recent years, as a result of urbanisation, growing community and family disintegration, economic development and unemployment especially after the crisis.

Ngan's chapter (Chapter 8) goes further to present a concise comparison of the social security systems in five countries, namely Indonesia, Malaysia, the Philippines, Singapore and Thailand. He argues that expansion and thorough review of statutory social security are essential to protect the citizens, especially in view of the worst social impact made by the recent Asian financial crisis.

High investment in education to improve the quality of labour is a key factor to contribute to the so-called Asian Miracle. David Chan's chapter (Chapter 9) uses the trends, globalisation, marketisation, privatisation and decentralisation, to analyse the recent education reforms in education in Singapore and Thailand. He observes that governments have gradually transformed their roles as provider to regulator or service purchaser, but do not give up their control.

Kwok's chapter (Chapter 10) offers an account of the development of a disability movement, both at national and regional level, in Southeast Asia in recent decades. Disabled groups are one of the socially marginalised groups in the societies. The movement aims at promoting full equality and social inclusion through various strategies. While there are some improvements, the objectives are yet to be realised.

Hewison's concluding chapter (Chapter 11) offers a review of the debates on globalisation across Southeast Asia. Globalisation is a trend which impacts on national and regional social, political and economic development. Hewison argues that globalisation is both a threat and an opportunity to this region. Although globalisation is not entirely inevitable, and cannot be slowed or reversed, the issue of inequality and governance needs to be addressed in the debate in the future direction of Southeast Asian development.

Raymond K H CHAN
Kwan Kwok LEUNG
Raymond M H NGAN

Department of Applied Social Studies
City University of Hong Kong

July 2002

PART 1
SOCIETY AND POLITICS

1 Integrating ASEAN and Fragmenting ARF in a Subregional and Regional Context

KWAN KWOK LEUNG

Introduction

This chapter studies the opportunities and challenges of the Association of Southeast Asian Nations (ASEAN) and the ASEAN Regional Forum (ARF) in a subregional and regional context in the 21st century. It also investigates the perceived threatening strategic role of the People's Republic of China (PRC) as a dialogue partner of ASEAN and one of the founding participants of the ARF, in sustaining security in the two subregional and regional organisations. In addition, it examines the concerted ASEAN response to the Great Powers which affect the balance of regional power in the ARF where Australia, China, India, Japan, Russia and the United States assume increasing dominant roles. In the final analysis, the extent to which the development of the ASEAN and the ARF contributes to the integration or fragmentation of the Southeast Asian region will be addressed.

Similarities and disparities coexist in Southeast Asia. The ASEAN-10[1] share more or less a common experience: subjugation by Japanese occupation, struggle for nation-building and state-building, authoritarian legacy, and aspiration for economic modernisation. On the other hand, these nations differ in history, culture, language, ethnicity and religion.[2] It is surprising that a united ASEAN encompassing the entire region with a framework for 'One Southeast Asia' can be established in about half a century's time after the Second World War. Indeed, in spite of the disengagement of the Russian Federation in the Asia-Pacific, the military retreat of the United States from Southeast Asia, the upturn and downturn of economic growth in East Asia, the unification and liberalisation in Vietnam, democratisation in the Philippines, Thailand, Malaysia and Indonesia, the pro-democracy movements in Myanmar, the power replacement of Lee Kuan Yew with Goh Chok Tong in Singapore, the political stagnation in Brunei, and the turmoil in Laos and Cambodia, a new Southeast Asia was born.

Underlying these changes, however, there is a parallel development, the so-called 'China Threat'. The 'China Threat' is like a specter hunting the neighboring countries of the PRC especially the countries in East and Southeast Asia. The ASEAN was formed partly because of the infiltrating pressure from communist China in the 1960s, and one of the reasons for the establishment of the ARF was an unstable environment in the Asia Pacific area in the 1990s. The consensus model of the 'ASEAN Way' serves to integrate the members of the Association against the emerging China. However, the same type of consensus model serves to fragment the ARF because of the diversified interests of the Great Powers which participate in the Forum.

Consensus Politics in a Subregional Context

Upon gaining independence, Southeast Asian countries were preoccupied with state-building and connections were initially made with their ex-colonisers rather than among themselves. The Non-Aligned Movement initiated by India made further regional cooperation unlikely. Instead, subregional bilateral relations were maintained because of common interests and/or common needs. Vietnam and Indonesia, Indonesia and Malaysia, and Thailand and the Philippines, generally had good relations. However, conflicts did exist between the Philippines and Malaysia over the territorial claim of Sabah, between Malaysia and Indonesia over the establishment of a new federation, among most of the Southeast Asian countries over the division of the two Vietnams, and during Vietnam's invasion of Cambodia.

Efforts to seal the subregional and regional divisions initially had little effect. The eight-member Southeast Asia Treaty Organisation (SEATO) established in 1955 only included Thailand and the Philippines and was created by the extra-regional powers (the United States, the United Kingdom, France, Australia, New Zealand, and Pakistan).[3] The Association of Southeast Asia (ASA, including Malaysia, the Philippines, and Thailand) formed in 1961 and MAPHILINDO (Malaysia-Philippines-Indonesia) confederation in 1962-63 were abolished because of ceaseless conflicting interests among the member states.

Still, there were several reasons for the establishment, the development, and the strengthening of the ASEAN, in spite of diversified interests among the states in the region. In face of the communist challenge from the Soviet

Union and the PRC in the 1960s, Southeast Asian countries shared a common goal to establish a stable environment and counteract the internal subversion of their national solidarity. Subregionalism and regionalism[4] provided a political umbrella for the member states to negotiate with external powers so that individual members did not have to bargain with the Great Powers on their own. Likewise, external powers did not want to deal with the Association, but rather, to have separate bilateral cooperation with individual nations. After years of exploitation from their former colonisers, the member states decided to find an Asian way of governing which was different from the Western values and experience. Unlike the Western model which adopts an integrative approach in order to promote the collective institutionalisation of liberal democracy, the Asian model can retain the national identity of the sovereign state without sacrificing the opportunity for establishing mutualism. Apart from political independence, the Association promoted economic cooperation rather than military coalition. The leaders of the member states believed that security alliance would inevitably create antagonism among themselves and between the Association and external powers.

Instead of projecting a negative image for the security community in Southeast Asia by entering into military alliance, the ASEAN designed a positive measure to create a friendly, peaceful and unprejudiced area shared by all members. This was achieved through the mutual agreements in the Bangkok Declaration[5] in 1967, the Declaration on the Zone of Peace, Freedom, and Neutrality (ZOPFAN)[6] in 1971, the Treaty of Amity and Cooperation (TAC)[7] in 1976, the ASEAN Declaration on the South China Sea[8] in 1992, and the Treaty on the Southeast Asia Nuclear Weapon Free Zone (SEANWFZ)[9] in 1995. Based on these unique characteristics of the Association, Acharya invokes the concept of security community[10] to describe the ASEAN as 'groups of states which have developed a long-term habit of peaceful interaction and ruled out the use of force in setting disputes with other members of the group' (2001, p.1). This kind of consensus politics is commonly considered as the 'ASEAN Way' because it stresses 'informality, organisation minimalism, inclusiveness, intensive consultations leading to consensus and peaceful resolution of disputes'.[11]

However, there are also concerns that the emphasis of the ASEAN is on the 'process' and seldom on the 'product' (Acharya, 2001, p.201). In addition, there is a question whether the exercise of the principle of 'conflict avoidance' can lead to the successful implementation of 'conflict resolution'.[12] The concerns arise because many issues have been discussed but few have been resolved. Conflicts have been tentatively avoided but avoidance is also likely to develop into latent crises which might later become unpredictable clashes. A 'dialogue' approach has merit in resolving minor local or subregional issues before they surface as major regional or global conflicts. Harmonious subregional and regional politics can be maintained mainly because the political functions of the ASEAN are kept at a minimum. Instead, the focus is on the development of economic regionalism through participation in the Asia-Pacific Economic Cooperation (APEC) forum and the ASEAN Free Trade Area (AFTA). The integration of the ASEAN, in fact, contributes more to the settlement of non-political or sovereignty issues than to the betterment of the regional politics in Southeast Asia. However, after the Asian economic crisis, the ASEAN found it difficult to take uniform action against the globalised challenge which was undermining its integration.[13]

Great Power Politics in a Regional Context

Compared with the Asia Pacific region, Southeast Asia is only a subordinate region. ASEAN members are cautious about security matters within the subregion. Most of the intra-regional conflicts are settled by bilateral contacts so that the economic cooperation of the Association remains intact. However, in the post-Cold War period after the disintegration of the Soviet Union and the drastic transformation of Eastern Europe, there is a political vacuum in East Asia as American and Soviet influences diminish. Each country especially the weaker is looking for a protection to prevent itself from possible external threats. At the same time, stronger powers like China, India and Japan are seeking to exert more influence or intervention in the region. Against a backdrop of international instability, the regional security interests in the ASEAN leaders have been changing. As McClound (1995, p.308) observes, '... the ASEAN group defined three regional security strategies to include: (1) retaining the essential focus of each member state on its own national resilience and stability; (2) seeking assurance of an 'over-the-horizon' U.S. presence for security matters; and (3) addressing regional security issues through diplomacy'.

The ASEAN is aware of the limitation of 'Weak Power Politics'. The example of the conflict in Cambodia rings an alarm bell on the ideal practice of non-interference and non-use of force. It also demonstrates the incapability of the Association to prevent the intervention of Great Powers in regional affairs. The formation of the ARF[14] in 1993 as a regional multilateral security dialogue in the Asia-Pacific is a strategy designed to compensate the limitation of ASEAN in terms of its leverage over strong external powers. The ASEAN which originally dealt with subregional issues in Southeast Asia now acts as a 'driver'[15] of the ARF and expects to participate in the regional affairs of the Asia Pacific. While the ASEAN would like a balance of power in the region, the Great Powers like China, Japan, Russia and the United States are tilting the balance towards their own national interest at the expense of the ASEAN's control. Hence, as Neher observes, 'the future of Southeast Asia is inextricably tied to the policies of the great powers' (1999, p.245). The idea that the collective weak can win over the individual strong seems to be a wishful thinking of the ASEAN.

In general, three gradual evolutionary stages have been identified to achieve regional security cooperation by the ARF: (1) promotion of Confidence Building Measures (CBMs),[16] development of Preventive Diplomacy,[17] and development of Elaboration of Approaches to Conflicts (formerly called Conflict Resolution Mechanisms[18]). There are strengths and weaknesses in the feasibility of the CBMs and Preventive Diplomacy. On the one hand, both can be regarded as vehicles for the ASEAN 'to engage China and help induct it into a rule-based international system, to keep the United States involved, and to help ensure that Japan remains a constructive and positive factor in the changing Asia-Pacific security environment' (Singh, 1997, p.137). On the other hand, they are used as tools by the Great Powers to test the potential capability of the ASEAN and to monitor its maneuverability in the process of subregionalisation, regionalisation and globalisation. To a certain extent, the ASEAN can exploit the transitory absence of a dominant or hegemonic power in Southeast Asia by manipulating the balance of power in the regional politics. 'The Great Powers', as Tarling concludes, 'were beginning to see ASEAN as a political power bloc in its own right, and by the last decade of the [20th] century ASEAN was probably the most effective of Third World organisations' (1999, p.313).

The inclusion of Vietnam, Cambodia, Laos, and Myanmar in the late 1990s into the ASEAN not only shakes the integration of the Association but also accelerates the fragmentation of the Forum. The extended territorial lands of the ASEAN have reached those of China and India in the west and its original territorial waters in the east. The eastern frontier has already led to bitter disputes with China in the South China Sea. The potential conflicts between China and Japan, China and India, China and the United States, Japan and South Korea, North and South Korea, the Chinese mainland and Taiwan, and the stable alliances between China and Pakistan, India and the United States, the United States and Japan, Japan and Taiwan, Taiwan and South Korea, and North Korea and China, complicate the issues in the Asia-Pacific region in which no single Great Power nor the ASEAN alone can settle disagreements. The subregional and regional alignment and realignment based on changing national interest could endanger the potential for cooperation among the ASEAN member states as well as the ARF. The Southeast Asian countries will be differentiated by the Great Powers in relation to the Southeast Asia Nuclear Weapons Free Zone (SEABWFZ), the TAC, and the South China Sea. They may be further divided by their close bilateral relations with the Great Powers (such as the United Kingdom and Malaysia/Singapore, the United States and Thailand/the Philippines) when the common interest of the 'one Southeast Asia' vanishes. The complexity of subregional and regional interests will make future tension among the ASEAN and the ARF participants highly likely.

Subregionalisation and Regionalisation[19] in Southeast Asia

The centripetal force within the ASEAN is being counter balanced by the centrifugal force of the ARF. The subregional ASEAN states have to apply their survival skills among the regional Great Powers.

In the east, to maintain its economic and political interests in the East and Southeast Asia, the Japan-USA alliance seems indestructible. Indeed, the long-term protection by the United States of many of the Southeast Asian countries to a certain extent safeguards the stability of the region. These countries have their price to pay. They suffer from the partial loss of autonomy in dealing with the regional affairs in places under their sphere of influence. The retreat of the United States after the Vietnam War reinforces the consolidation of the ASEAN as a whole yet simultaneously Japan has been 'endorsed' by the United States to 'look after' the region. However, many Southeast Asian countries are hostile to Japan as a gatekeeper in the Asia-Pacific for historic reasons. Any move from Japan to interfere in Southeast Asian affairs will trigger a reaction within the ASEAN. The interplay between the regional bloc and the allying Great Powers is intricate and delicate.

In the west, after the disintegration of the Soviet Union and the withdrawal of the Russia from Southeast Asia, India's efforts to scramble for control in the region was temporarily curbed. As one of the nuclear powers in Asia, India is deemed a threat to its regional neighbors, particularly Indochina. Although political confrontation between the ASEAN and India is being diluted by economic cooperation, the former tend to be exploited by the latter as a leverage against another nuclear power, China. Any potential confrontation between India and China will definitely have an impact on the stability of Southeast Asia.

In the south, Australia plays a significant role in the APEC and the ARF. And it regards Southeast Asia as a stepping stone to the international theatre. However, a socially unstable, religiously passionate, politically undemocratic, and densely populated Indonesia makes Australia feel uneasy. To Australia, Indonesia is often a barrier to the vast blue sea and to the more friendly ASEAN states like Malaysia and Singapore. Geographical proximity coupled with political diversity may lead to potential conflicts if economic relations of the two countries deteriorate.

The situation in the north is more problematic. The political, economic and military expansion of the PRC poses a threat to the collective ASEAN. The ASEAN has always developed this ambivalence towards China. As an emerging economic giant, China provides many market opportunities for its neighboring countries. It is high time that the Southeast Asian countries revived their economy especially after the Asian Financial Crisis in the late 1990s. At the same time China can also check the possible aggression of Japan in the region. Still, China will exert its pressure on territorial claims in the South China Sea and attempt to dominate the political arena.

The South China Sea dispute is a flashpoint in the Asia-Pacific region. Since the 1970s, disputes over the territorial waters between the PRC and Brunei, Malaysia, Vietnam and the Philippines, have made the relations between China and the ASEAN tense. The Manila Declaration of 1992 led to a temporary agreement on the South China Sea dispute. It urges 'all parties concerned to exercise restraint in order to create a positive climate for the eventual resolution all disputes' and emphasises 'the necessity to resolve all sovereignty and jurisdictional issues about the South China Sea by peaceful means, without resort to force'.[20] China at the same time declares that it 'has maintained a highly restrained, responsible and constructive attitude on the issue of the South China Sea, adhering to friendly consultations in resolving disputes with the countries concerned'.[21] The Sino-ASEAN relations are to some extent in a deadlock over the South China Sea issue.

Moreover, there is more than one issue between the ASEAN and China. It involves the vested interest, sphere of influence, and rights of navigation claimed by the Great Powers. Most of the parties concerned, namely, China, India, Japan, North and South Korea, and the United States, are the members of the ARF. With the exception of China, all countries in the world would like to see the South China Sea turn into an international water. Therefore, rather than being a dispute between China and the ASEAN; it is one between China and the ASEAN supported by the Great Powers concerned. The ARF becomes a political arena for wrestling power.

Six approaches[22] for sustaining the dialogue between the ASEAN and China have been presented by various parties for consideration but none was accepted unanimously. While the ASEAN states subjectively hope to regionalise/internationalise the issue, China tries its best to subregionalise it in the hope that it will become more manageable. Regionalisation or internationalisation of the South China Sea dispute would help the ASEAN gain more political momentum and support any defense against China's claim. A concerted force may compel China to negotiate with the claimants one by one on a subregional basis.

However, the competence of the ASEAN to settle disputes with China is questionable.[23] Solidarity among the ASEAN member states is established on mutual understanding, mutual trust, and mutual compromise, assuming the conflicts among them are minor. Major political issues like the South China Sea dispute have usually stopped at the Elaboration of Approaches to Conflicts stage even if they have the chances to go through the earlier stages of CBMs and Preventive Diplomacy. A possible outcome is that the ASEAN may let external powers intervene so that it can fish in troubled waters. However, China is very firm on the territorial issue. While agreeing that the issue should be resolved by peaceful means, China has not conceded an inch of territorial water to neighboring countries. Foreseeing the dispute will be internationalised by the ASEAN, China has separated the issue into three components: (1) the waters can be internationalised for navigation in order to safeguard the Great Powers' interests and needs for communication and transportation; (2) the potential oil reserve in the South China Sea, if founded, can be mutually exploited and developed in cooperation with the neighboring countries so that the need of the claimants for scarce natural resources can be met; and (3) sovereignty is non-negotiable as far as China's military forces can manage to maintain.

The centrifugal effect of the major powers from the ARF make the centripetal effect of the ASEAN more shaky. On the one hand, it seems that the external pressure forces the ASEAN to become more consolidated. On the other hand, the continuous fragmentation will lead to the disintegration of the ARF and further endanger the endurance of the ASEAN as a whole.[24]

An Evaluation

The commonality of the Southeast Asian countries contribute much to the integration of the ASEAN: the Asian values, the autocratic regimes, the need for modernisation, and the challenge of common competitors. However, the integration is meeting the challenges of its dissimilarities: the developing and the underdeveloped, the communist versus the non-communist, and the inclusion versus exclusion of foreign engagements.

At the beginning of the millennium, both the ASEAN and the ARF entered a new international arena. The bipolar state of affairs rapidly metamorphosed into a hegemonic posture dominated by the United States. The supremacy is counteracted by the formation of subregional alliances and other Great Powers so that a balance of power can be maintained by a rule of plurality. The recent terrorist attack on the United States adds one more unpredictable factor in explaining the Southeast Asia affairs. Global economic turndown, racial cum religious conflicts, and the scramble for regional power are disturbing the two subregional and regional organisations. In the foreseeable future, the return of the military presence of the United States in Southeast Asia can be expected. The rivalry among the Great Powers in the region will become more intense. The power relations in the ASEAN and the ARF will undergo restructuring so that a new equilibrium can be reached. Under the realist approach, there is a slim chance for the weak though united ASEAN to resist the pressure constantly imposed by its surrounding Great Powers. The Association and Forum remain reactive rather than proactive mechanisms for seeking regional security. Paradoxically, an integrating ASEAN leads to a fragmenting ARF simply because the 'driver' does not take control and there is no committed Great Power to backup the Association which always argues for a neutrality in the region.

Globalisation is an irresistible trend in international relations. No sovereign state can stay detached without cooperation or alignment with other state(s). In the present dynamic international society, it is unrealistic to think of a self-contained security entity unrelated to other external powers. Subregional and regional configurations are for the purpose of association but not for isolation. The common aim for all countries in the world is to develop a sustainable security for the betterment of all human beings.

The author wishes to thank Gerald Chan, Glenn Drover, and Emily Leung for reading an earlier draft of this chapter.

Notes

1   ASEAN-10 are ASEAN-5 (Indonesia, Malaysia, the Philippines, Singapore, and Thailand joined in 1967), Brunei Darussalam (1984), Vietnam (1995), Laos and Myanmar (1997), and Cambodia (1999).
2   Southeast Asia is a region of divisions (McCloud, 1995, pp.8-11). Geographically, it is divided into the Indo-Pacific Peninsula and the Indonesian-Filipino Archipelago. Religiously, Buddhism is dominant in the Peninsula while Muslim in the Archipelago. Ethnically, four major groups can be identified, namely, the Sino-Tibetan group, the Austroasiatic group, the Thai, and the Malayo-Polynesian group.
3   This is sometimes called the 'hub and spokes' security structure, a system of bilateral defense treaties between the United States and some Southeast Asian countries, through which 'the United States sought to contain the spread of communism and Chinese (before the early 1970s) and Soviet power in the region' (Singh, 1997, p.119).
4   Regionalism is defined as 'the body of *ideas* promoting an identified geographical or social space as the regional project. Or it is the presence or the conscious construction of an identity that represents *one specific* region' (Stubbs and Underhill, 2000, p.72). Subregionalism can be regarded as 'new regionalism' which 'reflects a tendency to

emphasise subregions within nation-states and to give priority to building a network of transactions and collaboration across national boundaries between such subregions' (ibid.).

5   The first two aims of the Association stated in the Bangkok Declaration are: '(1) To accelerate the economic growth, social progress and cultural development in the region through joint endeavours in the spirit of equality and partnership in order to strengthen the foundation for a prosperous and peaceful community of Southeast Asian Nations; (2) To promote regional peace and stability through abiding respect for justice and the rule of law in the relationship among countries of the region and adherence to the principles of the United Nations Charter; ...' ('The ASEAN Declaration (Bangkok Declaration), retrieved in September 2001 from World Wide Web: http://www.aseansec.org/history/leader67.htm).

6   The Declaration of the ZOPFAN recognises 'the right of every state, large or small, to lead its national existence free from outside interference in its internal affairs as this interference will adversely affect its freedom, independence and integrity'; dedicates ' to the maintenance of peace, freedom and independence unimpaired'; and agrees 'that the neutralization of Southeast Asia is a desirable objective and that we should explore ways and means of bringing about it realization' ('Zone of Peace, Freedom and Neutrality Declaration', retrieved in September 2001, from World Wide Web: http://www.aseansec.org/politics/pol_agr1.htm).

7   The fundamental principles of the TAC are: '(1) Mutual respect for the independence, sovereignty, equality, territorial integrity and national identity of all nations; (2) The right of every State to lead its national existence free from external interference, subversion or coercion; (3) Non-interference in the internal affairs of one another; (4) Settlement of differences or disputes by peaceful means; (5) Renunciation of the threat or use of force; and (6) Effective cooperation among themselves' (see 'Basic Documents: Treaty of Amity and Cooperation in Southeast Asia (1976)', retrieved in September 2001, from World Wide Web: http://www.aseansec.org/menu.asp?action=2&content=1).

8   The ASEAN Declaration on the South China Sea emphasises 'the necessity to resolve all sovereignty and jurisdictional issues pertaining to the South China Sea by peaceful means, without resort to force', and urges 'all parties concerned to exercise restraint with view to creating a positive climate for the eventual resolution of all disputes' (see the 'ASEAN Declaration on the South China Sea' retrieved in September 2001, from World Wide Web: http://www.aseansec.org/politics/pol_AGR5.htm).

9   The Treaty on SEANWFZ determines 'to take concrete action which will contribute to the progress towards general and complete disarmament of nuclear weapons, and to the promotion of international peace and security' and convinces 'that the establishment of a Southeast Asia Nuclear Weapon-Free Zone, as an essential component of the ZOPFAN, will contribute towards strengthening the security of States within the Zone and towards enhancing international peace and security as a whole' ('Treaty on the Southeast Asia Nuclear Weapon-Free Zone', retrieved in September 2001, from World Wide Web: http://www.aseansec.org/politics/pol_agr7.htm).

10 The characteristics of a security community includes: '(1) Strict and observed norms concerning non-use of force; no competitive arms acquisitions and contingency-planning against each other within the grouping. (2) Institutions and processes (formal or informal) for the pacific settlement of disputes. (3) Long-term prospects for war avoidance. (4) Significant functional cooperation and integration. (5) A sense of collective identity' (Acharya, 2001, p.21).

11 Singapore's Foreign Minister S. Jayakumar, cited from Acharya (2001, p.63). Chin Kin Wah also lists 'seven pillars of resilience' of the ASEAN, namely, (1) 'a strong adherence to the international norms of seemly behaviour', (2) 'not premised upon the principle of supra-nationality or political union but regional co-operation', (3)

'characterized by consultation and consensus building, particularly on political matters', (4) 'handling of intramural conflict ... principally by way of conflict management or conflict avoidance, rather than conflict resolution', (5) 'grounded in the pragmatism of its political elites', (6) 'remarkably successful in forging common fronts and negotiating positions *vis-à-vis* the 'outside world' despite underlying differences in perspectives among its members', and (7) 'proven to be adaptable to change in its environment – even if it meant having to re-examine some long-held assumptions' (1997, pp.149-54).

12 Denoon and Colbert note that the 'ASEAN has contributed much more to *conflict avoidance* among its members than to *conflict resolution*' (1998, p.506).

13 Acharya remarks that 'ASEAN's trade with non-ASEAN members is significantly higher than intra-ASEAN trade. Moreover, the most important forces of economic integration in the region today have not resulted from conscious regional schemes pursued by ASEAN, but are rather a function of the national economic liberalisation programmes of the members and the increasing pace of economic globalisation' (2000, p.199).

14 The 23 participants are: ASEAN-10, Australia, Canada, China, India, Japan, European Union, Democratic People's Republic of Korea, Republic of Korea, Mongolia, New Zealand, Papua New Guinea, Russian Federation, and United States. Its objectives are: '(1) to foster constructive dialogue and consultation on political and security issues of common interest and concern; and (2) to make significant contributions to efforts towards confidence-building and preventive diplomacy in the Asia-Pacific region' ('The Objectives of ARF', retrieved in September 2001, from World Wide Web: http://www.aseansec.org/amm/objarf1.htm).

15 The ASEAN 'continued to play its leading role in the ARF ...' ('Chairman's Statement: The Eighth Meeting of the ASEAN Regional Forum, Hanoi, 25 July 2001, retrieved in September 2001, from World Wide Web: http://www.aseansec.org/view.asp?file=/amm/hanoi05.htm
Singh is right to observe that 'its leading role in the ARF is unavoidable at this stage because on other power or group is acceptable in the driver's seat to all members' (1997, p.138).

16 The immediate measures of the CBMs are to develop 'a set of basic principles to ensure a common understanding and approach to interstate relations in the region' and to adopt 'comprehensive approaches to security'. The medium and long term measures of the CBMs include: '(1) Further exploration of a Regional Arms Register; (2) Regional security studies centre/coordination of existing security studies activities; (3) Maritime information data bases; (4) Cooperative approaches to sea lines of communication, ...; (5) Mechanism to mobilise relief assistance in the event of natural disasters; (6) Establishment of zones of cooperation in areas such as the South China Seas; (7) Systems of prior notification of major military deployments that have region-wide application; and (8) Encourage arms manufacturers and suppliers to disclose the destination of their arms exports'. For the above information, see 'The ASEAN Regional Forum: A Concept Paper', retrieved in September 2001, from World Wide Web: http://www.aseansec.org./politics/arf_ch2c.htm

17 The definition of PD is 'consensual diplomatic and political action taken by sovereign states with the consent of all directly involved parties: (1) To help prevent disputes and conflicts from arising between States that could potentially pose a threat to regional peace and stability; (2) To help prevent such disputes and conflicts from escalating into armed confrontation; and (3) To help minimise the impact of such disputes and conflicts on the region' ('ASEAN Regional Forum (ARF): Concept and Principles of Preventive Diplomacy', retrieved in September 2001, from World Wide Web: http://www.aseansec.org/view.asp?file=/amm/arf8doc5.htm). The immediate measures of the PD are to '(1) Develop a set of guidelines for the peaceful settlement of

disputes, ...; (2) Promote the recognition acceptance of the purposes and principles of the TAC and its provisions for the Pacific settlement of disputes, ...; and (3) Seek the endorsement other countries for the ASEAN Declaration on the South China Sea in order to strengthen its political and moral effect ...'. The medium and long term measures of the PD are to '(1) Explore and devise ways and means to prevent conflict; (2) Explore the idea of appointing Special Representatives, in consultation with ARF members, to undertake fact-finding missions, at the request of the parties involved to an issue, and to offer their good offices, as necessary; and (3) Explore the idea of establishing, a Regional Risk Reduction Centre ... Such a centre could serve as a data base for the exchange of information'. For the above information, see 'The ASEAN Regional Forum: A Concept Paper', retrieved in September 2001, from World Wide Web:
http://www.aseansec.org./politics/arf_ch2c.htm

18 'The ASEAN Regional Forum: A Concept Paper' states: 'It is not envisaged that the ARF would establish mechanism conflict resolution in the immediate future. The establishment of such mechanisms is an eventual goal that ARF participants should pursue as they proceed to develop the ARF as a vehicle for promoting regional peace and stability' (retrieved in September 2001, from World Wide Web: http://www.aseansec.org./politics/arf_ch2c.htm). The change from Conflict Resolution Mechanisms to Elaboration of Approaches to Conflicts is an ASEAN's concession to China which disapproves the rapid institutionalisation of the ARF (Acharya, 2001, p.201).

19 Subregionalisation or regionalisation refers to 'the process that actually builds concrete patterns of transaction within an identified [sub/]regional space' (Stubbs and Underhill, 2000, p.72).

20 See 'Political and Security Cooperation', retrieved in September 2001, from World Wide Web: http://www.aseansec.org/view.asp?file=/politics/ov_psc.htm

21 See 'ASEAN Regional Forum: Annual Security Outlook 2000, China, retrieved in September 2001, from World Wide Web:
http://www.aseansec.org/view.asp?file=/amm/aso/aso_chi.htm.

22 They are: (1) South China Sea informal annual meetings organised by Indonesia, (2) establishment of an Eminent Persons Group (EPG), (3) third-party mediation, (4) multilateral talks between the ASEAN and China, (5) two-step approach – bilateral-first and multilateral-second negotiations, and (6) establishment of Joint Resource Development Authority. See The United States Institute of Peace, 'Special Report: The South China Sea Dispute: Prospects for Preventive Diplomacy', retrieved in September 2001, from World Wide Web:
http://www.usip.org/oc/sr/snyder/South_China_Sea1.html

23 As Acharya remarks: 'ASEAN's ability to handle what is essentially an extra-mural conflict may not only fail (although it might have a moderating effect on the conflict), but the [South China Sea] dispute may severely test intra-ASEAN solidarity, including its ability to offer a common position vis-à-vis external powers' (2000, p.5).

24 Some international politics scholars use a label 'fragmegration' to describe a situation in which 'the clash between that world [populated by authorities free from the domestic and international constraints and responsibilities of governments] and the world of sovereign states has produced integrative and fragmenting dynamics' (Earnest and Rosenau, 2000, p.90).

References

Acharya, A. (2001), *Constructing a Security Community in Southeast Asia: ASEAN and the*

Problem of Regional Order, Routledge, London.
Association of Southeast Asian Nations, World Wide Web: http://www.aseansec.org
Chin, K.W. (1997), 'ASEAN in the New Millennium', in S.Y. Chia and M. Pacini (eds), *ASEAN in the New Asia: Issues and Trends*, Institute of Southeast Asian Studies, Singapore, pp. 144-64.
Denoon, D. and Colbert, E. (1998), 'Challenges for the Association of Southeast Asian Nations (ASEAN)', *Pacific Affairs*, vol.71 no.2, pp. 195-214.
Earnest, D. and Rosenau, J. (2000), 'The Spy Who Loved Globalization: James Bond was wrestling with forces of integration and fragmentation decades before political scientists invented the ideas', *Foreign Policy*, no.120, pp. 88-90.
McCloud, D. (1995), *Southeast Asia: Tradition and Modernity in the Contemporary World*, Westview, Boulder, Colorado.
Neher, C. (1999), *Southeast Asia in the New International Era*, Westview Press, Boulder, Colorado.
Singh, D. (1997), 'ASEAN and the Security of Southeast Asia', in S.Y. Chia and M. Pacini, (eds), *ASEAN in the New Asia: Issues and Trends*, Institute of Southeast Asian Studies, Singapore, pp. 118-143.
Stubbs, R. and Underhill, G. (2000), *Political Economy and the Changing Global Order*, Oxford University Press, Oxford.
Tarling, N. (ed.) (1999), *The Cambridge History of Southeast Asia: Volume Four - From World War II to the Present*, Cambridge University Press, Cambridge.
United States Institute of Peace, World Wide Web: http://www.usip.org

2 Civil Society in Southeast Asia: Cases of Singapore and Malaysia

MING SING

Civil Society: Significance in Southeast Asia and in the World

After a century of inattention, the present-day discussion of civil society was invigorated in the struggles against authoritarian socialist states in Eastern Europe and, to a minor degree, military dictatorships in Latin America (Pelcynski 1988; Tismaneanu, 1992). Indeed, the 20th century has witnessed a significant decline of authoritarian states and expansion of democratically elected governments. In 1900, the states with restricted democratic practices were 25 in number and accounted for just 12.4 percent of the world population. In 2000, liberal and electoral democracies visibly prevail, representing 120 of the 192 existing countries and 62.5 percent of the global population (Lipset et al, 2000). Given the bourgeoning prevalence of democracies in the world today, it is of paramount significance to understand what make them emerge.[1]

While no single factor has yet been found to be necessary or sufficient for explaining democratisation, one of the most commonly mentioned one has been the vibrancy of pro-democracy movements from civil society (Huntington, 1991). Organised social movement organisations, encompassing labour unions, religious organisations, woman's associations, students unions and other intermediate groups in civil society, spanning from Poland, Hungary, Czechoslovakia and Yugoslavia in Eastern Europe, through Taiwan, South Korea, Philippines and Thailand in Asia, to those in Latin America and Southern Europe, have undermined the authoritarian states and enhanced democratisation (Nether, 1991; White, 1994).

In Asia, there has been a mounting literature on civil society too. Riker (1995) regards state-civil society relations as appearing in three differing phases in the region. At the first phase, i.e., by the mid-1980s, civil society groups were perceived by elites as having a complementary role in advancing development. Towards the start of the 1990s, the second phase of civil society development figured itself as some autonomous and countervailing power to various states, challenging them for greater freedoms and democracy. The third phase of civil society is marked by the incorporation of civil groups by Asian governments in response to the rising pressures from civil society groups as an instrument of states.

Given the potential political significance of civil society both globally and in Southeast Asia, the resurgence of interest in civil society of Southeast Asia has been especially obvious with the unfolding of the economic crises in 1997 (Zarsky and Tay, 2001). Side by side with the economic crises has been some gripping political transformations in a number of countries, including Malaysia and Singapore. Questions have been raised as to how the civil groups can contribute to their democratic development.

Singapore and Malaysia: Different Income Levels and Spectacular Economic Growth Rates

While the 'Asian economic miracles' have happened for a number of Asian countries, both Singapore and Malaysia stand out from the rest. Indeed, the two countries share a few practically important and theoretically interesting features. First, while Singapore and Malaysia has respectively belonged to the high-income and middle-income groups as defined by the World Bank for quite some time, their growth rates in GDP between 1990 and 1995 have been the fastest ones within their own income groups in the Pacific Region (Table 2.1) (Morley, 1999, p.5). They have also both been part of the 'tiger clubs', whose economies seem to have rebounded relatively faster than many other Southeast Asian countries (Case, 2001, p.43). Therefore, both countries have been exemplars for many developing countries, at least as far as economic development is concerned.

Second, while both countries have had formal electoral politics, they have never achieved full democracy (Morley, 1999, p.29). While Malaysia has been classified as 'pseudo-,' 'semi-,' 'quasi-democracy,' or 'authoritarian-democratic regime' (Case, 2001, p.43; Crouch, 1996, pp.3-13), Singapore has been labelled as 'soft-authoritarian' or 'authoritarian-democratic regime' (Means, 1996, pp.103-117; Morley, 1999, p.29). In other words, both countries have defied the global trend of democratisation and remained authoritarian. Different researchers have explained their lack of democracy either separately or together by different historical, political, social and economic factors (Ahmad and Alatas, 1999, pp.176-196; Case, 2001, pp.43-57; Lam, 1999, pp.255-275; Jesudason, 1995, pp. 335-56; Jesudason, 1996, pp. 128-160; Loh, 2000, pp.65-87; Rodan, 1996, pp.95-

127). This chapter will distinguish itself from the previous ones by focusing on the political weakness of their civil societies, and especially, their labour sectors. Why should we focus on the labour sector in Malaysia and Singapore?

Table 2.1 Average annual growth rates of GDP and population in the Asia-Pacific region (%)

	1965-80		1980-90		1990-95		1995-99	
	GDP	Pop.	GDP	Pop.	GDP	Pop.	GDP	Pop.
High-Income								
Japan	6.3	1.2	4.0	0.6	1.3	0.3	1.3	0.3
Singapore	10.1	1.6	7.1	1.7	8.5	2.0	5.9	2.6
Middle-Income								
Taiwan	9.8	2.3	7.9	1.3	6.6	0.9	5.9	2.2
South Korea	9.5	2.0	9.1	1.2	7.5	0.9	4.8	1.1
Malaysia	7.4	2.5	5.9	2.7	8.7	2.4	5.1	2.4
Thailand	7.2	2.9	7.9	1.8	8.4	0.9	1.4	0.7
Philippines	5.9	2.9	1.6	2.4	2.3	2.2	2.4	2.1
Indonesia	8.0	2.4	6.3	1.9	7.8	1.6	1.6	1.63
Low-Income								
China	7.4	2.1	9.1	1.5	12.3	1.1	8.8	1.01
Vietnam	-	-	-	-	-	-	7.5	1.6
Myanmar	-	-	-	-	-	-	6.0	1.2

Sources: Morley, 1999, p.5 and Table 1.2; The World Bank online sources; Asian Development Bank online sources

Why Focus on the Labour Activism in Malaysia and Singapore?

Popular protests in Spain of Southern Europe, in Peru and Argentina of Latin American, in South Korea of Asia, in Eastern Europe, and in the bulk of 42 African countries have not only facilitated the democratisation after the initiation of the process, but also directly contributed to the initiation of the entire process (Bratton and van de Walle, 1992; 1997, p.83; Collier, 1999, pp.110-114; Geddes, 1999, p.120; Kim, 2000, pp.137-150).

Those recent researches underscore popular mobilisations of different classes, especially the working class, in bringing about democratisation in Europe, Latin America, Asia and Africa (Adler and Webster, 1995, pp.75-106; Bellin, 2000, pp.175-205; Collier, 1999, pp.110-114; Kim, 2000, pp.93-

95; Manuel, 1998, p.133). Among those researchers, Samuel Valenzuela (1989, pp.447-50) has succinctly presented one of the few broadly comparative analyses of the labour movement during recent democratisation. He argued that the labour plays such a pivotal role among the multiple groups of civil society as that 'it should not be discussed simply on the same plane with other segments of society'. He claimed that the inimitable position of labour particularly within an authoritarian milieu lies in its unusual ability for mobilisation, its existing organisational network, and the association between 'labor demands and activity on the one hand and production and macroeconomic performance and policy on the other' (Collier, 1999, p.9).

Given the aforementioned cross-national contributions that labour can make in political mobilisation and democratisation, I will delineate the labour inactivism in both Singapore and Malaysia, especially centering around their weak unionism.

Singapore and Labour Inactivism

A Strong One-Party State with a Weak Civil Society

The hallmark characterising the prolonged governance of Singapore by its leading party, i.e., the People's Action Party (PAP), has been its sophisticated authoritarian control over social forces. The party has emphasised the technocratic nature of public policy at the expense of competitive politics, on the ground of benevolent autocracy, or some form of developmental paternalism (Deyo, 1997). The benevolent autocracy or developmental paternalism manifests itself in the presence of an efficient and effective ruling party, which has not only contributed to Singapore's continued economic success, but also avoided nepotism, corruption, ethnic conflicts, and maintained the overall political stability.

Despite the existence of parliamentary elections, the PAP has exercised extensive extraparliamentary influences, and blocked effective political opposition, as well as institutionalised PAP's world view on society (Rodan, 1992, p.3). The widespread quality of authoritarianism in Singapore has been backed up by a combination of sophisticated legal constraints on non-governmental organisations, and wide-ranging co-optive mechanisms to defuse political challenges through state-led organs. The suppression of an authentic civil society not only frustrates the PAP's formal political opponents, but also blunts political pluralism and interest group politics (Rodan, 1998, pp.63-66).

To exemplify the dominant state control over the civil society, the low level of labour activism in Singapore offers an excellent illustration. It will be seen that the state led by the PAP has managed to incorporate its largest labour federation, the National Trade Union Congress (NTUC) under its control. The incorporation finally results in subordination of labour unions to the state. Given that the NTUC represents one of the most mature and developed institutions of civil society (Rosa, 1990, p.492), the following explanation of the labour subordination illustrates significantly the presence of the strong state side by side with a weak civil society in Singapore.

A Weak Labour Participation and a Strong Union Federation

The coming sections will highlight the relatively low union density of both countries when compared with other industrialised countries. Then, it outlines the historical development of the major labour union federations in both countries and the dominance of the federation by the state.

Despite the advanced level of industrialisation and economic development that Singapore has achieved in the 1990s, the country has consistently scored a much lower level of union density than other western counterparts (Table 2.2).

Table 2.2 Unions membership, 1989-1999

	1989	1996	1997	1998	1999
Total Work Force ('000)	1,314.0	1,801.9	1,876.0	1,931.8	1,976.0
Employees' Trade Unions	83	83	82	80	76
Membership	212,874	255,020	260,130	272,769	289,707
Ratio	16.20%	14.15%	13.87%	14.12%	14.66%

Sources: Chew, 1991, p.3; Ministry of Manpower, Singapore Online Sources.

Noticeably, among those limited number of unions, the bulk of them have joint a labour union federation, the NTUC. For instances, in 1979, 94.7 percent of union members were affiliated with the NTUC, which grew to 96.8 percent in 1984 and 98 percent in 1986 (Leggett 1993b, p.123 and 127). Given the extremely high ratio of participation of Singaporean unionised workers in the NTUC, the history and the relationship between the NTUC and the state are worth examining.

National Trade Union Congress (NTUC)

The history of the NTUC can be traced back to the Singapore Trade Union Congress (STUC) founded in 1951 under the full support of the colonial government. The STUC was far from strong, given that only 28 out of 107 unions were affiliated with the STUC (Rosa, 1990, p.490).

In 1961, the STUC was split into the NTUC and SATU (Singapore Association of Trade Union), with the former led the PAP (Chew, 1991, p.33). In 1965, almost all of the trade unions in Singapore were affiliated with the NTUC (Chew, 1991, p.33). Then came the year of 1969, a milestone for the NTUC.

During 1969, the trade union movement began to develop a vision of acting in partnership with the state. Trade unions, shepherded by the NTUC, no longer confined themselves to the collective bargaining for the workers, but also attended to the overall economic growth, productivity and performance of the entire country (Chew, 1991, p.34). In other words, the 'the labor movement in Singapore has successfully transformed from a wage-negotiating unit to a nation-building institution (Chew, 1991, p.38).' Since then, the NTUC has become highly involved in many services, such as supermarket, income insurance, taxi, media and dental care service. (Tan, 1995, p.72 and 80-81; The homepage of NTUC, online sources).

Membership and Objectives

The members of the NTUC from 1964 to 2000 were listed in Table 2.3. The predominance of NTUC among labour unions in Singapore was testified, by instance that in 1988, 98 percent of the union members were affiliated with the NTUC (Leggett, 1993, p.231). In 1992, as many as 73 unions and three associations were affiliated with the NTUC. They represented 217,000 members or 22 percent of the bargainable workforce in Singapore (Tan, 1995, p.73). In 1999, 73 out of 82 employees unions affiliated with the NTUC (Department of State, 2000, p.10).

The NTUC, as revealed in its latest organisational chart, unveils three types of objectives:

1. To help Singapore stay competitive, and workers to remain employable for life.
2. To enhance the social status and well-being of workers.
3. To build a strong, responsible and caring labor movement (online source: website of NTUC).

Table 2.3 NTUC membership

Year	Number of Members
1964	101,800
1967	92,900
1970	85,400
1973	168,100
1976	212,000
1979	236,600
1982	203,100
1985	197,300
1988	209,100
1991	216,300
1992	230,400
1993	236,100
2000	316,000

Sources: Tan, 1995, p.78; The Straits Times, Singapore, January 17, 2001.

Table 2.4 The five largest unions in terms of number of members in Singapore as of December 1993

Union	Numbers of Members
United Workers of Electronic and Electrical Industries	35,076
Amalgamated Union of Public Employees	20,190
Food, Drink and Allied Workers' Union	12,520
Singapore Teachers' Union	11,981
Singapore Manual and Mercantile Workers' Union	13,492

How can those objectives be achieved? The NTUC tries to realise them by 1) helping 'the government to implement polices to maximise economic growth for Singapore', and 2) 'achieving growth with equality in Singapore via a strong labor movement.' (Chew, 1991, p.2). In particular, the close collaboration between the PAP and NTUC, manifest in terms of overlapping leadership, facilitates the attainment of those objectives. It is not uncommon for leaders to move between leadership in government, unions and the civil service. The relationship is secured by a PAP/NTUC liaison committee, and there are specified Labor Members of Parliament to relay information in both directions between the NTUC and the PAP (Goh and Green, 1997, p.232). In view of their close cooperation, I will argue below for the subordination of the labour federation and sector to the state in Singapore.

Subordination of the NTUC to the PAP: their Inter-Penetration and Collaborationist Stance of NTUC

The state has long played an important role in NTUC through provision of funds, personnel and policy initiatives. Inter-penetration has been the appropriate concept to describe the relationship between the state and the federation. The state opened some areas of the state, such as tripartite institutions, parliament and the civil servants, to assist the federation to formulate wage claims and collective bargaining (Rosa, 1990, p.492). What is more, PAP members always held the important post of secretary-general of the NTUC. Devan Nair, Lim Chee Onn and On Teng Cheong were of such examples (Chew, 1991, p.10). In 1997, 16 MPs have NTUC background. However, some of them joined the NTUC after they were elected (Singapore Straits Times, January 1, 1997), though the number dropped to six in 2000 (The Straits Times, Singapore, December 10, 2000).

Deputy Secretary-General released that there were 59 union representatives in 29 public institutions in the late 1980s (Rosa, 1990, p.492). Even in recent years, the NTUC and the government have still exchanged their officers. For example, in 1997, the director of the Legal Department of the NTUC, Halimah Yacob was transferred to the Ministry of Labor (MOL) and the labour relation officer of the MOL, Jeanette Har was seconded to the industrial relations department of the NTUC (The Straits Times, Singapore, December 17, 1997). The Young PAP, the young wing of the PAP, was a corporate member of the NTUC club (Singapore Straits Times, May 7, 1996). Such close inter - penetration seems to confirm Rosa's view that 'complete interpenetration between the NTUC and the government is regularly and openly publicised' (Rosa, 1990, p.492). The inter-penetration has no doubt fostered the collaborationist stance of the NTUC with respect to the state of Singapore. The stance can be illustrated as follows.

First, the NTUC has been highly committed to some important tripartite bodies, such as the National Wages Council (NWC) and the Skill Development Fund (Chew, 1991, p.10). Those tripartite bodies were set up to ensure full cooperation between labour and capital under the guidance of the state. In the late 1980s, the NWC was made up of 13 members, four from each of the NTUC, the government and the employers' organisations. The guiding principle for the NWC has been to avert the basic clash in interest between labour and capital by connecting wages with company profits (Rosa, 1990, p.493).

An Act of Parliament established another influential tripartite body, the Skills Development Council in 1979 to manage a central fund to which both employers and employees devote to promote training (Rosa, 1990, p.493). Under the context of the developmental state and the collaborationist union movement, the NTUC has pressured employers to sign up to collective agreements on training, and swayed workers to receive training (Goh and Green, 1997, p.230).

Second, in response to the economic recession in 1985, the NTUC supported the government to cut the labour cost. The employers' Central Provident Fund contribution rate was cut from 25 percent to 10 percent. When the recession was over, the government eventually raised this rate to 16 percent and lowered employees' contribution from 25 percent to 22 percent after the appeal of the NTUC (Chew, 1991, p.64).

Third, after the 1988 elections, the NTUC disallowed members that openly opposed the PAP to hold office, i.e., dissidents were expelled from the NTUC leadership. Leaders of the political opposition were forced to step down from the office of the union branches. Two taxi operators of the NTUC, for instance, who stood as opposition candidates, were forced to resign. However, such actions caused bitterness and apathy among some members. A survey of 105 workers conducted between 1988-89 indicated some popular beliefs among them, such as absence of freedom to push for issues unacceptable to the ruling party, and the belief that the PAP and government interests become dominant (Chew 1991, p.64; Rosa, 1990, p.494).

Fourth, the NTUC has not raised strong objections to some draconian laws that restricted the workers' rights to strikes or the autonomy of labour unions. For instances, under the Industrial Relations Ordinance, any strike of workers in essential services would be regarded as illegal. Strikes in non-essential services would also be illegal if the Industrial Arbitration Court that consisted of representatives of government, workers and management 'has taken cognizance of the dispute'. Without the government approval, strike has been impossible (Rosa, 1990, pp.494-495). Since 1986, strike has disappeared in Singapore (Department of State, 2000, p.10). Under the same Act, promotions, transfers, hiring, firing and redundancy were defined as managerial prerogatives and hence non-negotiable, save in the case of dismissal without just cause or excuse (Woodiwiss, 1998, p.238).

Also, under the Trade Unions Ordinance, the state has been empowered 'to grant or deprive trade unions of recognition; to supervise their handling of their fund; to influence the selection of their leaders and to decide upon the right of representation before state and employers' (Rosa, 1990, p.496).

Under the Trade Unions Act, registration of trade unions is compulsory, and that a registered trade union can, at any time, be de-registered if found to conduct activities other than those stated in its constitution (Chew, 1991, p.2). Besides, if the trade union seeks to represent an employee or a group of employees, the trade union must either get the recognition and acceptance of the employer or the approval of the majority of the employees through secret ballot (Anantaraman, 1990, pp.105-117; Chew, 1991, p.2).

In short, instead of describing the PAP-NTUC relationship as a symbiotic one like Leggett (1993) and Tan (1995) did, there has been a clear subordination of the labour federation and workers to the state in Singapore, and that their relationship required 'a clear loyalty commitment to the PAP from NTUC affiliates' officials and employees' (Leggett, 1993, p.124). Indeed, as opposition MP Chiam See Tong criticised, there was no real tripartite relationship in Singapore because the PAP controlled the labour movement. Some PAP's Members of Parliament responded to this critique not by a denial of the subordinate relationship, but on the pragmatic ground that close relationship could bring the voice of workers to the Parliament and the cabinet (The Straits Times, Singapore, January 16, 1998). The leaders of the NTUC not only recognised the subordination relationship but took pride in it as well. Lim, the NTUC chief, for instance, pointed out that the relationship 'enabled the NTUC to do so much for workers, such as setting up NTUC FairPrice, INCOME, Comfort, NTUC Pasir Ris Resort and the Orchid Country Club' (Singapore Straits Times, April 4, 1997, November 29, 1995). The Country Reports on Human Rights Practice published by the US Department of State described the PAP-NTUC relations as symbiotic as well (US Department of State, 1997).

The NTUC unabashedly acknowledges that its interests are closely linked with those of the ruling PAP, a relationship often described by both as 'symbiotic'. For example, the NTUC secretary general (SG), Lim Boon Heng, a PAP M.P., is Minister without Portfolio and was formerly Second Minister for Trade and Industry. His predecessor, Ong Teng Cheong, the country's first elected President (1993-99) was simultaneously NTUC Secretary-General and Deputy Prime Minister. It is common for your PAP's Members of Parliament to be given leadership positions in the NTUC or a member union. NTUC policy prohibited union members who actively support opposition parties from holding office in affiliated unions. While the NTUC is financially independent of the PAP, with income generated by NTUC-owned businesses, the NTUC and the PAP share the same ideology and work closely with management in support of non-confrontational labour relations (US Department of State, 1997).

General Satisfaction with NTUC and Unions Among Singaporeans

There is little threat to the tight bondage of the PAP-NTUC, as there has been a general satisfaction with the NTUC among Singaporeans. Chew's (1991) survey conducted between late 1985 and early 1987 showed that:

78% of the general public 'believed that the NTUC and the unions had been able to improve the wages, working conditions and job security of workers'.... 72% of the respondents 'felt that the close relationship between the NTUC and the government had been an asset to the labor movement.' Only 10% disagreed.... 73% of the respondents answered 'the NTUC leaders had lived up to their expectation and only 2% said that they had not'.... 62% of the respondents answered, 'unions members were better off as a result of joining a union and only 2% said that they were worse off' (Chew, 1991, p.189).

The positive attitudes did not wane with time. In another survey done on union members conducted between December, 1989 and February, 1990 (Tan, 1995) similar favorable findings towards unions were found.[2] Labour unions were regarded effective in the following areas:

1. Protecting members against unfair treatment (80%)
2. Providing social, welfare and recreational activities (80%)
3. Securing better terms and conditions of service (79%)
4. Securing better wage (76%)
5. Solving members' grievances (75%) (Tan, 1995, p.69)

In short, unlike South Korea, Taiwan and Hong Kong, Singapore has a 'labor movement that is able to comply with government directives and yet, ...successfully socialise and resocialise the workforce from which it must draw its vitality (Leggett in Rodan, 1993b, p.117)'. What are the important underlying causes of the labour subordination to the state in Singapore?

First, the PAP has been highly committed to the formation of the NTUC and recognised its right to collective bargaining (Leggett, 1993a, p.244). The legitimacy of the NTUC was just enhanced by the state's recognition of those rights.

Second, the opposition to the PAP was unable to mobilise support among the workers since the mid-1960s (Leggett, 1993a, p.244). Constraints in laws and resources have dampened the performance of the opposition and the enthusiasm of workers to seek alternative political backing from the opposition forces (Deyo, 1997, p.2). Besides, the electoral manipulation and the intolerance of the PAP-NTUC of 'deviant' analyses of industrial relations, have deprived the workers the access to alternative views on policy choices (Leggett, 1993a, p.244).

Third, the PAP government has been highly successful with its economic development policies, that enabled the NTUC leaders to have earned credibility by association. The workers have also been frequently reminded that the survival and prosperity of the nation depend on the quality of the human resources (Leggett, 1993a, pp.244-245).

Fourth, the socialisation through national service in armed force and moral education in school has reinforced the subordination of unions to the state (Leggett, 1993a, p.245). Next, we turn to examine the situation in Malaysia.

Malaysia and Labour Inactivism

A Pseudo-democracy Maintained by Resilient Forces

Malaysia has been dubbed as a resilent pseduo-democracy, and its political structure has been propped up by opposing historical and socio-economic forces, with some facilitating democracy and others promoting authoritarianism (Case, 2001, p.45; Crouch, 1996). The British legacy of respect for 'meritocracy', 'rule-of-law', and party and electoral politics, alongside with the social mobilisation brought by socio-economic development, have laid premium for a democratic push. However, the aforementioned pro-democratic structural forces are also beset with some countervailing ones, such as the state-dependent bourgeoisie and middle class, who have been cautious of the working and agrarian classes, and an ethnic cleavage between Malays and Chinese. The high suspicion between the two ethnic communities has arguably lent themselves to the manipulation of the authoritarian elites and strengthened their acquiescence in authoritarian controls (Case, 2001, p.45; Loh, 2000).

Indeed, one of the greatest manipulations of the Malaysian state has been towards its civil society. Those manipulations have emasculated the social groups in developing their organisational and ideological capacities to limit the power of the authoritarian elites (Jesudason, 1995, p.336). One important sector in which the state's manipulation and dominance can be vividly illuminated has been the labour sector, i.e., the one that theoretically promises big potential as a key agent in promoting democracy. It will be shown below that many state policies and legislations have enfeebled labour unions and labour activism in Malaysia.

Low Union Density and Competitive Labour Federations

In Malaysia, the workers in Malaysia have shot up spectacularly from 5.6 million in 1985 to 7.9 million in 1995. And in 2000, it reaches 9.3 million (Department of Statistics Homepage online sources) in the wake of rapid economic development. The unions have however remained politically feeble and been vulnerable to state control (Suaram, 1998, p.46).

Between 1957 and 1990, the average membership of unions was less than 2,000 (Table 2.5). In 1988, only 612,000 employees that constituted 18 percent of the total wage earners were union members (Levine, 1997, p.367). The unionisation dropped further to 10 percent of labour or 706,253 members in 1995 (Saravanamuttu, 2000, p.14). In 1994, there were 1272 registered labour organisations, but most of them were small and either enterprise or industry based (Arudsothy and Littler, 1993, p.108; Levine, 1997, p.343; Wong, 1993, p.229).

There were three federations of trade unions, namely, Malaysian Trade Union Congress (MTUC), Malaysian Labor Organisation (MLO) and the Congress of Unions of Employees in the Public and Civil Service (CUEPACS). The colonial government sponsored MTUC and CUEPACS. Therefore, they were far from militant (Crouch, 1996b, p.89). The three federations have competed for the positions in the tripartite bodies and the status as the representative for the workers (Levine, 1997, pp.368-370). In Malaysia, the state tightly controlled the labour organisations through legal and political means.

Table 2.5 Union strength of Malaysia, 1957-2001

	No. of Union	Average membership of unions
1957	168	888
1965	286	1,146
1970	251	1,475
1975	267	1,992
1980	290	1,868
1985	296	1,920
1990	322	1,778
1999	551	1,317
2000	577	1,273
2001	587	1,255

Sources: Arudsothy and Littler 1999, p.110; The Ministry of Human Resources, Malaysia, online resource

Legal Constraints Dampens Labour Activism

The Trade Unions Act of 1959 and the Societies Act of 1966 were the two major legal means to regulate the formation and activities of the labour organisations. Under the Trade Unions Act of 1959, workers belonging to the essential services, such as 'confidential, managerial, executive, or security' categories as defined by the government are not allowed to join unions. In the same fashion, non-clerical police and military personnel are also disallowed to join unions and confined to in-house style unions (Saravanamuttu, 2000, p.14). What is more, after a strike of an airline in 1979, the amended Industrial Relations Act of 1967 has empowered the minister of labour to treat any industrial or service as 'essential', thus disallowing unions in the so-called 'essential' services. The Act also enabled the government to suspend unions for half a year in case the government felt that they were against the national interest (Kuruvilla, 1995, p.51).

The Director-General of Trade Unions has the power to permit and withdraw the registration of the trade unions (Levine, 1997, p.330 and 343). Moreover, the Malaysian government dampens the formation of national unions. Under the Trade Unions Act, the trade union can only represent workers in a particular trade or industry or similar trades or industries, otherwise its registration will not be approved. The Electrical Industry Workers Union has tried to form a national union but opposed by the government on the ground that the electrical industry and electronic industry were not similar (Levine, 1997, p.330 and 343). Such regulations have clearly limited the size and power of the trade unions.

Because of this regulation, the MTUC and the MLO have been only registered under the Societies Ordinance. The registration prevents the MTUC from joining any wage negotiations or assisting in any industrial action (Arudsothy and Littler, 1993, p.119). Therefore, the politically weak federation of the MTUC has concentrated its energies on worker education and pushing for the reform of labour laws (Silva, 1998, p.37). In short, general federations are prohibited, since union members have to be employed in a similar trade, occupation or industry (Silva, 1998, p.119).

In addition, the Industrial Relations Act has forbidden the unions to represent the managerial ranks workers to negotiate with the employers if managerial ranks workers do not constitute their majority membership. It discouraged the workers from joining unions that have broader membership (Arudsothy and Littler, 1993, p.123).

Also, the Trade Unions Ordinance has prevented office bearers or employees of political parties from holding office in trade unions (Crouch, 1996, p.90). This measure has weakened any possible political integration between political parties and labour unions. In particular, the Essential (Trade Unions) Regulations promulgated in 1969 and consolidated in an ordinance of 1980 forbad a union to use funds for political objectives (Crouch, 1996, p.90).

Moreover, the Industrial Relations Act (1967) has restricted the collective bargaining of the labour. Data from 1981 to 1986 indicated that the labour minister has increasingly taken up an activist stance, and attempted to settle disputes through its referrals to the Industrial Court

(Kuruvilla, 1995, pp.52-53). Such increasing referrals have effectively reduced the free collective bargaining. As a result, the influence of unions in private sectors has been waning when measured in terms of the overall trend of collective bargaining. The agreements of collective bargaining fell from 137 in 1983 to 105 in 1986 for instance (Arudsothy and Littler, 1993, p.127).

Regarding labour strikes, any strike in Malaysia requires the approval of two-thirds of the affected workers and must inform the Director General of Trade Unions seven days before the event. The Minister of Human Resources has the power to end the strike and arrange a compulsory arbitration in the industrial court. The minister, for instance, indeed exercised this power in 1990 on the strike of the National Union of Plantation Workers over a wage dispute (Saravanamuttu, 2000, p.14).

Another important constraint has been that the government employees were only allowed to join the unions which excluded non-government workers (Arudsothy and Littler 1993, p.120). In statutory bodies, the employees are permitted to participate in the in-house unions only. Moreover, different unions represent different categories of employees (Arudsothy and Littler, 1993, p.121). Besides, their right to strike in the public sector has become largely illusionary, with the shifting to a more paternalistic system of industrial relations in the public sector (Arudsothy and Littler, 1993).

Apart from the above controls, the state has also thwarted the unions to be political oppositions. The Minister of Labour and Manpower has been given the power to suspend any trade union used for political purpose or deemed a threat to the national security and public order (Levine, 1997, p.43). Also, although union officers are permitted to act as an opposition in the parliament, they are forbidden to serve as the political party leaders at the same time (Levine, 1997, p.343). Having finished the discussion of legal constraints, we next move to the political controls over unions.

Political Constraints on Labour Activism

The government's resolve to split the labour movement has been evinced by the formation of the state-sponsored and compliant MLO in 1989. The MLO has been a rival federation to the MTUC since then (Kuruvilla, 1995, p.55). As mentioned, the government encouraged the formation of the MLO. The MLO rapidly gained a membership of 100,000 through defections from the MTUC, but the numbers have remained steady since then, and it was finally dissolved in 1996 (Saravanamuttu, 2000, p.14).

Besides, the government has used the Internal Security Act (ISA), a draconian law to control the society and undermine the opposition force

(Crouch, 1996a, p.118). For instance, in 1987, the government detained 106 anti-government activists, including some unionists, without trial under the Internal Secret Act (Loh, 2000, p.77). Judging by the marked decrease in the number of activists in human rights work compared to the pre-ISA days, evidence suggests that the ISA has played a part in deterring Malaysian dissidents (Weiss, 1999, p.24).

Last but not the least, the government has also used some more subtle means of control, such as excluding the MTUC from a number of tripartite bodies, like the National Labour Advisory Council (NLAC) and the board of the Employees' Provident Fund (Jesudason, 1996, p.144). Besides the legal and political constraints from the state, the political strength of labour unions in Malaysia was also undermined by the following constraints.

Other Constraints on Labour Activism

All major unions have been faced with financial problem. For example, the MTUC raised the affiliation fees in 1989 in order to avoid bankruptcy, and the National Union of Plantation Workers was compelled to mortgage part of its assets. The debts owed by unions to the government-funded trading banks have simply increased the vulnerability of the unions (Arudsothy and Littler, 1993, p.127).

Last but not the least, though the society of Malaysia is stratified, the ethnic identity is so strong that the class tension does not enter into the formation of personal identity (Boulanger, 1992, p.322). The labour union movement simply lacked political cohesion as its members were incorporated from different racial communities (Couch, 1996b, p.90).

Conclusion

Some theorists favoring democratic transition have argued civil society in at least three ways: 1) 'as the state withdraws economically, associations aid in meeting the needs of the poor and reducing the demands on the state.' 2) 'In tems of sheer numbers, civil society comprises increasing voices pressuring the state for a decentralisation of decision-making powers.' 3) 'Civil society plays a critical role in organising and demanding policy changes' by projecting an alternative vision and organisation of society. Their participation can promote a democratic political culture (Kleinberg and Clark, 2000, p.3).

To reduce the bottom-up pressures from labour sectors for democratisation, both governments in Singapore and Malaysia have however attempted to nip the buds in their early phase, by exerting legal and political maneuvers on their unions and labour federations. In the context of the sustained and high-speed economic development and the concomitant rising living standards for the two countries, those maneuvers have been so far successful. Yet, the state repressions of civil society in general, and of labour unions in particular, have been constrained by state elites' need to avoid provoking civil unrests with some excessively repressive measures (Kleinberg and Clark, 2000, p.291). Besides, public support for civil society can also expand during sustained economic downturn, and worsening abuses of power and corruption. Under those circumstances, the allegiance held by the public to the pseudo-democracies or soft-authoritarianism in Singapore and Malaysia will be put to severe test. Civil society, including labour sector, can then have a more positive role to play for replacing the authoritarian institutions with more fully democratic ones.

Notes

1 Definitions of democracy abound. Dahl's, the most popular version, can be crystallised into political opposition, political participation in selecting leaders and policies via elections and enjoyment of basic civil and political liberties. Democratisation means the process of building up democracy. See O'Donnell, G.A., Schmitter, P.C. and Whitehead, L. (eds) (1986), *Transitions from Authoritarian Rule: Prospects for Democracy*, Johns Hopkins University Press, London. For Robert Dahl's definition, see (1971), *Polyarchy: Participation & Opposition*, Yale University Press, New Haven.
2 Number of interviews: 1044 (20% officials / 80% rank-and-file members) (Tan, 1995).

References

Newspapers:

The Strait Times, Singapore. 1980s-2000.

Other References:

Adler, G. and Webster, E. (1995), 'Challenging transition theory: the labor movement, radical reform, and transition to democracy in South Africa', *Politics & Society*, vol. 23, pp. 75-106.

Ahmad, Z.H. and Alatas, S.M. (1999), 'Malaysia: In an Uncertain Mode', in J.W. Morley (eds), *Driven By Growth: Political Change in the Asia-Pacific Region* (revised edition), M. E. Sharpe, New York.

Anantaraman, V. (1990), *Singapore Industrial Relations System*, McGraw Hill, Singapore.

Arudsothy, P. and Little, C.R. (1993), 'State Regulation and Union Fragmentation in Malaysia', in S.F. Ithaca (ed.), *Organized Labor in the Asia-Pacific Region*, ILR Press, Ithaca, New York.

Bellin, E. (2000), 'Contingent Democrats: Industrialist, Labor, and Democratization in Late-Developing Countries', *World Politics*, vol. 52, pp. 175-205.

Boulanger, C.L. (1992), 'Ethnic Order and Working Class Strategies in West Malaysia',

Journal of Contemporary Asia, vol. 22, pp. 322-39.
Bratton, M. and van de Walle, N. (1992), 'Popular Protest and Political Reform in Africa', *Comparative Politics,* vol. 24, pp. 419-42.
Bureau of Democracy, Human Rights, and Labor (1999), *1999 Country Reports on Human Rights Practices,* U.S. Department of State, February 25, 2000, Washington D.C.
Case, W. (2001), 'Malaysia's Resilient Pseudodemocracy', *Journal of Democracy,* vol.12, pp. 43-57.
Chew, S.B. (1991), *Trade Unionism in Singapore,* McGraw Hill, Singapore.
Collier, R.B. (1999), *Paths Towards Democracy: the Working Class and Elites in Western Europe and South America,* Cambridge University Press, Cambridge.
Crouch, H. (1996), 'Malaysia: Do Elections Make a Different?' in R.H. Taylor (ed.), *The Politics of Elections in Southeast Asia,* Woodrow Center Press & Cambridge University Press, Cambridge, New York and Melbourne.
Deyo, F. (1997), 'Labor and Post-fordist Industrial Restructuring in East and Southeast Asia', *Work & Occupations,* vol. 24 no. 1.
Geddes, B. (1999), 'What Do We Know About Democratization After Twenty Years?' *Annual Review of Political Science,* vol. 2, pp. 115-44.
Jesudason, J.V. (1995), 'Statist Democracy and the Limits to Civil Society in Malaysia', *Journal of Commonwealth & Comparative Politics,* vol. 33 no. 3, pp. 335-56.
Jesudason, J.V. (1996), 'The Syncretic State and the Structuring of Oppositional Politics in Malaysia', in G. Rodan (ed.), *Political Oppositions in Industrializing Asia,* Routledge, London and New York.
Kim, S.H. (2000), *The Politics of Democratization in Korea: the Role of Civil Society,* University of Pittsburgh Press, Pittsburgh.
Kleinberg, R.B. and Clark, J.A. (2000), *Economic liberalization, democratization, and civil society in the developing world,* St. Martin's Press, New York.
Kuruvilla, S. (1995), 'Industrialization Strategy and Industrial Relations Policy in Malaysia', in S. Frenkle and J. Harrod (eds), *Industrialization & Labor Relations: Contemporary Research in Seven Countries,* ILR Press, New York.
Lam, P.E. (1999), 'Singapore: Rich State, Illiberal Regime', in J.W. Morley (ed.), *Driven by Growth: Political Change in the Asia-Pacific Region* (revised edition), M. E. Sharpe, New York.
Leggett, C. (1993a), 'Corporatist Trade Unionism in Singapore', in S. Frenkel (ed.), *Organized Labor in the Asia-Pacific Region,* ILR Press, Ithaca, New York.
Leggett, C. (1993b), 'Singapore's Industrial Relations in the 1990s', in G. Rodan (ed.), *Singapore Changes Guard: Social, Political and Economic Directions in the 1990s,* Longman Cheshire and St. Martins Press, Melbourne and New York.
Lipset, S. M. et. al, (2000), *Democracy's Century,* Freedom House, New York.
Loh, F.K.W. (2000), 'State-Societal Relations in a Rapidly Growing Economy: The Case of Malaysia, 1970-97', in R.B. Kleinberg and A. Janine (eds), *Economic Liberalization, Democratization & Civil Society in the Developing World,* St. Martin's Press, New York and London.
Manuel, P.C. (1998), 'Civil society and democratization in Europe: Comparative Perspectives—Introduction', *Perspectives on Political Science,* vol. 27 no. 3, p. 133.
Means, G.P. (1996), 'Soft Authoritarianism in Malaysia and Singapore', *Journal of Democracy,* vol. 7, pp. 103-17.
Morley, J.W. (1999), *Driven by Growth: Political Change in the Asia-Pacific Region* (revised edition), M.E. Sharpe, New York.
Pelczynski, Z.A. (1988), 'Solidarity and the rebirth of civil society in Poland, 1976-81', in J. Keane (ed.), *Civil society and the State,* Verso Press, London.
Riker, J. (1995), 'Reflections on Government-NGO Relations', in N. Heyzer, J. Riker and A. Quizon (eds), *Government-NGO Relations in Asia,* Macmillan, London, pp. 194-96.

Rodan, G. (1992), 'Singapore's Leadership Transition: Erosion or Refinement of Authoritarian Rule?' *Bulletin of Concerned Asian Scholars*, vol. 24 no. 1, pp. 3-17.
Rodon, G. (1996), 'State-society Relations and Political Opposition in Singapore', in Gary Rodan (ed.), *Political Oppositions in Industrializing Asia*, Routledge, London and New York.
Rodan, G. (1998), 'The Internet and Political Control in Singapore', *Political Science Quarterly*, no.113, pp. 63-89.
Rosa, L. (1990), 'The Singapore State and Trade Union Incorporation', *Journal of Contemporary Asia*, vol. 20 no. 4, pp. 487-508.
Saravanamuttu, J. (2000), *The Non-State Sector: Rise of Human Rights Activism – Labor*. Retrieved in May 1, 2001, from the World Wide Web: http://www.malaysia.net/lists/sangkancil/2000-06/msg00163.html
Silva, S.R. (1998), *Elements in the Shaping of Asian Industrial Relations*, International Labor Organization, Geneva.
Tan, C.H. (1995), *Labor Management Relations in Singapore*, Prentice Hall, Singapore.
Tismaneanu, V. (1992), *Reinventing Politics: Eastern Europe After Communism*, Free Press, New York.
U.S. Department of State (1997), *Singapore Country Report on Human Rights Practices for 1996*, Bureau of Democracy, Human Rights, and Labor, Department of State, Washington D.C..
Valenzuela, J.S. (1989), 'Labor movements in Transitions to Democracy: A Framework for Analysis', *Comparative Politics*, vol. 21 no. 4, pp. 445-72.
Weiss, M.L. (1999), 'What Will Become of Reformasi? Ethnicities and Changing Political Norms in Malaysia', *Contemporary Southeast Asia: A Journal of International & Strategic Affairs*, vol. 21, pp. 424-50.
Woodiwiss, A. (1998), *Globalization, Human Rights and Labor Law in Pacific Asia*, Cambridge University Press, Melbourne.
Zarsky, L. and Tay, S.S.C. (2001), 'Civil Society and the Future of Environmental Governance in Asia Singapore Institute of International Affairs April 2000', in D. Angel and M. Rock (eds), *Asia's Clean Revolution: Industry, Growth and the Environment*, Greenleaf Publishing, Sheffield.

3 Constructing the 'China Circle' in China and Southeast Asia: State Policy, the Presence of Chinese Overseas and Globalisation

PAK NUNG WONG

Introduction

In recent years, due to the fact that the Asia/Pacific region has become a major centre of global capital accumulation, there have been numerous scholarly works devoted to the phenomenon of the China Circle or Greater China (e.g. Hsing, 1994; Naughton, 1994; Sung, 1994; Shambaugh, 1995). What is the China Circle or Greater China? Sociologist Manuel Castells describes the China Circle as,

> ... the powerful networks of ethnic Chinese capital, connecting Hong Kong, Taipei, Singapore, and 'overseas' Chinese business groups (often operating through Hong Kong), all of them with direct linkages to China, forming what observers are calling the 'the China Circle' (Castells, 1996, p.109).

At approximately the same time, in Greater China: the next superpower?, Shambaugh (1995, p.2) asserts that Greater China is 'an adequate term to describe the activities in, and interactions between, mainland China, Hong Kong, Macao, Taiwan and the offshore islands, and overseas Chinese.' According to Harding (1995, p.9), the term refers to economic, cultural, and political processes in the region. The above definitions suggest that the China Circle and Greater China refer to the same phenomenon, so I will use the term China Circle in the following discussion. The term is meant to convey a complex and multidimensional phenomenon and to refer to a geographical region that extends beyond the national boundaries separating China and Southeast Asian nations. It also refers to those economic, political, and cultural activities conducted by those involved in this process of extension. These processes constitute a 'powerful network' in Manuel Castells' words. The China Circle is so powerful and its economic growth has been so rapid in recent years that some predict it will overtake Japan as the dominant regional power (Shambaugh, 1995, p.1).

The China Circle deserves our attention because it involves one of the biggest remaining socialist states in the world, China, and a minority of economically powerful 'outsiders' – the Chinese overseas in Southeast Asia (Chirot and Reid, 1997). China has experienced dramatic changes since the late 1970s when it adopted an open-door policy to attract foreign investment as part of its economic reform. China's recent rapid economic growth has been primarily attributed to its governmental strategy, which regarded as been dubbed 'the China miracle' (see Lin, Cai, and Li, 1996). One of the main initiatives of the economic reform is to attract foreign investment by setting up Special Economic Zones (SEZs) in south China such as Shenzhen in Guangdong province and Xiamen in Fujian province. SEZs enjoy relative autonomy from central government to determine their own policies. As the *qiaoxiang* (homeland for Chinese overseas), southeastern region of Fujian, notably the city of Xiamen, has attracted overseas Chinese capital to support the economic reform since its formulation. The first part of this paper reviews the contribution of this policy to the formation of the China Circle by bringing Chinese capital from overseas to China. I argue that the policy encouraged the awakening of a sense of identity among Chinese overseas, and led further ethnic tensions in Southeast Asia.

The second part of this paper reviews recent developments in the experience of Chinese overseas particularly in terms of economy, that have been noted in widely circulated literature. I argue that by framing Chinese overseas as a formidable ethnic group struggling for hegemony in a regional economy, the region has been 'Orientalised' by discourses of power/knowledge. Notwithstanding the counter-Orientalists' attempt to restrain this development, 'self-orientalisation' has prevailed (Szanton Blanc, 1997; Yao, 1997). Given that China will be more open to foreign markets after it joins the World Trade Organisation (WTO), and Chinese overseas are perceived as engaging in a hegemonic pursuit of the global economy, the concept of globalisation will be examined to see if it can shed light on our understanding of Chinese overseas. Global capitalism has replaced the Cold-War antagonism as the new world order (or disorder?) and is regarded as the dominant force of globalisation (Sklair, 2001). If the overseas Chinese entrepreneurs are emerging as an increasingly cohesive entity that transcends political boundaries in the Asia/Pacific geo-political region (as I shall suggest later), this phenomenon deserves greater attention. I see the phenomenon as constructed, first, by the policy regarding Chinese overseas of the Chinese government and, second, by the portrayal of Chinese overseas in recent, highly circulated literature. I suggest that ethnic Chinese entrepreneurs are emerging as a cohesive globalising force. This paper contains a synthesis of relevant literature, and material from the author's fieldwork in the Philippines and Fujian, China, in 2000.[1]

State Policy: Chinese Overseas Investment and its Impacts

China's Chinese Overseas Policy as Economic Policy

After Mao Zedong died, Deng Xiaoping adopted a series of reforms that quickly reversed the direction of the faltering Chinese economy. The economic reforms in the later 1970s clearly represented a shift in the strategy of the Chinese government by prioritising economic development in the first place. Deng's pragmatic approach was translated into theories such as *you zhongguo tese de shehuizhuyi* (socialism with Chinese characteristics). The economic reform inaugurated a process of selective decentralisation. In the early 1980s, the Chinese reformers encouraged a form of regional decentralisation that presaged a radically new theory of development for the nation, and one that owed little to Mao (Sklair, 1995, p.217). The radical reformers departed from their predecessors by proposing the use of foreign direct investment (FDI) to, first, raise technological and managerial expertise, and, second, to promote exports and stimulate the domestic economy (Howell, 2000, p.120).[2] The SEZs were then established to respond to the political sensitivity within the Chinese Communist Party (CCP). These SEZs are still 'in the experimental stage', but proudly announce annual economic growth figures. The dramatic economic success of the Xiamen SEZ may be attributed to the contribution of Chinese overseas (Howell, 2000, pp.128-129; Hsiao, 1998, p. 2). For instance, since Lee Kuan Yew's visit to Fujian in 1980, many ethnic Chinese tycoons in Southeast Asia of Fujian origin have made substantial investments in Fujian (e.g., the Philippines' Lucio Tan, Indonesia's Liem Sioe Liong, and Malaysia's Robert Kuok). Using the Philippines as an example, I am going to show that China's policy regarding Chinese overseas is an economic strategy to attract FDI from the Southeast Asian Chinese. Focusing on Filipinos' reactions to their country's tycoons' investments in China, I will show the increase in ethnic tension in Southeast Asia. As the discussion will show, ethnic tension and an awakening of Chinese identity and its subsequent process of 're-sinification' are the impacts of Chinese-Filipino investments in China.

Deng's foreign policy, unlike Mao's, encouraged contacts with foreigners in general, which led to business links with Chinese overseas. Deng also noticed the fact many Chinese in Southeast Asia are originally from Fujian. An estimated 90 percent of Chinese in the Philippines are of Fujian origin and, of these, 78 percent of them come from Minnan (the south Fujian) region including Jinjiang, Xiamen and Quanzhou as well as Zhangzhou (Yeung, 2000, p.6). These Chinese occupy the upper economic stratum in local societies. Although Ang See (1995) maintains that the Chinese only represent approximately 1.3 percent of the total population of the archipelago, in early 1980s, Chinese-owned banks possessed 45.4 percent of the total assets of private domestic banks in the Philippines (Suryadinata, 1995). Recent estimates of the Chinese share of the economy by Philippine researchers range from 25 percent to 50 percent, most often in 25 to 35 percent range (Wickberg, 1998). Foreign estimates are sometimes over 50 percent, such research led Chinese reformers to realise that Fujian, with its concentration of *qiaoxiang*, could serve China by spearheading economic reform and modernisation (Chan, 2000, p.62).

In order to embrace this mission, the Overseas Chinese Affairs Office (OCAO) was established at both national and provincial levels to direct the affairs of Chinese overseas. According to a publication edited for the OCAO cadres school, OCAO's functions include,

1. Helping the CCP to devise sound and feasible overseas Chinese policy.
2. Supervising lower levels of government in implementing overseas Chinese policy.
3. Promoting and protecting interests and welfare of overseas Chinese so that their patriotism and love for the nation can be maintained.
4. Encouraging and mobilising overseas Chinese to work for China's reform and modernisation.
5. Contributing to the four modernisations and unification of Hong Kong, Macau and Taiwan (Chan, 2000, pp.64-65).

Under the OCAO, the 'Southern Fujian Triangle Open Area',[3] 'Overseas Chinese Farms', 'Overseas Chinese Factories,' and 14 'Overseas Chinese Economic Development Zones' have been developed to establish economic connections with these Chinese overseas and to attract capital for China's economic development. It is clear that Chinese overseas are, according to Deng's agenda, viewed pragmatically, as a means to develop China's economy. In order to facilitate the contribution of Chinese overseas to China's economy, appropriate social and political programmes have been designed to enhance social ties and political intimacy (Chan, 2000, p.67). These programmes have been subtle in formulation and low-key in execution. Examples are ethnic associations; official visits abroad to build formal links, and the circulation of regular publications such as the *Fujian Qiaoxiang Bao*.

In the opening ceremony of a Fujianese ethnic association in the district of North Point, Hong Kong, which is named *Xianggang Yongning Tongxianghui*, an approximately 50-table banquet was organised for 600 people, including Chinese officials from the provincial, township, and village levels from Fujian and some prominent community leaders and businessmen from the Philippines to celebrate New Year's eve, 2000. During the ceremony, they sang the song of the ethnic association in the Hokkien dialect. They were so accustomed to using their dialect that some kept speaking Hokkien to the waiters and waitresses, though they spoke only Cantonese. The ethnic association serves the function of consolidating the identity of Fujianese overseas and establishing connections across political boundaries.

Although Deng died in 1997, his successor Jiang Zemin continued Deng's economic policy direction. During an official visit to Southeast Asia in 1999, Chinese premier, Zhu Rongji, stated that China's long-term development will follow three strategies:

1. Continue to expand domestic demand and boost economic growth by increasing both investment and consumption.
2. Make a strategic readjustment of our national economic structure and rigorously promote optimisation and upgrading of the industrial pattern.
3. Implement the strategy for all-out development of western China and speed up the development of its central and western region (Zhu, 2000, pp.18-21).

China's policy towards Southeast Asian nations resembles its national policy of economic development. Zhu urges entrepreneurs in Southeast Asia to recognise that 'the great business opportunities in China are within the reach not only of Chinese entrepreneurs but also of those foreign business people who have the courage, vision and aspiration to make investment in China. China welcomes ASEAN entrepreneurs to China for economic, trading, and investment activities, and in particular the all-out development strategy of China's western regions' (Zhu, 2000, p.23 and 27).

Researchers commonly point out that the role of Chinese overseas has contributed significantly to China's economic growth since Deng introduced economic reform to attract FDI. Chinese overseas policy was then adjusted to conform the general development policy of China so that the substantial capital possessed by Chinese overseas could be used to benefit China's economic development. Among the Chinese overseas policies, a set of economic, social, and political programmes were designed to receive ethnic Chinese capital. After the death of Deng, it seems China is pursuing a course to further optimise the use of this resource. What will be the consequences of more interaction between China and Chinese overseas in the China Circle? Two effects emerge: ethnic tension and re-sinification of ethnic Chinese cultural identity.

Impacts: Ethnic Tension and Re-sinification

Lim and Gosling (1997, pp.292-293) maintain that Southeast Asian Chinese investment has been encouraged by several factors: the domestic financial liberalisation of host countries, a strategy of business diversification, China's attraction as a lucrative market, and a sentiment for the motherland, especially on the part of those from the home provinces of Fujian. Although these appear to be fairly understandable reasons for investment in China on the part of Chinese overseas, if we look into the original ethnic dynamic (particularly between Chinese and non-Chinese), we will also understand why transnational investment in China creates ethnic tension. The most obvious source of tension is the perception that there is a diminishing loyalty on the part of the ethnic Chinese to the host nations. This is usually accompanied by the perception of their correspondingly greater attachment to their regional economic interests, which leads to a further consolidation of a common ethnic identity of Chinese overseas across the region - re-sinification.

Philippines researcher Theresa Carino found the Chinese-Filipinos' loyalty to the host nation is suspected (Carino, 1998, p.188). In the case of the Philippines, Chinese-Filipinos, like other Southeast Asian Chinese are economically powerful. Wickberg (1998) found that the poorest 10 percent of Chinese-Filipinos are richer than the poorest 10 percent Filipinos. With the economic disparities between the ethnic Chinese and the majority of the Filipinos, it is not surprising that Carino (1998, p.87) reports that there are 'Filipino nationalists who take every opportunity to raise alarm bells about the "Chinese control of the economy"'. When President Fidel Ramos, was accompanied by six ethnic Chinese tycoons (Alfonso Yuchengco, Lucio Tan, John Gokongwei, Henry Sy, George Ty and Andrew Gotianun) toured to China in early 1993, the six tycoons were told to invest in the Philippine infrastructure. They were then targeted for taxation investigation. A government spokesman, while denying that only Chinese were targeted, responded to the question 'What do you want the Filipino Chinese to do?'

with the comment 'They're already in a position of advantage. They should invest more in the Philippines rather than outside. The country should not be a milking cow' (quoted in Wickberg (1997, p.153). This puts the Chinese in a no-win situation: if they expand their businesses in the archipelago, they are accused of 'excessive control'; if they invest outside of the country, they are guilty of engaging in 'capital flight.' Lim and Gosling (1997) suggest that this is one of the reasons that the Southeast Asian Chinese choose to spread their businesses across various countries.

When the ethnic Chinese diversify their investment in a number of countries, local investments inevitably decrease. In 1993, when Lucio Tan established a commercial bank in Xiamen SEZ, Fujian, (the first Philippine-based bank granted authority to operate in China (Rivera, 1997, p.106)), there was a reported decline of shares in Chinese banks in the Philippine commercial bank system, which was attributed to investment in China (Go, 1995, pp.89-90). Nevertheless, the ethnic Chinese have been enlarging their investments in China (Ang See, 1997b). Willy Laohoo (1995) conducting an exploratory survey, interviewed 66 Filipinos regarding their attitude to Philippine Chinese investments in China. Some of the findings are reproduced in Table 3.1.

Although this survey suffers from flaws including sampling undersize, it gives us some indication of the reaction of Filipinos to Chinese-Filipino investments in China. To briefly summarise, these findings show that the loyalty of Philippine Chinese is seriously questioned and that Filipinos have a generally negative views of Chinese investment abroad, which is considered harmful to the Philippine national economy.

Regarding the increasing ethnic tension, Philippine scholar Theresa Carino comments,

> This of course requires skilful handling on the part of government and greater sensitivity on the part of the ethnic Chinese to long-standing attitudes towards the Chinese among non-Chinese Filipinos. Accusations of divided political loyalties have to be addressed. Myths and stereotypes about the Chinese have to be abolished. This is a serious challenge not only to government and media but also to the academe (Carino, 1995, p.3).

Wickberg (1997, p.177) realistically points out that for Chinese, the 'long-standing association of interest in Chinese culture with loyalty to China will not be dissipated overnight'; the same logic applies to the Filipinos' perception of Chinese-Filipinos. The interest in Chinese culture and emotional attachment to China are both associated with the re-sinification of Chinese overseas ethnic identity.

Inter-ethnic tension between Chinese Filipinos and non-Chinese Filipinos is also related to the issue of re-sinification arising from their investments in China. One of the functions of the OCAO is 'promoting and protecting the interests and welfare of overseas Chinese so that their patriotism and love of nation can be maintained'; the Chinese overseas are maintained to be 'patriotic' to mainland China, which results in an increase in ethnic tension. However, the process of re-sinification may be confined to ethno-cultural identity and not extend to politico-national identity (Ang See, 1998). By definition, 're-sinification' refers to the process of subjective re-identification and attachment with China as a cultural entity and relearning things that reinforce one's Chinese cultural identity.

During my fieldwork in Manila, I had the opportunity to meet with representatives of the Federation of Filipino-Chinese Chamber of Commerce and Industry Inc. (FFCCCII), which represents all chambers within the archipelago. According to Wickberg (1998), the FFCCCII has more influence in the community than any of its predecessors and it has used its influence to negotiate with the Philippine government to mitigate the effects of policies. During my visit in July 2000, and my informant showed me photos taken by the FFCCCII when the Chinese Premier Zhu Rongji visited them in November, 1999. My informant told me that, during the official visit, Zhu encouraged Chinese-Filipino entrepreneurs to conduct *aiguo touzi* (patriotic investment) in China, especially after the opening of western China. I asked for his view of *aiguo touzi*. My respondent thoughtfully replied, 'I am a Philippine citizen. And frankly speaking, I don't believe in *aiguo touzi*. If there is no profitability, how can a businessman invest?'

Table 3.1 Filipino reactions to Chinese-Filipino investment in China

	Emotional attachment to their former homeland is the primary reason why ethnic Chinese are investing in China.		The pursuit of profit is the primary motivation for ethnic Chinese investment in China.	
Response	No.	%	No.	%
Agree	33	50.00	42	63.64
Disagree	12	18.18	8	12.12
Don't Know	21	31.82	16	24.24

	By investing in China, the ethnic Chinese are diverting much needed capital out of the Philippines.		Ethnic Chinese investments in China are strengthening the mainland Chinese economy at the expense of that of the Philippines.	
Response	No.	%	No.	%
Agree	45	68.18	38	57.58
Disagree	12	18.18	19	28.79
Don't Know	9	13.64	9	13.64

	The ethnic Chinese should be discouraged from investing in China; instead they should be encouraged to invest in the Philippines.		Ethnic Chinese investment in the People's Republic is not all bad as it opens the mainland Chinese market to Philippine export.	
Response	No.	%	No.	%
Agree	37	56.06	41	62.12
Disagree	25	37.88	17	25.76
Don't Know	4	6.06	8	12.12

Source: Laohoo, 1995

His response highlighted an important issue: ethnic Chinese's transnational investment in China involves the re-sinification of ethno-cultural identity but less of politico-national identity. Transnational investment could be evidence of 'flexible citizenship' – 'the cultural logics of capitalist accumulation, travel, and displacement that induce subjects to respond fluidly and opportunistically to changing political-economic conditions' (Ong, 1999, p.6). Identities become negotiable and are contextually exploited, according to the actors' intentions. My informant's response shows that he may be primarily interested in economic profits. As a way of acquiring prestige and establishing necessary networks which are beneficial to his investment in China, my informant told that he would choose to donate money for repairing roads, building bridges and schools in his homeland in Fujian. Re-sinification is an active identity negotiation process in which capitalist accumulation remains essential. The Chinese overseas have formed an 'imagined community' in which they share a common Chinese ethnic identity; this community allows them to transcend political boundaries and invest in the China Circle.

As China's economic power grows and its international prestige increases, there are more reasons to be proud to be Chinese. Theresa Carino (1998, pp.188-189) has observed that a positive perception of the Chinese has resulted in a growing desire to be identified as Chinese among Chinese-Filipinos. This is manifested in the increasing interest in learning Putonghua/Mandarin on the part of younger Chinese. As China grows as a centre for business, they realise that their ethnicity and linguistic capacity will give them a competitive edge. Ethnic Chinese youth therefore seek to acquire such symbolic and cultural capital. Their re-sinification is, again, more cultural than political. Theresa Carino stresses that,

> ... there appears to be identification with China and Chinese culture to the extent they represent modernity and economic progress and to the extent they are internationally regarded as symbols of success. Among the Chinese Filipinos and presumably among most Southeast Asian Chinese, there is no clear linkage between ethnic identity and Chinese nationalism or patriotism (Carino, 1998, p.189).

Hence, we may only claim that re-sinification has stirred some degree of ethnic pride in being Chinese. Another source of ethnic pride is the significance of the Chinese economy and the emerging transnational economy in the Asia-Pacific region in which they play a part. As the FFCCCII observes, 'the network of Entrepreneurship that the overseas Chinese have woven through East Asia, the Pacific and – in fact – The World, makes them an economic power in themselves' (FFCCCII, 1994, p.35).

Re-sinification signifies a process of subjective re-identification and attachment with China as a cultural entity, which, in turn, reinforces the Chinese ethnic identity of Chinese overseas. Cultural re-identification and acquisition of linguistic capability are forms of symbolic and cultural capital that can be used in transnational investment in China and other parts of the region. Re-sinification encourages increasing ethnic pride in

'Chineseness', which stems from Chinese economic success in Southeast Asia. In the last decade, there has been a flood of publications portraying the view that ethnic Chinese entrepreneurs are a significant economic power in the Asia/Pacific region.

Framing The 'Overseas Chinese': From Culturalist Explanation To Orientalism

The ethnic Chinese in Southeast Asia are perceived as a formidable ethnic group of entrepreneurs who are claiming hegemony in the region, as the term 'China Circle' implies. This view has been widely circulated in the past decade (see, for example, Kotkin, 1995; Haley, Tan and Haley, 1998; Weidenbaum and Hughes, 1996; Seagrave, 1995). According to Hodder (1996), as a form of cultural determinism, the culturalist explanation of Chinese economic success refers to the reduction of Chinese culture into a few traits that are believed to be so distinctive that they unidimensionally contribute to good economic performance. This section of the paper will examine these claims and show how the ethnic pride of the Chinese overseas is reinforced by the above belief, with reference to Edward Said's 'Orientalism'.

Ethnic Chinese economic success has drawn attentions in the past decade. For instance, to Sterling Seagrave (1995), the Chinese overseas are the 'Lords of the Rim' who own an 'Invisible Empire.' Seagraves starts,

> 'Be so subtle that you are invisible. Be so mysterious that you are intangible. Then you will control your rivals' fate.' - Sun Tzu, The Art of War. When the 1990s began, the West was so spellbound by the economic threat of Japan that it took a while to realize there were more important things happening next door in China (Seagraves, 1995, p.1).

What enables these 'mysterious' and 'intangible' people to threaten and spellbind the West? Haley et al (1998) characterise the overseas Chinese by referring to firstly their Confucian cultural roots and then elucidate how overseas trade and economies are influenced by this inheritance. A second characteristic is role of family in Chinese business; for Chinese, 'the family is a business'. Finally, the importance of *guanxi* (personal relationship) contributes to their cultural uniqueness. These cultural explanations are also found in The Bamboo Network; where Weidenbaum and Hughes (1996, p.52) believes that 'because of their shared culture, ethics and language,' the ethnic Chinese have an 'inherent advantage' over Western investors in the China Circle.

What is misleading in culturalist explanation is the deterministic notion that economic success is the result of a few cultural traits. Social scientists studying the development of capitalism in East and Southeast Asia have investigated these factors to determine their relation to economic success. Wong (1988, 1991) has written on Chinese familism and business trust; Tan (1994), on Chinese socio-cultural resources and adaptability; Redding (1993), on 'spirit of Chinese capitalism', White and Wade (1988), on the role of the government in economic development; Hamilton (1991), and Biggart and Hamilton (1997) on organisational and institutional factors. While these perspectives and approaches cannot offer a definite account of the economic success of the Chinese overseas, without these works, we cannot see the whole picture of this complex phenomenon. The danger of confining oneself to one set of factors is to reduce a world of variables, systems, and interrelationships into a deterministic and unidimensional world, which may 'therefore serve as a template upon which other explanations of other phenomena (economic success) can be hammered out' (Hodder, 1996, p.13). As discourses of power/knowledge, cultural explanations could also serve the purpose of 'Orientalism'.

According to Edward Said (1995), Orientalism refers to the theories and practices that are used by the 'West' to exercise hegemonic control or cultural domination over the 'Orient' and identify themselves vis-à-vis the Orient. Although Said originally conceived Orientalism in the West-Islam context, Orientalism is not confined to the Middle East but exists anywhere there is an unequal power relationship. To summarise, according to Said, Orientalism is first an academic practice to know the 'Orient' – through study at an institutional level. Second, it is a way of thought, which involves a 'binary opposition' and 'exteriority' in which the West is opposed to the Orient (Said, 1995). Third, Orientalism is a corporate institution for dealing with the 'Orient' – making statements about it, authorising views of it, describing it, by teaching it, settling it, and ruling over it. In short, Orientalism is the Western strategy to dominate, restructure and have authority over the Orient (Said, 1995, p.3). Incorporating Foucault's concept of power/knowledge and Gramscian notion of hegemony, Orientalism is also a practice of the discourse of power/knowledge to claim truth-effect for hegemonic purposes. In the 'China Circle', the West encounters the 'Chinese overseas' and regards them as an Oriental subject. We have seen in the foregoing discussion that ethnic Chinese economic success has been attributed to 'culture'. Does this relate to 'Orientalism' as a theory and practice to exert hegemonic control? There cannot be a better answer than Seagrave's warning to the West:

The longer-term outlook is that the Overseas Chinese will greatly increase their commercial lead over the rest of the world – and if the West does not prepare for that possibility, it is in for a major shock (Seagrave, 1995, p.5).

Rupert Hodder (1996, p.14) puts it even more plainly that he sees these views actually serve the purpose of portraying 'Chinese as a single body working in unison towards a common goal and thereby to create a imaginary economic and military threat.' Weidenbaum and Hughes articulate this threat:

> In the case of China, its massive size threatens to alter fundamentally the world balance of economic, political, and military power. Fitting Greater China into a club of large developed nations will not easy. Mutual accommodations will have to be reached. Sooner or later, Western nations will have to accept the realities of a new world economy with three distinct trading regions: North America, Europe, and East Asia (Weidenbaum and Hughes, 1996, pp.195-196).

The Orientalist discourses on Chinese overseas have received critical attentions, notably by Wang Gungwu. Wang (1999) meticulously examines the quoted figures and claims regarding the ethnic Chinese economic success. He notes that the exaggerated and one-sided notion of Chinese economic success is 'the makings of either a larger myth which reinforces the image of Chinese hegemony or a self-fulfilling prophecy' (Wang, 1999, p.16). Those holding an Orientalist point of view see the ethnic Chinese economic success as a threat to the West. Such notions are reminiscent of Samuel Huntington's 'clash of civilisations' thesis (Huntington, 1996). They seem to share the assumption that there are impenetrable cultural faultlines between cultural groups in the post-Cold War era, and that unity within these groups is unquestioned. These fault-lines are viewed as the source of conflict of all kinds. However, one of the great advances of in modern cultural theory is to realise that cultures are hybrid and heterogeneous. In Culture and Imperialism, Said (1994) suggests that cultures and civilisations are actually interrelated and interdependent as well as inter-diffusing; 'uniqueness' is hardly possible due to centuries of migration, colonialism, trade, and, now, globalisation. Andrew Nathan (1993) also observes that the distinctiveness of Chinese culture is a matter of degree relative to that of another culture; there is no absolute, distinctive Chinese culture. Ong (1999, p.190) regards Huntington's notions as Orientalist because Huntington 'dramatises non-West's cultural threat, which the West, especially the United States, must test its mettle against'. Nonetheless, one of the effects of the Orientalist points of view, which anthropologists have noted, is that the Asian subjects (particularly the

Chinese overseas) have absorbed and internalised the construction, a process referred to as 'self-orientalisation' (Ong, 1999; Szanton Blanc, 1997; Yao, 1997).

According to Aihwa Ong (1999, p.81), although self-orientalisation has arisen in a world of Western hegemony and Asian voices are unavoidably inflected by Orientalist essentialism, Asian subjects are still active agencies in receiving and manipulating meanings. Nonini and Ong (1997) suggest that a new social movement is emerging in the ethnic Chinese entrepreneurial community in the China Circle. This movement, could be seen, from the Orientalist point of view, as a hegemonic project for controlling and accumulating capital. After my informant shared his experience at the World Chinese Entrepreneurs Convention in 1999, he told me that, when asked to express his opinion about China's future after joining WTO, he said,

> The WTO is a tool for strong Western nations to take advantage of the others. Big fish eat small ones. We are going to takeover them [WTO]. We still see there are lots of business opportunities for us in China.

Self-orientalisation is the recognition of Orientalist essentialism, leading to pursuit of a possible Chinese hegemony in the China Circle. On one hand, the ethnic pride of overseas Chinese stems from their economic success and China's entry into the global market. On the other hand, ethnic pride may also be related to self-orientalisation. Given that Chinese overseas are overly-represented in the business sector in Southeast Asia, it is not surprising that their ethnic pride would have a reinforcing effect on the actualisation of further capital accumulation and the desire to claim for hegemony in the region. In the global era, their transnational success would transform public opinion and challenge the perception that overseas Chinese are an economically powerful minority who are uninterested in politics.

Conclusion: 'China Circle' in Action – Ethnic Chinese Entrepreneurs and Globalisation

Chinese overseas have long been perceived as economically powerful but uninterested in politics. However, when ethnic Chinese entrepreneurs mobilise resources to respond to changing political-economic conditions, especially those imposed by local and overseas nation states, the politics of economic power will come into play. Given their elite economic status and emerging political power, I suggest that ethnic Chinese entrepreneurs' globalisation would shed light on our understanding of the Chinese overseas.

In the case of the Philippines, when a Chinese-Filipino entrepreneur, who was once mayor in a North Luzon city, was asked why he ran for mayor, he replied, 'When the business was becoming bigger and bigger, more difficulties were caused by the rivals. If you still want to do business, you will need political power.' Rivera (1997, pp.106-109) observes that the politics of economic power relies on the development of partnerships with local elites that the leading Chinese families have cultivated through years of business. The partnerships provide links to politicians, well-placed government officials, and military generals. Chinese-Filipino entrepreneurs have shown a remarkable degree of social and political skills that have enabled them to operate effectively in the transnational context. One of the fieldwork informants in Manila, originally from Jinjiang, Fujian, is now serving as the head of the Philippine Jin Jiang General Association Inc. (PJJGAI). He maintains that the PJJGAI is mainly responsible for coordinating relationships between Chinese-Filipino investors and Chinese government officials and other local bodies in Jinjiang, Fujian. As an entrepreneur who owns canned food and metal factories, he also mediates his Filipino fellow citizens and Chinese officials when there are 'disputes' or 'complaints'.

Ethnic pride, re-sinification, economic success and self-orientalisation all contribute to the pursuit, on the part of ethnic Chinese entrepreneurs, of a hegemonic project in the global economy. The ethnic Chinese have identified with other Southeast Asian Chinese who are playing a key role in globalisation. In 1991, the First World Chinese Entrepreneurs Convention in Singapore attracted about 800 delegates from 30 countries. In their study of Chinese transnationalism, Nonini and Ong quoted the chairman's welcoming speech:

> Today, there are some 25 million ethnic Chinese outside of China, the bulk of whom are concentrated around the fast-growing Pacific Rim. Individually and collectively, they are well-placed to play a key role in realising the potential and promise of globalisation, particularly in making the Pacific Century come true (quoted in Nonini and Ong, 1997, p.4).

In the same year, *Yazhou Zhoukan,* which claims to be 'the only international Chinese weekly' held the first annual *Guoji Huashang 500* (International Chinese Merchants 500). Like *Fortune's* Global 500, *Yazhou Zhoukan's Guoji Huashang 500* lists the 500 most financially successful Chinese companies in Asia/Pacific region. Although these companies' financial profiles are dwarfed by those listed in *Fortune's* Global 500, it is clear that an increasingly cohesive Chinese transnational entrepreneurial community will have global implications.

In his study of Fortune's Global 500, sociologist Leslie Sklair defines 'globalisation' by distinguishing 'transnational' and 'global' (Sklair, 2000, pp.2-3). 'Transnational' refers to 'forces, processes, and institutions that cross borders but do not derive their power and authority from the state'; 'global' refers to 'the goals to which processes of globalisation are leading. The most important of these goals are the establishment of a borderless global economy, the complete denationalisation of all corporate procedures and activities, and the eradication of economic nationalism.' Whilst the global is the goal, the transnational is the attempt to transcend nation-states in an international system. Sklair also suggests that the Transnational Corporations (TNCs) and an increasingly cohesive Transnational Capitalist Class (TCC) are the major 'globalisers' who conduct transnational practices to achieve a borderless global economy. Social movement is conventionally perceived to be revolutionary and anti-establishment in nature. Unlike this conventional understanding, the globalisers' transnational hegemonic pursuit is termed as the 'elite social movement', which can maintain and transform the status quo (Sklair, 1997). In the Asia-Pacific context, with their elite economic status and emerging political power, the ethnic Chinese entrepreneurs are emerging to be an increasingly cohesive globalising force to establish a regional economy in the China Circle.

Follow the opening of China, as the biggest potential market in the world, will there be an ethnic fault-line between Fortune's Global 500 and *Yazhou Zhoukan's Guoji Huashang 500* in their hegemonic pursuit of global capitalism? In the foregoing discussions, I have suggested that the China Circle is constructed by China's policy towards Chinese overseas, re-sinification of ethnic Chinese identity as a result of ethnic pride, and the vision of Chinese hegemony in the Asia-Pacific region induced by self-orientalisation. Transnational activities will follow the further opening of the biggest potential market in the world when China joins the WTO. The question of whether ethnic faultline will remain in the context of global capitalism will require further empirical investigation.

The author would like to thank Frank Pieke and Brian Alleyne for their reading and commenting on the early draft.

Notes

1 Fieldwork details: south-eastern Fujian, China (2 weeks in February, 2000); Manila, Luzon and Visayas, the Philippines (2 weeks in July, 2000).
2 Encouraging FDI is only one of the reform programmes; for reform details, results and figures, see Lin, Cai, and Li, 1996, Chapters 6 and 7.
3 According to Chan (2000, p.68), a recent survey shows that the triangle area contains the largest number of Fujianese overseas in Fujian.

References

Ang See, T. (1995), 'The Chinese in the Philippines: Continuity and Change', in L. Suryadinata (ed.), *Southeast Asian Chinese: The Socio-Cultural Dimension*, Times Academic Press, Singapore.
Ang See, T. (1997a), *Chinese In the Philippines: Problems and Perspectives (Volume I)*, Kaisa Para Sa Kaunlaran Inc, Manila.
Ang See, T. (1997b), *Chinese In the Philippines: Problems and Perspectives (Volume II)*, Kaisa Para Sa Kaunlaran Inc, Manila.
Biggart, N.W. and Hamilton, G.G. (1997), 'Explaining Asian Business Success: Theory No. 4', in N.W. Biggart, G.G. Hamilton and M. Orru (eds), *The Economic Organisation of East Asian Capitalism*, Sage, Thousand Oaks, CA.
Carino, T. (1995), 'China, Taiwan, and the Ethnic Chinese in the Philippine Economy: An Overview', *Chinese Studies Journal*, vol. 5, pp. 1-3.
Carino, T. (1998), 'Philippine-China Relations and the Philippine Chinese', in G. Zhuang (ed.), *Ethnic Chinese at the Turn of the Centuries (Volume II)*, Fujian Renmin Chubanshe, Fuzhou.
Castells, M. (1996), *The Rise of Network Society*, Blackwell, Oxford.
Chan, C. Y. (2000), 'The Overseas Chinese', in Y.M. Yeung and D.K.Y. Chu (eds), *Fujian: A Coastal Province in Transition and Transformation*, The Chinese University Press, Hong Kong.
Chirot, D. and Reid, A. (eds) (1997), *Essential Outsiders: Chinese and Jews in the Modern Transformation of Southeast Asia and Central Europe*, University of Washington Press, Seattle.
Federation of Filipino-Chinese Chambers of Commerce and Industry Inc. (1994), *40 Years Ruby Anniversary Commemorative Album*, Federation of Filipino-Chinese Chambers of Commerce and Industry Inc., Manila.
Go, B. J. (1995), 'Ethnic Chinese in Philippine Banking', *Chinese Studies Journal*, vol. 5, pp. 85-91.
Haley, G.T., Tan, C.T. and Haley, U.C.V. (1998), *New Asian emperors: The Overseas Chinese, Their Strategies And Competitive Advantages*, Butterworth Heinemann, Oxford.
Hamilton, G. (1991), 'The Organisational Foundations of Western and Chinese Commerce: A Historical and Comparative Analysis', in Hamilton, G. (ed.), *Business Networks And Economic Development in East and Southeast Asia*, Centre of Asian Studies, University of Hong Kong, Hong Kong.
Harding, H. (1995), 'The Concept of "Greater China": Themes, Variations and Reservations', in D. Shambaugh (ed.), *Greater China: The Next Superpower?*, Oxford University Press, Oxford.
Hodder, R. (1996), *Merchant Princes of the East: Cultural Delusions, Economic Success and the Overseas Chinese in Southeast Asia*, John Wiley and Sons, Chichester.

Howell, J. (2000), 'The Political Economy of Xiamen Special Economic Zone', in Y.M. Yeung and D.K.Y. Chu (eds), *Fujian: A Coastal Province in Transition and Transformation*, The Chinese University Press, Hong Kong.

Hsiao, H.H.M. (1998), *Social Transformation, Nascent Civil Society and the Taiwanese Capital in Fujian. (Occasional Paper No. 84)*, Hong Kong Institute of Asia-Pacific Studies, The Chinese University of Hong Kong, Hong Kong.

Hsing, Y.T. (1994), *Blood Thicker than Water: Networks of Local Chinese Officials and Taiwanese Investors in Southern China*, paper delivered at the conference on The Economies of the China Circle, Hong Kong, September 1-3, 1994, University of California Institute on Global Conflict and Cooperation.

Huntington, S. P. (1996), *The Clash of Civilisations and the Remaking of World Order*, Simon and Schuster, New York.

Kotkin, J. (1992), *Tribes: How Race, Religion and Identity Determine Success in the New Global Economy*, Random House, New York.

Laohoo, W. L. (1995), 'Filipino Reactions to Philippine Chinese Investments in China: An Exploratory Survey.' *Chinese Studies Journal*, vol. 5, pp. 31-45.

Lim, L.Y.C. and Gosling, L.A.P. (1997), 'Strengths and Weaknesses of Minority Status for Southeast Asian Chinese at a Time of Economic Growth and Liberalisation', in D. Chirot and A. Reid (eds), *Essential Outsiders: Chinese and Jews in the Modern Transformation of Southeast Asia and Central Europe*, University of Washington Press, Seattle.

Lin, J.Y., Cai, F. and Li, Z. (1996), *The China Miracle: Development Strategy and Economic Reform*, The Chinese University Press, Hong Kong.

Nathan, A. (1993), 'Is Chinese Culture Distinctive? - A Review Article.' *The Journal of Asian Studies*, vol. 52 no. 4, pp. 923-36.

Naughton, B. (1994), *Increasing Economic Interaction in the China Circle in the Context of East Asian Growth*, paper delivered at the conference on The Economies of the China Circle, Hong Kong, September 1-3, 1994, University of California Institute on Global Conflict and Cooperation.

Nonini, D.M. and Ong, A. (1997), 'Introduction: Chinese Transnationalism as an Alternative Modernity', in D.M. Nonini, and A. Ong, A. (eds), *Ungrounded Empire: The Cultural Politics of Modern Chinese Transnationalism*, Routledge, New York.

Ong, A. (1999), *Flexible Citizenship: The Cultural Logics of Transnationality*, Duke University Press, Durham.

Redding, S.G. (1993), *The Spirit of Chinese Capitalism*, Walter de Gruyter, Berlin.

Rivera, T.C. (1997), 'The Leading Chinese-Filipino Business Families in the Post-Marcos Era: a Socio-Political Profile', *Chinese Studies Journal*, vol. 7, pp. 103-10.

Said, E. (1994), *Culture and Imperialism*, Vintage, London.

Said, E. (1995), *Orientalism: Western Conceptions of the Orient*, Penguin, London.

Seagrave, S. (1995), *Lords Of The Rim: The Invisible Empire of the Overseas Chinese*, G.P. Putnam's Sons, New York.

Shambaugh, D. (ed.) (1995), *Greater China: The Next Superpower?*, Oxford University Press, Oxford.

Shambaugh, D. (1995), 'Introduction: The Emergence of "Greater China"', in D. Shambaugh (ed.), *Greater China: The Next Superpower?*, Oxford University Press, Oxford.

Sklair, L. (1995), *Sociology of the Global System (second edition)*, The Johns Hopkins University Press, Baltimore.

Sklair, L. (1997), 'Social Movements for Global Capitalism: the Transnational Capitalist Class in Action', *Review of International Political Economy*, vol. 4, pp. 514-38.

Sklair, L. (2001), *The Transnational Capitalist Class*, Blackwell, Oxford.

Sta. Romana, C. (1997), 'Chinese Politics in the Post-Deng Era: Challenges and Scenarios', *Chinese Studies Journal*, vol. 6, pp. 5-24.

Sung, Y.W. (1994), *Hong Kong and the Economic Integration of the China Circle*, paper delivered at the conference on The Economies of the China Circle, Hong Kong, September 1-3, 1994, University of California Institute on Global Conflict and Cooperation.
Suryadinata, L. (1995), 'Southeast Asian Chinese Society and Culture: an Introduction', in L. Suryadinata (ed.), *Southeast Asian Chinese: The Socio-Cultural Dimension*, Times Academic Press, Singapore.
Szanton Blanc, C. (1997), 'The Thoroughly Modern 'Asian': Capital, Culture, and Nation in Thailand and the Philippines', in D.M. Nonini and A. Ong (eds), *Ungrounded Empire: The Cultural Politics of Modern Chinese Transnationalism*, Routledge, New York.
Tan, C.B. (1994), 'Culture and Economic Performance with Special Reference to the Chinese in Southeast Asia', in T. Ang See and B.J. Go (eds), *The Ethnic Chinese: Proceedings of the International Conference on: Changing Identities and Relations in Southeast Asia*, Kaisa Para Sa Kaunlaran Inc, Manila.
Wang, G. (1999), *China and Southeast Asia: Myths, Threats and Culture*, Singapore University Press, Singapore.
Weidenbaum, M. and Hughes, S. (1996), *The Bamboo Network: How Expatriate Chinese Entrepreneurs are Creating a New Economic Superpower in Asia*, The Free Press, London.
Wickberg, E. (1997), 'Anti-Sinicism and Chinese Identity Options in the Philippines', in D. Chirot and A. Reid (eds), *Essential Outsiders: Chinese and Jews in the Modern Transformation of Southeast Asia and Central Europe*, University of Washington Press, Seattle.
Wickberg, E. (1998), 'The Philippines', in L. Pan (ed.), *The Encyclopedia of the Chinese Overseas*, Chinese Heritage Centre, Singapore.
White, G. and Wade, R. (1988), 'Developmental States and Markets in East Asia: An Introduction', in G. White (ed.), *Developmental States in East Asia*, St. Martin's Press, New York.
Wong, S.L. (1988), 'The Applicability of Asian Family Values to other Socio-cultural Settings', in P. Berger and H.H.M. Hsiao (eds), *In Search of an East Asian Developmental Model*, Transaction Books, New Brunswick.
Wong, S.L. (1991), 'Chinese Entrepreneurs and Business Trust', in G. Hamilton (ed.), *Business Networks and Economic Development in East and Southeast Asia*, Centre of Asian Studies, University of Hong Kong, Hong Kong.
Yao, S. (1997), 'The Romance of Asian Capitalism: Geography, Desire and Chinese Business', in M.T. Berger and D.A. Borer (eds), *The Rise of the East Asia. Critical Visions of the Pacific Century*, Routledge, London.
Yeung, Y.M. (2000), 'Introduction', in Y.M. Yeung and D.K.Y. Chu (eds), *Fujian: A Coastal Province in Transition and Transformation*, The Chinese University Press, Hong Kong.
Zhu, R. (2000), *China and Asia in the New Century*, Institute of Southeast Asian Studies, Singapore.

4 Gender and Development in Post-Crisis Southeast Asia
VIVIENNE WEE

How has the Asian Economic Crisis impacted on Women?

Since the Economic Crisis began in July 1997, the East Asian 'miracle' has become the East Asian 'debacle'. The region descended suddenly and rapidly into economic chaos, out of which it has yet to emerge. As a result of the Crisis, by 1998, the GNP of Malaysia had fallen by more than 8 percent, that of Thailand by nearly 8 percent and that of Indonesia by as much as 20 percent (UNIFEM, 2000, p.32). About 20 million were added to the 30 million already below the poverty line in the affected countries. Eighteen million more people became openly unemployed in Indonesia, Thailand and Korea. Real wages fell by 10 percent in Thailand and by 40 to 60 percent in Indonesia (see World Bank, 1998).

This paper does not deal with the causes of the Asian financial crisis, or with its financial and political consequences.[1] Instead, the paper focuses on the impact of the Crisis on women in Southeast Asia. It compares their situation before and after the Crisis, and examines some implications for future development trajectories.

The Crisis has impacted not with equal force on all the ten countries that make up Southeast Asia – namely, Brunei, Myanmar, Cambodia, Indonesia, Laos, Malaysia, Philippines, Singapore, Thailand, and Vietnam. Nevertheless, throughout the region, women have been among the hardest hit by the economic chaos. The burden of the economic 'debacle' is falling forcefully on women through mass unemployment, devalued currencies, food shortages, pharmaceutical shortages, rising crime rates, cutbacks in social services, and worse. Millions of women have been affected in one way or another.[2] This chapter cites examples from Indonesia, Malaysia, Thailand, Vietnam and the Philippines, which are among the countries most seriously affected by the Crisis.

Evidence of the impact of the Crisis on women in Southeast Asia is scattered. Nevertheless, an understanding of the impact may be discerned from the following examples.

Unemployment

In Indonesia, women made up 40 percent of the labour force but 50 percent of the openly unemployed.[3] Of the estimated 13 million unemployed in Indonesia due to the crisis, 43 percent are women, according to the Jakarta Office of the International Labour Organization (ILO).[4] The Indonesian textile industry, which employs mostly women, has already laid off more than half a million workers, while footwear manufacturers have laid off about 10,000 workers (The Straits Times, March, 17, 1998). In the Philippines, the number of unemployed reached 3.9 million in 1999, with 40 percent being women (The Philippine Star, June, 12, 1999). According to the 1999 figures of the International Labour Organisation (ILO), women's unemployment rose to 15 percent, compared to 12 percent for men.[5] In Thailand, women comprise 80 percent of unskilled labour laid off in the manufacturing sector (Bangkok Post, February 22, 1998).

Table 4.1 Lay-offs by sector and sex in Thailand, January 1997 - February 1998

Sector	Women	Men
Garments	2,120	648
Textiles	3,032	1,025
Shoes, leather products	1,533	521
Food processing	1,803	836
Finance	3,337	2,622
Electrical, electronic	3,025	1,854

Source: ILO, 1998, pp.19-20

Illegal Labour Migration

There has been a tenfold increase in the number of women attempting to leave Indonesia illegally to seek work abroad, according to the non-governmental organisation called Women's Solidarity for Human Rights (The Straits Times, June 11, 1998).

Dropping out of School

The number of children dropping out of elementary school in poor areas of Indonesia doubled in 1998, with girls forming the great majority of the dropouts (International Herald Tribune, June 12, 1998).

Poverty and Malnutrition

In Indonesia and the Philippines, half the population are now living on less than US$2 a day.[6] Women comprise the most vulnerable part of this population. 'About 40 percent of 15 million Indonesian female workers lack adequate nutrition, many suffer from malnutrition which also reduces their productivity'.[7] Karlina Leksono and Gadis Arivia of the University of Indonesia said, 'We saw poor mothers in the slum facing a critical situation of life and death. We could be on the way to losing a generation from malnutrition' (Newsweek, March 9, 1998). Women home workers in Thailand require loans during the crisis period to tide them over several problems such as receiving less orders, late payments, and lower piece-rate wages. But moneylenders are charging exorbitant interest rates of 20 percent per month'.[8]

Family Stress and Domestic Violence

Women suffer when husbands and fathers are unable to cope with the stress caused by the crisis. In Thailand, 'men are ... killing themselves for fear of growing debts. Others have turned to using drugs and worse, abusing their own children' (Bangkok Post, March 8, 1998). 'The evidence is anecdotal but the strains of financial hardship are leading to more violence at home. "If I don't have enough food in the house, my husband hits me", says a woman selling chillies in a city market in Indonesia' (International Herald Tribune, June 12, 1998).

Many more examples can be added to those mentioned above. When women are unable to sustain their everyday livelihoods, it signals the emergence of the following dangers:

1. A lack of food security
2. A lack of employment in the formal sector
3. A lack of income-generation opportunities in the informal sector
4. A rise in prostitution and sexual exploitation
5. A rise in the trafficking of girls and children
6. And consequently, a collapse of family and community structures

Given the disproportionate impact of the Asian Economic Crisis on women, would it not be the case that they would be the ones to benefit most from economic recovery? To answer this question, we need to consider their economic role prior to the Crisis, as well as the gender implications of economic recovery.

What was Women's Economic Significance in the East Asian 'Miracle Economies'?

During the heyday of the 'miracle', the countries of East and Southeast Asia achieved record levels of growth based largely on the labour of women workers in the export industries. Women workers dominated the export sector. For example, in Malaysia in 1993, women accounted for 71.3 percent of the workf :ce in the manufacture of electrical machinery (ILO, 1999, Table 6.9). According to the 1995 figures of the ILO, in East and Southeast Asia, women accounted for more than 80 percent of the work force in the export zones.[9]

Alexander (1999, p.31) points out that it was women's cheap labour that gave Southeast Asia's export industries a 'competitive edge' in the global market. But we should ask why women should have constituted the workforce of choice. On the relatively positive side, women were perceived as skilled, patient and painstaking. On the relatively negative side, however, women were seen as cheaper, more compliant, not unionised, and easier to dismiss using life-cycle events such as marriage and childbirth. It was thus women's supply of cheap 'flexible' labour that enabled the export industries to compete globally.

The flexibility of women's labour is associated with the casualisation of labour – for example, part-time work, piece-rate contracts, sub-contracting and home-based work. This is rooted in the gender division of labour in everyday life, such that women in most societies are allocated the responsibility of caring for the dependent members of the community – the young, the old, the sick and the disabled. Because of their gender role in society, women tend to enter the workforce with a propensity to seek casualised forms of employment that would enable them to combine their income-earning activities with their caring activities.

Women's gendered propensity for casualised labour meshed with the demand of companies to maximise profits through lowering labour costs. As a result, even in the heyday of industrial growth, women became an expendable workforce that could be flexibly hired and fired to meet the needs of external competitiveness. It is this expendable workforce that has been worst hit by the economic contraction brought about by the financial crisis.

In the entire Southeast Asian region, women have come to comprise a major share of the labour force in most sectors:

Table 4.2 Women's percentage share in economic sectors in ASEAN[10]

Sectors	Percentage
Wholesale, retail trade	51
Manufacturing	46
Community and personal services	45
Agriculture	37
Finance, business services	35

Source: ASEAN, 1997[11]

This increase in women's percentage share of the workforce is, however, a mixed blessing. On the one hand, it has increased women's labour force participation rate and concomitantly, their income-earning capacity. But on the other hand, women's entry into the labour force has been on less than equitable terms. As pointed out by Benaria (1989, p.249), 'there is little variation in the fact that female occupations are paid less and that, when a male occupation becomes feminised, relative wages tend to decline'. Given existing gender inequities, the increasing feminisation of the workforce is also indicative of economies that have become increasingly reliant on a cheap and flexible workforce.

This trend is not limited to Southeast Asia alone. As shown by Standing (1996), there is 'global feminisation through flexible labour'. He relates this to the rise of the 'supply-side politico-economic agenda that has dominated policy making in most of the world in the 1980s' (Standing, 1996, p.405).

> The supply-side model entails a global strategy of growth based on open economies, with trade liberalisation as vital and export-led growth as the only viable development strategy. As such, cost competitiveness is elevated to utmost significance, and from that, labour market regulations become 'rigidities', which raise costs and thus harm living standards and employment. An irony is that in the 1980s many of the previous objectives of economic growth, notably a whole set of labour and social rights, became perceived increasingly as costs and rigidities....
>
> The global pursuit of flexible low-cost labour has encouraged industrial

enterprises everywhere to reduce their fixed wage labour force, make payment systems more flexible, and use more contract workers, temporary labour, and out-sourcing through use of homeworking or subcontracting to small informal enterprises, that are not covered by labour or other regulations and that bear the risks and uncertainty of fluctuating business. That is the context in which to assess the changing labour market position of both men and women in many parts of the world (Standing, 1996, p.406 and 408).

As noted by Alexander (1999, p.31), the World Bank's book The East Asian Miracle (1993), like most accounts, makes frequent reference to the 'competitive edge' in cheap and efficient labour that many Asian countries have employed in breaking into world trade:

> In effect, we can understand the term 'competitive edge' as a code name for the vital yet unacknowledged role that Asian women have played, as their countries have become world leaders in growth and key members of an increasingly integrated global workforce. The rate of entry of women into the industrial labour force in Asia over the past decade has been higher than that of men. They have performed as a cheap labour pool in the export manufacturing industries and in the burgeoning service industries in finance and information technology....
>
> No country that has expanded its export manufacturing capacity has done so without drawing an increasing proportion of women into industrial waged employment Alexander (1999, p.31 and 36).

Table 4.3 below shows the extent to which the increase in manufacturing capacity is correlated with increased female employment in the manufacturing sector. These figures show that in the early 1990s, for the five ASEAN countries listed, women accounted for more than 40 percent of the manufacturing work force, while manufacturing accounted for more than 20 percent of GDP. From 1970 to 1992, women's employment in this sector rose from an average of 40.3 percent to 46.7 percent. Concurrently, the manufacturing sector's share of GDP rose from an average of 13.8 percent to 25.8 percent.

Table 4.3 Women's share of manufacturing employment and manufacturing's share of GDP in five ASEAN countries, 1970-1992

Country	Women's share of manufacturing employment (in %)			Manufacturing sector as % of GDP	
	1970	1980	1992	1965	1991
Indonesia	42.6	42.2	46.6	8	21
Malaysia	29.0	39.1	47.7	9	27 *
Philippines	53.4	40.3	45.6	20	26
Singapore	33.6	46.0	43.9	18	29
Thailand	42.7	45.4	49.9	14	27

* Figure of 1992
Sources: Praparpun, 1998, p.126 and *Asia Business Network* at http://www.abisnet.com/malaysia_1.htm

Joekes (1995) shows a direct link between trade in export-oriented manufactures and women's employment.

> Industrialisation under a strategy of national autarky provides 'jobs for the boys', i.e., for a male 'labour aristocracy', whereas the types of industry that expand in response to foreign market opportunities in an open trading regime rely heavily on the use of female labour. In the contemporary era, no strong export performance in manufactures by any developing country has ever been secured without reliance on female labour.
>
> The breakthrough into exports of manufactures typically begins for a low-income country with exports of clothing, footwear and processed foods, followed (if diversification takes place) by production of micro-circuits and electronic products for consumer or business use. In both of these broad product categories women workers constitute the majority of the manufacturing sector workforce. [12]

Benaria (1989, p.248) confirms this linkage:

> Important changes have taken place, particularly...in the shift in employers' preference from men to women in some industrial production processes. This preference-shift has been amply documented for the case of labour intensive, cheap labour, export-processing industries associated with transnational capital...and also with national capital.... It is well known that the proportion of women in many of the world's export processing zones can be as high as 80-90 percent.

According to UNCTAD's 1994 study of 200 export-processing zones employing about two million workers in 50 countries, 80 percent of the workers are women, mostly between 16 and 25 years of age. These workers work hours that are 25 percent longer than schedules prevailing in other firms; the women are paid 20 to 50 percent less than men working in the same zones. There is considerable literature about the exploitative and inequitable conditions of employment suffered by women in these export-processing zones.[13]

Benaria (1989, pp.246-247) points out that the direct employment of women by multinational firms represents only a small fraction of women's employment globally—perhaps no more than 0.5 percent as reported by UNTC/ILO in 1985. However, she notes, 'multinationals generate a multiplier effect through subcontracting chains, linking them with domestic firms of all sizes; women's employment is generated particularly in labour-intensive production' (Benaria, 1989, p.247).

In Southeast Asia, many of these domestic firms are small and medium Enterprises (SMEs).[14] In Thailand in 1995, SMEs accounted for 90 percent of total registered businesses, employing 73.8 percent of the total work force (Praparpun, 1999, p.126). This profile applies beyond Southeast Asia to APEC.[15] Within APEC, SMEs make up over 95 percent of all enterprises and provide 32 to 84 percent of employment (Lee et al, 1994). Women form the majority of the work force of SMEs.

> Although it seems that the number of SMEs is increasing as a result of global trading trends, these SMEs operate on a very small scale as sub-contractors within the informal sector. These small businesses are attractive to large numbers of female entrepreneurs and workers. This is because small, informal businesses are easy to enter, hours are flexible, much work can be done at home, high skills are not required, etc. These factors permit, indeed encourage, the entry of low-skilled women workers. (Praparpun, 1999, p.126)

Praparpun (1999, p.125) also notes that 'many SMEs operate within the informal sector and are thus unregistered, having no legal status'. This also means that their workers are unregistered workers in the informal sector. Women are the majority of such workers. For example, women engaged in informal economic activities, such as homeworking, food processing and petty trading are estimated as constituting 65 percent in Indonesia (according to UN figures, 1995) and 62 percent in the Philippines (according to ESCAP figures, 1996).[16]

Standing (1996, p.411) argues that there is an increasing global trend towards women working in export-oriented manufacturing in the informal sector:

[The] female proportion of productive wage workers rose in all countries that had set up large Export Processing Zones—the Dominican Republic, El Salvador, Honduras, Hong Kong, Republic of Korea, Malaysia, Mexico, the Philippines, Puerto Rico, Singapore, Sri Lanka and Thailand. Productive employment, of course, covers only direct wage earners, and there is growing evidence that...much of the employment connected with export industries...is indirect, if not concealed altogether. A very good example comes from a study in Mexico that should be replicated in many more countries. This study showed that production was organised through a complex process of subcontracting, with the labour-intensive, low-paid, more informal activities being put out to women workers, many of whom were not recorded in the workforce. This is a classic instance of 'modern' production relying on what is depicted as 'premodern', or informal, labour relations. The pressure to avoid overhead and other indirect labour costs in the quest for competitiveness has surely accentuated such tendencies.

The point is: women's economic role in the heyday of the East Asian 'miracle' was part of a larger picture of the global restructuring of capital, labour and profits. In the export industries in Southeast Asia (and other developing countries), there was a convergence between the flexibilisation of labour and the feminisation of labour. The gender division of labour in society, which predisposes women to favour forms of casualised labour (e.g. part-time, home-based) created a source of cheap labour supply for the export industries. The demand of industries for cheap casualised labour of this sort has brought about mode of production that is organised through a complex process of subcontracting, with the labour-intensive, low-paid, more informal activities being put out to undocumented women workers.

Standing (1996, p.405) relates this development to the rise of the 'supply-side politico-economic agenda that has dominated policy making in most of the world in the 1980s'.[17] US economists have tended to discuss supply-side economics in terms of tax cuts (see Krugman, 1994). But as argued by Standing (1996), in many developing countries, including those of Southeast Asia, the supply-side agenda was operationalised through the deregulation of labour. This was the context for the massive entry of women as the workforce of choice for the export industries. The result was the so-called 'miracle' of export-led growth in Southeast Asia, founded as it was on a regime of feminised, cheap and flexible labour.

Economic Recovery for Whom?

Despite their vital economic significance, women were generally invisible in policy discourse during the heyday of the 'miracle'. After the crisis of

1997, they have become even more marginalised. This increased marginalisation from mainstream discourse and decision-making means the omission of women's livelihoods in any rescue package or recovery strategy.

The Asian economic crisis is not just a crisis for the financial sector, but also a livelihood crisis for vulnerable sectors of society, especially women. The World Bank has acknowledged that 'this is a financial crisis and a human crisis – and both dimensions need to be addressed':

> Civic groups are beginning to report how these issues [of unemployment, shortages of food and medical supplies, price increases, a squeeze on health and education programmes] are playing out in terms of people's lives:
> – Job losses linked to increases in crime and violence
> – A rise in the numbers of street children and prostitution
> – And women's roles in households and job markets coming under pressure. [18]

All these impact with gender-specific force on women. But there are no clear indications how women are to benefit from the economic recovery programme. No funds have been earmarked to address the gender-specific needs and realities of women bearing the brunt of the Asian economic crisis. Instead, women are likely to be doubly victimised. Not only are they likely to be the first to be fired, they are likely to be bypassed in the economic recovery process, as shown by their omission in programmes directed at job creation.

The main reason for this is their relative invisibility, first in the economic development of their countries, then in the economic recovery process. There is a critical information gap in the policy discourse that has become a gender gap. The gendered specificity of the 'human crisis' needs to be understood if the measures undertaken are to be appropriate for women's livelihood needs and realities.

For example, considerable sums of money have gone into public works programmes for job creation. But how many women are being included in these public works jobs? An instance of this is the World Bank's recovery package for Indonesia. On the one hand, as international donors at a World Bank meeting agreed, 'women and children would suffer in greater proportion as basic services are reduced by the expected major contraction in budgetary expenditures...[and there is]...the need to pay special attention to the needs of women'.[19]

On the other hand, the Bank's recovery package does not show any such 'special attention'. Instead, the Bank's loan of US$100 million to Indonesia to cushion the impact of the financial crisis was meant specifically for creating 75 million man-days of low-waged jobs in labour-intensive public works.[20] But there may not be even a single 'woman-day' of waged work through this recovery package.

I publicised the gender-inequitability of this particular recovery package on three occasions: first, in an earlier version of this paper presented to a Conference of the ASEAN Confederation of Women's Organisations (Singapore, 1998), then in a re-presentation of this paper to the APEC Women Leaders Network (Kuala Lumpur, Malaysia, September 1-2, 1998), then again in a revised version at a Conference on 'Democracy, Market Economy and Development', organised by the World Bank and the Government of Republic of Korea (Seoul, February 26-27, 1999).[21]

Gratifyingly, in August 1999, Indonesia's State Minister for the Role of Women, Tutty Alawiyah, picked up on this issue. She initiated an agreement between her Office with the Department of Public Works to set up a Special Initiative for Women's Unemployment, which would allocate to unemployed women 15 percent from the total amount of Social Safety Net Funds earmarked for the public works sector. This amounted to some 150 billion Indonesian rupiah (approximately US$14 million), aimed at generating employment for 5 million women, with 50 percent of these funds to be used for the women's wages and the rest for working costs. The local media reporting on this event expressed surprise at the Minister's choice of the Department of Public Works as a partner, noting that this was the very first time that the Office of the Role of Women had established a programme using funds from Public Works. Furthermore, the Coordinating Minister of Community Welfare, Taskin Haryono Suyono, was reported as saying that in 1999-2000, the government would ensure that 50 percent of Social Safety Net Funds that go to Public Works would be allocated for women (Dewi, 1999).

It cannot be proven that there is a direct causal link between my earlier publicisation of the gender-inequitability of the World Bank's recovery package for Indonesia and Tutty Alawiyah's initiative, which obtained US$14 million for unemployed women, though she was certainly present and active in various ASEAN and APEC fora on women.[22] Nevertheless, this example possibly illustrates the role of research as a performative practice, whereby research produces not just a reflection of the world as is, but rather, knowledge on which the world to come is shaped.[23]

The Relevance of 'Gender and Development' in Shaping the Economic Future of Southeast Asia

The discourse of 'gender and development' contains a performative aim. It is a critique of gender inequities with a view of contributing to the development of a more gender-equitable world. In the 1960s, the 'Women in Development' (WID) approach saw women as a sub-group with special needs to be addressed, separately from mainstream development processes (see Kabeer, 1994, pp.2-39). This was followed in the 1970s by the Women and Development (WAD) approach, which gave greater prominence to the significant role played by women in development, but still considered women as adjunct to 'larger' development processes. In the 1980s, the Gender and Development (GAD) approach acknowledged that women could not be seen in isolation, and therefore focussed instead on gender relations as an integral part of the development process itself.

As shown above, women's gender role in society brought about their propensity to seek casualised labour. This gendered propensity then became an economic resource that gave export industries in Southeast Asia a competitive edge in the global market. The 'and' in 'Gender and Development' is not a trivial link. Indeed, the development process that brought about the East Asian miracle is gendered development, where gender as such has been a factor of production through the supply of a specific type of labour.

In the aftermath of the Asian economic crisis, women in Southeast Asia found themselves having to devise their own coping strategies. Despite the exceptional initiative of Tutty Alawiyah in Indonesia, women have not received adequate attention in any rescue strategy put forward by international financial institutions and national governments. With massive unemployment, company bankruptcies and the closure of factories, women have had to seek alternative means of making a living. These may be listed as follows:

1. Rural subsistence
2. Making and selling cultural products, e.g. hand-woven cloth
3. Sex work
4. Migrating to work in other countries, e.g. as domestic helpers

After the Crisis, one million unemployed workers in the cities of Thailand returned to their villages of origin in a massive urban-rural migration (see Immigration Laws, 1998; and Richburg, 1998). Many of them were women. But how well has the rural sector coped with this massive influx of returning migrants?

According to Peter Heller (1999), Deputy Director of the Fiscal Affairs Department in the International Monetary Fund, the rural sector is coping well in the aftermath of the crisis:

> Witness how the first impressions of the human impact of the crisis have had to be revised. Only several months ago, the World Bank and International Labour Organisation were suggesting that in Indonesia, the number of poor would almost double. Now, the evidence suggests that poverty rates in Indonesia may not increase so dramatically. It is the urban poor and middle class that now appear to have been most affected, with rural food producers largely protected, if not benefiting.

But other reports indicate the contrary. According to Jones (1998):

> Violence linked to land disputes may...increase, as hundreds of thousands of construction workers, food vendors and petty traders return from depressed urban areas to their homes in the countryside. The chief of Thailand's irrigation department announced on January 2 that the irrigation system would not be able to cope with the expected number of people returning to farming as a way of survival. In Indonesia, drought has devastated rural Java, making a mass influx of sacked workers even more insupportable. When decreasing availability of money, land and water is combined with an increasing demand, the prospect for violence is high.

How is this contradiction to be resolved? Booth (1999) notes that 'rural producers of export crops such as rubber, coffee and pepper gained from the post-crisis currency devaluation which led to a rapid increase in local prices for these crops'.[24] Indeed, it would seem that while rural producers of export crops have been able to market more of their produce, thereby earning more income, subsistence farmers may not have done as well, given the increased pressure on land, water and food.

Where are women positioned in this context? The Food and Agriculture Organisation (FAO) of the United Nations has provided ample documentation of the gender division of labour among rural producers worldwide:

> Men tend to do the work of large-scale cash cropping, especially when it is highly mechanized, while women take care of household food production and small-scale cultivation of cash crops, requiring low levels of technology.... Men tend to grow cash crops and keep the income, while women use their land primarily for subsistence crops to feed their families.[25]

According to the International Federation of Agricultural Producers, worldwide, 'women own only 2 percent of the land, and receive only one percent of all agricultural credit'.[26] Southeast Asia does not deviate from this global pattern. It is likely that women are not the producers of export crops that are now marketed in abundance. Rather, they are likely to be subsistence farmers or landless rural workers, who are struggling to make ends meet.

The second coping strategy listed above is 'making and selling cultural products – e.g. hand-woven cloth'. For centuries, women in the rural sector have been engaged in craft production, both for domestic use and for earning cash income in the market. In the rural sector, this has long been a supplementary activity to food production. Worldwide demand for Southeast Asian crafts has been rising. From Vietnam alone, exports are said to have reached US$75 million in the first half of 1999 (see Alderman, 2000). Annual global trade in crafts is estimated at US$30 billion annually (see Smith and White, n.d.).

Cohen (2000, pp.23-24) observes the following change in the craft sector in Thailand, before and after the crisis:

> Thailand enjoyed for the last three decades an almost continuous boom.... The younger generation in many craft villages...sought employment in new, urban occupations, despising work in crafts.... The economic crisis of 1997 reversed this situation to some extent.... As growing numbers of unemployed urban migrants begin to return to their villages, some may engage in crafts production as a temporary expedient, even while domestic demand for crafts diminishes, as the urban middle classes experience the crisis in sharply reduced disposable incomes. However, with the drastic fall in the exchange value of the Thai currency, which in 1998 stabilised around at a rate of about 60 percent lower than before the crisis (at around 40 baht for one US$ as against 25 baht previously), the competitiveness of Thai crafts on the world market improved considerably. Insofar as the baht prices of crafts will remain stable, a growing reorientation of craft production to the foreign tourist, and especially the export market, will be necessary to keep up even the level of production prior to the crisis. It is questionable, however, whether under the present depressed conditions the necessary entrepreneurship will emerge to create the mechanisms for such a reorientation of production in the craft villages, the great majority of which have not been involved with exports, and many of which did not produce primarily even for the foreign tourist market.

Where are women positioned in craft production? Women certainly constitute a major proportion of craft producers. 'According to the United Nations, 90 percent of all women in the developing world are engaged in some craft activity' (Smith and White, n.d.). However, most of these women are likely to lack the capital and time resources to develop craft entrepreneurship successfully. As noted by Cohen above, entrepreneurship is necessary to develop appropriate mechanisms for orientating craft production for the export market. An indicator of women's lack of financial resources may be discerned from the following figures for six Southeast Asian countries:

Table 4.4 Unpaid male and female family workers as a proportion of male and female labour force (%), 1990

Countries	Male	Female
Brunei Darussalam	< 1	1
Indonesia	9	34
Malaysia	3	14
Philippines	9	18
Singapore	1	2
Thailand	16	44

Source: UNIFEM, 2000, p.87

The preponderance of unpaid female family workers is likely to be particularly true of women in the rural sector. Furthermore, it has been estimated that women account for 65 percent of food production in Asia and that they may spend up to five hours a day collecting fuel wood and water, and four hours a day on cooking (see Brown, Feldstein and Haddad, 2001, pp.207-208). This does not leave them with much time for craft production, particularly production that is oriented towards an export market.

As a result, left to their own limited resources, most rural women would produce craft items primarily for their own use and secondarily for local markets. Even access to local markets may be more available to those living near roads and towns, and less available to those living in remote areas.

In this context, the role of some non-governmental organisations (NGOs) in Southeast Asia has been significant. These NGOs provide critical entrepreneurial support to rural craft producers in terms of capital, logistical support, market intelligence, design inputs and quality control. Examples of such NGOs are ThaiCraft in Thailand, Craft Link in Vietnam, Lao Handicraft Group in Laos. Furthermore, higher-level regional networks of such NGOs have been formed through regional organisations such as ENGENDER (based in Singapore) and AHPADA (based in Bangkok).[27]

While further research needs to be done on the increase in revenue earned by rural craft producers as a result of NGO activities, my own research on craft communities in Southeast Asia indicates a significant financial improvement among those working with them. For example, in Laos, women weavers working with the Lao Handicraft Group could earn up from US$50 (400 thousand *kip*) to US$200 (1.6 million *kip)* per month. Such incomes compare favourably with the salaries of government employees who earn only about US$10 (80 thousand *kip*) per month.

Nevertheless, it is questionable whether there are sufficient NGOs to service all the rural craft producers of Southeast Asia, in terms of developing their export capacity. It has been estimated that 70 percent of Southeast Asia's population is rural (FAO, 1994, p.2). The estimated population of Southeast Asia is about 500 million.[28] There are thus about 350 million rural villagers who produce craft, at least for their own use – for example, woodwork, metalwork, hand-woven cloth, and baskets.

What magnitude of capital, infrastructural development, logistical and marketing support is needed to enable these craft producers to export their crafts? This would require major inputs and supportive policies from governments, over and above the efforts of NGOs. In this context, UNIFEM's Women's Economic Empowerment Programme is significant. Its current pilot phase includes the women weavers of Laos; pending the success of its pilot phase, this programme could eventually include more countries and women. As an inter-governmental, multilateral organisation, UNIFEM may be able to leverage with governments for the magnitude of support required to empower women craft artisans to access export markets.

In the absence of adequate support and in the face of livelihood difficulties, many women in Southeast Asia have had to turn to sex work as a major coping strategy. Figures on women and girls involved in sex work are difficult to obtain. Prior to the Economic Crisis of 1997, significant numbers were already involved in the sex industry. The International Labour Organization estimates that in Indonesia, Malaysia, Philippines and Thailand, 'anywhere between 0.25 percent and 1.5 percent of the total female population are engaged in prostitution'.[29]

> Estimates made in 1993/4 suggest that there were between 140,000 to 230,000 prostitutes in Indonesia. In Malaysia, the estimated figures for working prostitutes range from 43,000 to 142,000, but the higher figure is more probable, according to the ILO analysis. In the Philippines, estimates range from 100,000 to 600,000, but the likelihood is that there are nearly half a

million prostitutes in the country. In Thailand, the Ministry of Public Health survey recorded 65,000 prostitutes in 1997 but unofficial sources put the figure between 200,000 to 300,000. There are also tens of thousands of Thai and Filipino prostitutes working in other countries....

The sex sector in the four countries is estimated to account for anywhere from 2 to 14 percent of Gross Domestic Product (GDP).... Government authorities also collect substantial revenues in areas where prostitution thrives, illegally from bribes and corruption, but legally from licensing fees and taxes on the many hotels, bars, restaurants and game rooms that flourish in its wake. In Thailand, for example, close to US$300 million is transferred annually to rural families by women working in the sex sector in urban areas.... For the 1993-95 period, the estimate was that prostitution yielded an annual income of between US$22.5 and 27 billion. In Indonesia the financial turnover of the sex sector is estimated at US$1.2 billion to US$3.3 billion per year, or between 0.8 and 2.4 percent of the country's GDP, with much of prostitutes' earnings remitted from the urban brothel complexes they work in to the villages their families live in. In the Jakarta area alone, there is an estimated annual turnover of US$91 million from activities related to the sale of sex.[30]

The United Nations Development Fund for Women (UNIFEM) reports the following of Thailand:

> Estimates of the numbers of prostitutes in Thailand vary widely, depending on the source of the figures and the method of estimation. In 1995, the Public Health Ministry estimated that there were 81,384 Commercial Sex Workers (CSWs) of whom 16,383 were direct CSWs and 65,001 indirect CSWs. The total number of brothels was reported as 6,563—1,799 of these being outright brothels and the remainder, places where prostitutes were available but not the main business. These figures were based on a twice-yearly survey of sex establishments related to surveillance of venereal diseases.
>
> The Police Department provides the highest estimate of the numbers of CSWs— 500,000 based on the number of registered entertainment places. The National Commission on Women's Affairs estimated the number to be 150,000 to 200,000, of whom not more than 20 percent were thought to be children. Academics from the Population and Social Research Institute of Mahidol University estimated the numbers to be between 200,000 and 300,000.[31]

The non-governmental organisation Gabriela estimates that there are approximately 600,000 prostitutes in the Philippines, with 50,000 to 60,000 of them being children forced into prostitution.[32] The Asian economic crisis has led not only to an increase of sex work by women within one country, but also to an increase in the sex trafficking of women and children. The magnitude of the latter is hard to ascertain but there are some indications to be noted.

> For instance, the Ministry of Education estimates that in Thailand there are half a million children who have dropped out of school. According to Professor Lae Dilokvidhayarat from Chulalongkorn University, there has been a 10% decrease in the school enrolment at the primary school level in Thailand since 1996. Due to increased unemployment, children cannot find work in the formal sector, but instead are forced to 'disappear' into the informal sector. This makes them especially vulnerable to sexual exploitation. Also, a great number of children are known to travel to tourist areas and to big cities hoping to find work.[33]

As noted above, girls form the majority of school dropouts. The CIA (1999) estimates that approximately 30,000 women and children are trafficked annually to the United States of America from Southeast Asia, as compared to 10,000 from Latin America, 4,000 from the Newly Independent States and Eastern Europe, and 1,000 from other regions.[34]

Apart from sex work, increasing numbers of women have also been seeking employment as domestic helpers in foreign countries. Exact figures are difficult to obtain. A relatively conservative estimate by Heyzer et al (1994) was that over one million women from sending countries, such as Bangladesh, India, Pakistan, Sri Lanka, Indonesia and the Philippines, were working as domestic helpers, legally and illegally, in receiving countries, such as Hong Kong, Singapore, Taiwan, Malaysia and the Middle East.

Other estimates give much higher numbers. For example, the Philippines is said to be the world's second largest exporter of labour, next to Mexico, with an estimated 7 to 8 million Filipino workers abroad (see Gabriela, n.d.; Varona, 2001).

> About 60 to 80 percent...of...Filipino overseas workers are women who work as domestic helpers or entertainers. They are found in 168 countries in seven continents. In the first ten months of 1998, 640,054 Filipinos left the country to work abroad. In 1998, an increase of 3.5 percent was noted in the number of domestic helpers who left for abroad compared to the previous year (Gabriela, n.d.).

Based on this estimate, there are 4.2 to 6.4 million women working outside the Philippines either as domestic helpers or as entertainers. If this number were halved for each of these two occupations, there would be 2.1 to 3.2 million domestic helpers from the Philippines working abroad.

I have discussed these four coping strategies of women in Southeast Asia at some length to show the magnitude of their livelihood problems in a situation where they are left largely to their own devices. Four years after the crisis, 'women continue to be the worst affected by the region's economic downturn' (Gill, 2000). The gendered inequities that already existed have been aggravated by the 1997 crisis.

How then are these worsening conditions to be addressed? UNIFEM (2000, p.9) points out:

> Running through the commitments that governments made at Beijing [The Fourth World Conference on Women, 1995] and Copenhagen [The World Summit on Social Development, 1995] is a paradox: the commitments reflect an expectation that governments are responsible for implementing policies to improve the well-being of women, especially poor women, but they do not effectively address the ways in which market liberalisation and privatisation may undermine the capacity of governments to discharge these responsibilities, especially to poor women.

The Asian economic crisis is a case in point. If in the heyday of the Asian 'miracle economies', governments lacked the political will to be responsive to the needs of women, the crisis may now have deprived them of their political capacity to be responsive. This has resulted in many millions of women struggling to make a living through labour migration, prostitution and sex trafficking, as shown above. Even if these women are able to survive in the short term through these means, in the long run, these cannot be considered as sustainable development strategies for society as a whole. As noted above, when large numbers of women face livelihood difficulties, it signals the collapse of family and community structures.

Indeed, far from being responsive to women's needs, some Southeast Asian governments have become reluctant to intervene on behalf of women citizens. For example:

> When things go wrong, governments of the labour surplus countries are sometimes reluctant to criticize the government of the receiving country because they fear jeopardizing their country's ability to export more workers. For example, Vietnamese migrants in American Samoa, a US protectorate, complained that they were confined to their barracks next to a garment factory and not paid promised wages. The factory ultimately declared bankruptcy and closed, but the women, many of whom paid [US]$8,000 in fees to land the jobs, complained that Vietnam did not support their quest for justice for fear of jeopardizing future labour exports.[35]

So what would constitute a sustainable development strategy, from a gendered perspective? What kind of development trajectory would best serve women's interests in the long run? Would a return to the pre-1997 conditions of the 'miracle economies' be the best option for women?

It has been argued that the Asian economic crisis was really 'a growth crisis' (Delhaise, 1998, p.1). At the top, the 'growth' was pumped up by large inflows of foreign capital. At the bottom, it was propped up by cheap labour, provided largely by women as a flexible and expendable workforce that was employed under exploitative and inequitable conditions of employment. Do women really want to go back to a situation of economic vulnerability to be subjected to forces beyond their control -- either as cheap flexible labour for 'growth' or as survivors of 'crisis'? And if they do not, then what are the alternatives?

To answer this, let us consider just one of the alternatives that have arisen after the crisis -- localism. The aftermath of the crisis has seen a resurgence of localism as a political response to the crisis of capitalism. This has emerged particularly in Thailand, Indonesia and the Philippines. Connors notes that the key principle of localism is to root development in local communities, which are seen as having the capacity to be self-reliant and self-sustaining:

> Developmental activists have noted...the capacity of some communities to sustain their livelihoods and remain strong on the basis of self reliance and alternative forms of economy. Such strength, and the attempt to reciprocate it elsewhere, has become the political project of localists (2001, p.3).

In Thailand, for example, the discourse of localism, which first arose in the late 1970s, came to be known as 'community culture' (*watthanatham chumchon*). Following the crisis, the notion of self-reliant and self-sustaining communities has been valorised as the ideal type on which to re-organise the whole of society and economy (See Phongpaichit and Baker, 2000, pp.195-199).

This process of valorising local communities is also occurring in Indonesia, where 'customary societies' (*masyarakat adat*) are increasingly claiming sovereignty over 'customary territory, rights of upholding a value system, ideology and customs and traditions, economic rights, and, most importantly, the political right of customary societies to defend and develop their special cultures' (Acciaioli, 2001, p.2).

Where are women positioned in local communities? As shown above, women are very often unpaid family workers in local communities. The strength of local communities in sustaining their livelihoods is derived from women's unrecognised and unremunerated work in producing food, managing household resources and providing caring services. This very gender division of labour created the cheap and flexible labour force that has become such an asset under capitalist conditions of production.

Furthermore, as noted above, many rural communities have become dependent on the remittances of family members working in urban areas. As cited above, 'in Thailand, for example, close to US$300 million is transferred annually to rural families by women working in the sex sector in urban areas'.[36] Rural communities that depend on such remittances are clearly not self-sustaining.

As noted above, one of women's coping strategies after the Crisis has been to return to rural subsistence, but often on inequitable terms of land ownership. The idealisation of local communities, without a critical appraisal of their internal inequities, only reinforces these inequities, without providing any grounds for reform. Localism of this nature is of no advantage to women.

Hewison (2001, p.232) argues:

> There is often a naïve assumption that the local is about peace, togetherness and community. But communities are divided.... Civil society reflects the class condition of society at large, as well as local arrangements of power and wealth that are inequitable.... There is clearly a need to disaggregate this category and to be more critical of the functioning of 'communities'.

I would develop this argument further by pointing out that it is vitally important to disaggregate 'communities' in terms of gender. Without such gender-disaggregation in our understanding of 'communities', fundamental gender inequities would simply be ignored and, worse still, reproduced in the name of an ideal-type localism.

It is evident that there is a shortage of viable ideas for development alternatives. This is a massive challenge for all concerned, including governments, scholars and activists. This paper does not presume to propose a development alternative. But as I have demonstrated in this paper, any proposed development trajectory must be analysed through a 'gender lens'. A 'gender and development' approach would make transparent the labour subsidy provided by women, as a result of the gender division of labour. Only then can steps be taken to ensure gender equity in development. Otherwise, this gendered labour subsidy would simply be appropriated – be it by transnational corporations, small and medium enterprises or local communities – and exploited in ways that are detrimental to the long-term development of women and society.

Notes

1. For more information about the Asian Economic Crisis, see, for example, Robison et al (2000), Delhaise (1998), or Agenor et al (1999).
2. An example of a budgetary cutback with gendered implications is the Thailand Ministry of Public Health, which cut its AIDS budget by 24.7 percent in 1998 compared to a 5.5 percent cut for the non-AIDS budget (see UNFPA and ANU, 1999, p.136). As noted by UNIFEM, HIV/AIDS is a gender issue for the following reasons:
   1. The underlying causes and consequences of HIV/AIDS infections in men and women vary, reflecting differences in biology, sexual behaviour, social attitudes, economic power and vulnerability.
   2. Inequality between the sexes limits women's access to care and services. It also reduces both men and women's opportunities to acquire knowledge about safer sexual practices, and to develop skills to protect themselves from HIV.
   3. There is a large difference in attitudes towards men's and women's sexuality, both within and outside of marriage. Promiscuity in men is much more acceptable. This exposes men to an increased risk of infection, and increases the possibility that they will transmit HIV/AIDS to their partners.
   4. Women known to have HIV/AIDS are more likely to be rejected by their family, denied treatment, care and basic human rights. Yet women and girls tend to bear the main burden of caring for sick family members, including men living with HIV/AIDS.

    See World Wide Web: www.unifem-eseasia.org/Resources/GenderAids/genderaids1a.htm
3. See the Indonesia Government's *Labour Force Survey* (1997), cited from World Wide Web: www.unifem-eseasia.org/Resources/GlobalEconomy/Section4.html
4. See *Women Envision*, May-June 1998, No. 57-58.
5. See World Wide Web: www.unifem-eseasia.org/Resources/GlobalEconomy/Section4.html
6. See World Wide Web: www.worldbank.org/eapsocial/sector/poverty/povcwp3.htm
7. Bogor Nutrition Research and Development Centre, Indonesia (December 1997), cited from World Wide Web: www.unifem-eseasia.org/Resources/GlobalEconomy/Section4.html
8. Personal communication to UNIFEM from the Justice and Peace Commission of Thailand (1998), see World Wide Web: www.unifem-eseasia.org/Resources/GlobalEconomy/Section4.html
9. Cited from World Wide Web: www.unifem-eseasia.org/Resources/GlobalEconomy/Section2.html
10. ASEAN is the Association of Southeast Asian Nations, which currently includes ten countries – namely, Brunei, Myanmar, Cambodia, Indonesia, Laos, Malaysia, Philippines, Singapore, Thailand, and Vietnam.
11. See World Wide Web: www.unifem-eseasia.org/Resources/GlobalEconomy/Section2.html
12. See World Wide Web: www.unrisd.org/engindex/publ/list/opb/opb5/opb5-04.htm#TopOfPage
13. See, for example, Heyzer (1984); Nash and Fernández-Kelly (1983); Safa (1981).
14. SMEs have been defined as having between ten and fifty employees and a cottage industry as having between one and nine employees (see James and Akrasanee, 1986).
15. APEC is the Asia-Pacific Economic Cooperation forum established in 1989 to 'promote economic integration around the Pacific Rim and to sustain economic

growth'. It has 21 members: Australia; Brunei Darussalam; Canada; Chile; People's Republic of China; Hong Kong, Indonesia; Japan; Republic of Korea; Malaysia; Mexico; New Zealand; Papua New Guinea; Peru; the Philippines; Russia; Singapore; Chinese Taipei; Thailand; USA; Vietnam.

16 See World Wide Web: www.unifem-eseasia.org/Resources/GlobalEconomy/Section2.html

17 'Supply-side economics' has been defined as:
'A school of thought within the economics profession emphasizing that the main source of a country's economic growth is constant improvement in the efficiency with which resources are allocated for production.... Supply-side policy analysts focus on barriers to higher productivity—identifying ways in which the government can promote faster economic growth over the long haul by removing impediments to the supply of, and efficient use of, the factors of production.... Supply-side policy recommendations typically include deregulation of heavily regulated industries, promotion of greater competition through lowering protectionist barriers to international trade, and measures to repeal special subsidies and tax loopholes targeting particular industries in favour of lower and more uniform tax rates across the board' (World Wide Web: www.auburn.edu/~johnspm/gloss/index.html), or alternatively, as: 'economic theory that concentrates on influencing the supply of labour and goods as a path to economic health, rather than approaching the issue through such macroeconomic concerns as gross national product' (World Wide Web: www.encyclopedia.com/articlesnew/12489.html).

18 Speech by Sven Sandström, Managing Director of the World Bank, February 13, 1998; see World Wide Web: www.worldbank.org/html/extdr/extme/ss3speech.htm

19 See the World Bank's Press Release (April 1, 1998) at World Wide Web: www.worldbank.org/html/extdr/extme/1713.htm

20 See World Wide Web: www.worldbank.org/html/extdr/extme/1654.htm

21 The title of the earlier version of this paper is 'Women's coping strategies in the financial crisis: partnerships for community livelihoods'.

22 See, for example, World Wide Web: www.aseansec.org/function/pr_asw18.htm

23 See Gibson-Graham, 2000, pp.95-101 on performative research.

24 See World Wide Web: www.id21.org/insights/insights31/insights-iss31-art06.html

25 See World Wide Web: www.fao.org/Gender/en/lab-e.htm

26 See World Wide Web: www.rural-womens-day.org

27 ENGENDER is the Centre for Environment, Gender and Development. AHPADA is the ASEAN Handicraft Promotion and Development Association.

28 See World Wide Web: www.aseansec.org/news/camb_adm.htm

29 See World Wide Web: www.ilo.org/public/english/bureau/inf/pr/1998/31.htm

30 See World Wide Web: www.ilo.org/public/english/bureau/inf/pr/1998/31.htm

31 See World Wide Web: www.unifem-eseasia.org/Gendiss/Gendiss2.htm

32 See World Wide Web: members.tripod.com/~gabriela_p/8-articles/990601_prose.html

33 See World Wide Web: www.ecpat.net/eng/Ecpat_inter/IRC/articles.asp?articleID=143&NewsID=21

34 See World Wide Web: usinfo.state.gov/topical/global/traffic/report/chapt02.htm

35 See *Migration News* at World Wide Web: migration.ucdavis.edu/mn/Archive_MN/apr_2001-15mn.html

36 See World Wide Web: www.ilo.org/public/english/bureau/inf/pr/1998/31.htm

References

Acciaioli, G. (2001), 'Revitalising custom, reasserting sovereignty: opposition and alliance in Indonesia's Customary Society Movement', paper presented at The Symposium *Political fault-lines in Southeast Asia: movements for ethnic autonomy in nation-state structures*, October 15-16, 2001, Southeast Asia Research Centre, City University of Hong Kong.

Agenor, P.R., Miller, M. and Vines, D. (eds) (1999), *The Asian financial crisis: causes, contagion and consequences*, Cambridge University Press, Cambridge.

Alderman, L. (2000), *Handicrafts have become a $100 million export business*, available at World Wide Web: www.viam.com/archive/2000/02/crafts.htm

Alexander, P. (1999), 'Miracle women: the new trade agenda, jobs and transitions in Southeast Asia', in V. Wee (ed.), *Trade liberalisation: challenges and opportunities for women in Southeast Asia*, UNIFEM and ENGENDER, New York and Singapore.

Benaria, L. (1989), 'Gender and the global economy', in A. MacEwan and W.K. Tabb (eds), *Instability and change in the world economy*, Monthly Review Press, New York.

Booth, A. (1999), 'Stormclouds over Asia: signs of a silver lining?', *Insights*, issue 31, available at World Wide Web:
www.id21.org/insights/insights31/insights-iss31-art06.html

Brown, L. R., Feldstein, H. and Haddad, L. (2001), 'Generating food security in the year 2020: women as producers, gatekeepers and shock absorbers', in P. Pinstrup-Andersen and R. Pandya-Lorch (eds), *The unfinished agenda: perspectives on overcoming hunger, poverty, and environmental degradation*, International Food Policy Research Institute, Washington D.C.

CIA (1999), *Briefing on global trafficking in women and children: assessing the magnitude*, Central Intelligence Agency, Washington D.C.

Cohen, E. (2000), *The commercialised crafts of Thailand: hill tribes and lowland villages*, Curzon Press, Richmond.

Connors, M.K. (2001), *Ideological aspects of democratisation in Thailand: mainstreaming localism*, City University of Hong Kong Southeast Asia Research Centre, Working Papers Series No. 12, Hong Kong.

Delhaise, P.F. (1998), *Asia in crisis: the implosion of the banking and finance systems*, John Wiley and Sons, Singapore.

Dewi, K. (1999), 'Tutty Alawiyah controls Rp 150 billion', *Kapital: the Indonesian news*, PT. Bajomas Nusapermata, Jakarta.

FAO (1994), *Environment, women and population*, Food and Agricultural Organisation, Bangkok.

Gabriela (not dated), *Stop sex trafficking of Filipino women and children! A primer on sex trafficking*, available at World Wide Web:
members.tripod.com/~gabriela_p/8-articles/990601_prose.html

Gibson-Graham, J. K. (2000), 'Post-structural interventions', in E. Sheppard and T.J. Barnes (eds), *A companion to economic geography*, Blackwell, Oxford, pp. 95-101.

Gill, T.A. (2000), 'Asian crisis hits women hardest', *Asia Times Online*, June 6, 2000, available at World Wide Web: www.atimes.com/asia-crisis/BF06Db01.html

Heller, P. (1999), '*Human dimensions of the Asian Economic Crisis*', speech to World Bank Regional Meeting on Social issues arising from the East Asia Crisis and policy implications for the future, January 21, 1999, Bangkok.

Hewison, K. (2001), 'Nationalism, populism, dependency: Southeast Asia and responses to the Asian Crisis', *Singapore Journal of Tropical Geography*, vol. 22, no. 3, 2001, pp. 219-36.

Heyzer, N. (1984), 'From rural subsistence to an industrial peripheral work force', in L. Benaria (ed.), *Women and development: the sexual division of labour in rural societies*, Praeger, New York.

Heyzer, N., Nijeholt, G.L. and Weerakoon, N. (eds) (1994), *The trade in domestic workers: causes, mechanisms and consequences of international migration*, Asian and Pacific Development Centre, Kuala Lumpur and Zed Books, London.

ILO (1998), *The social impact of the Asian financial crisis*, Technical report for discussion at the High-level Tripartite Meeting on social responses to the financial crisis in East and Southeast Asian countries, April 22-24, 1998, ILO Regional Office for Asia and the Pacific, International Labour Organization, Bangkok.

ILO (1999), *Impact of flexible labour market arrangements in the machinery, electrical and electronic industries*, Report for discussion at the Tripartite Meeting on the impact of flexible labour market arrangements in the machinery, electrical and electronic industries, October 26-30, 1998, Geneva, International Labour Office, Geneva.

Immigration Laws, October 1998, no. 15, 'Asia: urban-rural, economy', available at World Wide Web: www.migrationint.com.au/news/luxembourg/oct_1998-15mn.html

James, K. and Akrasanee, N. (eds) (1986), *Small and medium business improvement in the ASEAN region: financial factors*, Field report series No. 16, ASEAN Economic Unit, Institute of Southeast Asian Studies, Singapore.

Joekes, S. (1995), *Trade-related employment for women in industry and services in developing countries*, The United Nations Research Institute for Social Development (UNRISD), Geneva.

Jones, S. (1998), 'Social cost of Asian crisis: the region's economic upheaval may lead to a human rights disaster', *The Financial Times*, London, January 26, 1998.

Kabeer, N. (1994), *Reversed realities: gender hierarchies in development thought*, Verso, London.

Krugman, P. (1994), *Peddling prosperity: economic sense and nonsense in the age of diminished expectations*, W.W. Norton, New York.

Lee, C.J., Li, C.K. and Hwang, T.S. (1994), *The APEC survey on small and medium enterprises*, APEC Secretariat, Singapore.

Migration News. April 2001, vol. 8, no. 4., 'Southeast Asia', available at World Wide Web: migration.ucdavis.edu/mn/Archive_MN/apr_2001-15mn.html

Ministry of Labour (1997) *Labour Force Survey 1997*, Government of Indonesia, Ministry of Labour, Jakarta.

Nash, J. and Fernández-Kelly, M.P. (1983), *Women, men and the new international division of labour*, State University Press, Albany, NY.

Phongphaichit, P. and Baker, C. (2000), *Thailand's crisis*, Silkworm Books, Chiang Mai.

Praparpun, Y. (1999), 'Small and medium enterprises in Thailand: the effects of trade liberalisation on SMEs and women workers', in V. Wee (ed.), *Trade liberalisation: challenges and opportunities for women in Southeast Asia*, UNIFEM and ENGENDER New York and Singapore, pp. 119-28.

Richburg, K.B. (1998), 'For migrant workers, path from boom to bust leads home', *Washington Post*, September 8, 1998.

Robison, R., Beeson, M., Jayasuriya, K. and Kim, H.R. (eds) (2000), *Politics and markets in the wake of the Asian crisis*, Routledge, London and New York.

Safa, H. (1981), 'Runaway shops and female employment: the search for cheap labour', *Signs* vol. 7, no. 2, pp. 418-33.

Smith, N. and White, M. (not dated), '*Freedom to craft a future? The impact of trade liberalisation on grassroots craftswomen*', Available at World Wide Web: www.craftscenter.org/advocacy/women.html

Standing, G. (1996), 'Global feminisation through flexible labour', in K.P. Jameson and C.K. Wilber (ed.), *The political economy of development and underdevelopment*, McGraw-Hill, New York, pp. 405-30.

UNCTAD (1994), *World Investment Report 1994*, United Nations Conference on Trade and Development (UNCTAD), New York.

UNFPA and Australian National University (1999), *Southeast Asian populations in crisis—challenges to the implementation of the ICPD Programme of Action*, United Nations Population Fund (UNFPA), New York and Australian National University, Canberra.

UNIFEM (2000), *Progress of the World's Women 2000: a new biennial report*, The United Nations Development Fund for Women (UNIFEM), New York.

Varona, R. (2001), 'Trends in the Asian migration map', paper presented at the seminar *On the Philippine migration trail: migration and reproductive health*, February 2001, Bangkok, Thailand.

Wee, V. (1998), '*Women's coping strategies in the financial crisis: partnerships for community livelihoods*', paper presented to the APEC Women Leaders Network, 1-2 September 1998, Kuala Lumpur, Malaysia.

Women Envision, May-June 1998, no. 57-58, Isis International, Manila.

World Bank (1993), *The East Asian miracle*, Oxford University Press, New York.

World Bank (1998), *Global economic prospects*, Clarendon Press, Oxford.

PART 2
ECONOMY AND LABOUR

PART 4

5 Emergence of a Global Economy in Southeast Asia: 1990s and Beyond

MOHA ASRI ABDULLAH
RAYMOND K H CHAN

Many have referred to globalisation as a world with a 'total system'. The system consists of many elements - physical and biological - that cannot be isolated from the political, economical, social and cultural aspects, that in turn, are directly and indirectly correlated to the processes of communication and evolution over the years. In many ways, the world system in the late twentieth century resembled the world economy as a world system that has been in existence for a very long time. It originated from Euro-centred mercantile adventurers of the sixteenth and seventeenth century. Through the early years of exploration and exploitation of mercantile, it led to the agrarian and industrial revolutions in Western Europe that paved the way for imperialist expansion to many underdeveloped countries. In other words, this phenomenon led to the beginning of so-called 'modern capitalism' (Wallerstein, 1974).

Though, it is seldom recognised that there was a phase of globalisation which began two centuries earlier, *circa* 1870, it gathered momentum until 1914 and then came to an abrupt end with the outbreak of the First World War. However, there had been a marked acceleration in this process of modern capitalism during the last quarter of the twentieth century with a progressive international economic integration since 1950. This modern capitalism flourishes in regions including Asia with former 'communist influence' and Latin America formerly under dictatorship rule. It is a globalising process that free market socialism is using to open up the 'closed-economies' in Eastern Europe, and in many parts of Asia such as China, India and Indo-China.

There are dimensions of this phenomenon that can be further presented in view of the accelerating process of trade, investment and finance across national borders reaching a point where a small movement anywhere in the globe can trigger a stock market crash, a recession, or massive movement of capital and foreign exchange from one border to another (Ohmae, 1990). It is important to emphasise that globalisation and openness is not simply confined to trade flows, investment flows and financial flows. It also extends to flows of services, technology, information, ideas and persons across national boundaries. Even though economic forces in a global marketplace are multi-centred and dominated by the interlinked economies of the USA, Western Europe and Japan, communication revolution and information technology have proceeded even more rapidly, enlarging the scope of global economy involving more countries that were formerly known as 'the peripherals' of the world system.

In past decades the economies of Southeast Asia have increasingly become more global and more integrated into this global system. Many of these countries which had been previously claimed as 'peripheral economies' 'have emerged as the most dynamic component of the global economy' (Dixon and Drakakis-Smith, 1993, p.1). The pattern of economic development and expansion in the Southeast Asia has seemed to gradually evolved in the region, if not fully transferred, since the 1960s (Gibney, 1992).

The World Bank (1993), for example, noted that most of the so-called 'miracle economies' of the world are concentrated in this region. This modern 'miracle' is also referred to for many reasons. Key economic indicators revealed a splendid economic performance particularly in terms of their sustainable-annual economic growth rate (Islam and Chowdhury, 1997). Indeed, the emergence of the East Asia economies, which also include some countries from Southeast Asia, are something of a miracle, considering that they occupy a pivotal role in the global and world economy. While globalisation has taken place and the economic integration is becoming more important to the region, the individual economies are considerably varied and complex, but linked together by rapidly changing structures.

Nonetheless, many seemed to agree that regional definition is notoriously hard to establish. It seems a lack of consensus emerged largely due to their confused character in the process from the periphery into the transitional zones, in which boundaries between zones are already hard to define.[1] In this chapter, Southeast Asia will be taken to mean the region that includes the Newly Industrialised Economy (NIE) of Singapore and the ASEAN-4, consisting of Malaysia, Thailand, the Philippines and Indonesia.

Since the economies of this region are highly heterogeneous[2] rather than homogenous, the splendid but differential growth in the past decades cannot be explained in simplistic terms. Such phenomena require a careful analysis of the specific tools in which the changing global context of the growth economies of this region have been experiencing. The focus of this chapter, therefore, is to describe and analyse the extent to which one is witnessing the emergence of an increasingly global and integrated Southeast Asia economy. In attempting to illuminate the key developments in its economic performance, including the wake of Asian financial crisis and its recovery, the chapter would be selective, rather than comprehensive in its nature of coverage, given such diversity does not permit the limited space on a chapter to provide in a holistic manner.

The Emergence of the Southeast Asia Economies

Most Southeast Asia economies experienced rapid growth especially from the 1970s. As a group, the regional economies have grown well above the world average. Compared to the other region's economies in the rest of the world, resilience was a common feature of the economic growth record in this region (Western, 2000), thus very much validating the popular perception of the emergence and dynamism of the region's economic performance as a 'miracle'. Though the economic growth started well before 1970s, during the 1971-1992, the NIEs, ASEAN-4 and China, compiled as a collective entity, experienced a growth rate of 7.7 percent, during which the world economy experienced a growth rate of 2.9 percent. In addition, the World Bank (1993) in its effort to measure the growth rate of the individual economy compiled a list of the 20 fastest growing economies in the world using per capita GDP growth rate over the period of 1965 to 1985. This compilation reveals that all of the Asia-Pacific economies, except the Philippines, are included in the list of the top 20 with the highest average growth rate.

The average annual growth performance experienced by the countries in the region in 1970s and 1980s can be seen in Table 5.1. It indicates that countries in the region experienced different rates of growth, at different phases. The Philippines experienced the highest growth among the four countries in the 1950s. Since then, all except Philippines since the 1980s, experienced a constant rate of rapid growth. The Philippines suffered a recession in the 1980s and only managed to perform a 1.0 percent growth during the 1980s.

Table 5.1 Average growth rate of GDP (%), 1950-2000

	Indonesia	Malaysia	Philippines	Singapore	Thailand
1950-1960	4.0	3.6	6.5	n.a.	5.7
1960-1970	3.9	6.5	5.1	8.8	8.4
1970-1980	7.6	7.8	6.3	8.5	7.2
1980-1990	6.1	5.3	1.0	6.6	7.6
1991	8.9	8.6	-0.6	6.7	8.5
1992	7.2	7.8	0.3	6.3	8.1
1993	7.3	8.4	2.1	10.4	8.3
1994	7.5	9.4	4.4	10.3	8.8
1995	8.2	9.4	4.8	8.9	8.7
1996	8.0	8.6	5.5	6.9	5.5
1997	4.7	7.5	5.2	8.0	-1.8
1998	-13.2	-7.5	-0.5	1.5	-10.4
1999	0.2	5.8	3.2	5.4	4.1
2000	4.0	8.5	3.8	5.9	4.5

Sources: Lim, 2001, Table 2.3; World Development Reports, various issues; Asian Development Outlook, various issues. Department of Statistics 2001

Their annual growth rates reached an incredible high that surpassed the rate experienced by OECD to as much as twice, in addition to the relatively low rates of inflation and unemployment. This made most economies in the region more robust in the 1990s. Singapore grew at around 8 percent, while the ASEAN-4 growth was rather remarkable, ranging from around approximately 4 percent to 8 percent. The overall growth record of the economies has been consistently good.

The relative size of the economies may be usefully determined by observing a 'market size' measurement. The measure can be calculated using the proportion of each economy's share in regional and world market over the year. According to Dixon and Drakakis-Smith (1993), there is a remarkable improvement of the economies in this region. The finding provides a simple indication of the perception of an emerging center of economic power in the region. Moreover, rapid economic growth experienced by the countries in the region in the 1990s has been kept within a controllable rate of inflation and observably low unemployment rate. Understandably, inflation can be influenced by many factors including rising prices of oil and other commodities, loose credit policies, and possibly poor fiscal management. While currency instability resulted from weak economic management and external forces, in many cases this may also generate inflation.

However, countries in the region seemed to have avoided any serious inflation during the 1990s. In the reverse, the rate of inflation has evidently been subdued generally. With the exemption of Indonesia and the Philippines that scored a high rate in 1998 (60.0 percent and 9.4 percent respectively), other countries have maintained their considerably low rate during the 1990s (Table 5.2).

With the exception of the Philippines and Indonesia also, the high growth rates experienced by the economies in the region have been followed by the relatively low unemployment rate of below 4.5 percent. Indeed, the economies in this region emerged as the most dynamic component of the global economy. The development of the region, may be slightly different in terms of economic growth rates, inflation and unemployment rates, their homogenous trend in general is often more recognisable as a group. Their spectacular growth in the past few decades cannot be explained in simplistic terms. It may not be precise, internal and external forces within a global economic integration of national economies through spatial movements in goods and services, finance, investment, technology and international migration may provide the impetus for such a regional growth performance in Southeast Asian countries.

The Structural Change in the Southeast Asia Economies

The rapid economic development experienced by many countries in this region has transformed their structural or sectoral shares of Gross Domestic Product (GDP). This economic transformation has been noted with the steadily decreasing share of GDP of their agriculture sectors, while other sectors in the economy, notably services and manufacturing, have been becoming progressively more dominant.

Table 5.2 Inflation and unemployment rates, 1991-2000

	Indonesia	Malaysia	Philippines	Singapore	Thailand
1991-95					
Inflation rate	10.5	4.0	9.7	3.1	4.8
Unemployment rate	3.9	3.3	8.7	2.5	1.6
1996					
Inflation rate	6.5	3.5	8.4	1.4	5.8
Unemployment rate	4.9	2.5	7.4	2.0	1.1
1997					
Inflation rate	11.6	2.6	5.1	2.0	5.6
Unemployment rate	4.7	2.6	7.9	1.8	0.9
1998					
Inflation rate	60.0	5.3	9.4	2.1	4.8
Unemployment rate	5.5	4.9	9.6	3.2	3.4
1999					
Inflation rate	20.7	2.8	6.7	0.0	0.3
Unemployment rate	6.4	3.4	9.4	4.6	3.0
2000					
Inflation rate	3.8	1.6	4.4	1.3	1.6
Unemployment rate	6.1	3.1	10.1	4.4	2.4

Sources: Asian Development Outlook, various issues; ADB, 2001

The structural change in the economies of the ASEAN-4 is clearly indicated in the Table 5.3 with the tendency in the increased share of the industrial sector in the GDP and decreased share of the agriculture sector, while the share of the services sector has been significantly rather unchanged. Two classic examples were Thailand and Indonesia from 35.0 percent and 30.2 percent of the agriculture shares of the GDP in 1970 to 17.6 percent and 12.2 percent in 1993 respectively. In the reverse, the contribution of the industrial sector's share of the GDP increased from 28.0 percent and 25.7 percent to 42.1 percent and 40.9 percent respectively during the same period.

Table 5.3 Structural change in the GDP (%), 1970, 1980 and 1993

Countries	Agriculture			Industry			Services		
	1970	1980	1993	1970	1980	1993	1970	1980	1993
Indonesia	35.0	24.4	17.6	28.0	41.3	42.1	37.0	34.3	40.3
Philippines	28.2	23.5	22.7	33.7	40.5	34.4	38.1	36.0	42.9
Malaysia	30.8	22.9	15.8	13.4	35.8	44.2	45.7	41.3	40.0
Singapore	2.2	1.1	0.2	36.4	38.8	36.5	61.4	60.0	63.3
Thailand	30.2	20.2	12.2	25.7	30.1	40.9	44.1	49.7	46.9

Source: Asian Development Outlook, 1994, Table A6

Malaysia, in particular, experienced phenomenal economic growth rates. During the period of 1971 to 1990, the Malaysian economy had expanded at an average rate of 6.7 percent per annum, while the annual rate increased to 8.4 percent between 1990 and 1995. The continuing increase in the manufacturing sector output surpassed other sectors, over the last two decades it has consequently transformed the structure of the Malaysian economy. This transformation can be observed from the declining share of the agriculture sector in the GDP i.e., from 30.8 percent in 1970 to about 14.9 percent in 1994 and 16.4 percent in 1995. On the contrary, the share of the manufacturing sector in the GDP had increased substantially from 13.4 percent to 31.4 percent during the 1970-1995 (Moha Asri, 1998). Singapore is said to be rather more urbanised in nature than other economies, however, there has been a structural change from manufacturing towards services sector.

The rapid growth of the economies has been underpinned by a rather stable current account deficit, as it can be seen in the relatively low proportion to the GDP (relatively below the danger mark of 8 percent of the GDP). Even though these were relatively higher for Malaysia in 1995, and Thailand in 1995 and 1996, it is pertinent to argue that such relatively high proportion of current account deficits was the importation of capital goods for economic development of respective countries in general. Table 5.4 illustrates that even with the advent of the crisis of 1997, financing the current account deficit did become a problem, nonetheless, many governments in the region have taken a prudent budget policy that forced a reduction in domestic absorption with the intent of curtailing imports. This, among others, provides more room for avoiding the unnecessary current account deficit.

Table 5.4   Current account deficit of the Southeast Asia countries (% of GDP), 1992-1998

	1992	1993	1994	1995	1996	1997	1998
Indonesia	-2.0	-1.3	-1.6	-3.5	-3.4	-3.6	4.1
Philippines	-1.9	-5.5	-4.6	-2.7	-4.7	-4.0	9.1
Malaysia	-3.8	-4.5	-5.9	-10.2	-4.9	-4.7	12.9
Singapore	11.3	7.3	16.2	18.0	15.0	15.2	20.9
Thailand	-5.7	-5.1	-5.7	-8.1	-7.9	-2.2	12.7

Sources: World Development Report, 1997; Asian Development Outlook, 1999

Moreover, the rapid growth rates of the Southeast Asian economies have been marked by very high savings and investment ratios. Table 5.5 reveals that saving rates in the 1980s ranged from 22.3 percent in the Philippines to 42.6 percent in Singapore, while the corresponding average investment rate ranged from 21.9 percent in the Philippines to 42.2 percent in Singapore. Overall, savings and investment rates for the region are well above the world norm which reflects a healthy economic growth. With the continued growth performance until mid-1990s, these healthy rates have been maintained.

Globalisation of Southeast Asian Economies

There is no doubt that globalisation has shaped and changed many economies in the Asia and Pacific region, if not all. To varying degrees, Southeast Asia economies have been gradually linked to the global market since the last quarter of the nineteenth century. Although the data is incomplete, an estimation made by the United Nations suggests that the stock of direct foreign investment in the world economy as a proportion of world output was 9 percent in 1913. The total stock of long-term foreign investment in the world reached US$44 billion by 1914, of which US$14 billion, about one-third, was direct foreign investment. At 1980 prices, total foreign investment in the world economy in 1914 was US$347 billion compared to the actual stock of direct foreign investment in 1980 at US$448 billion.

Table 5.5 Gross domestic saving rates (GDSR) and gross domestic investment rates (GDIR) (% of GDP), 1971-1995

Countries	1971-1980		1981-1990		1991-1993		1994		1995	
	GDSR	GDIR	GDSR	GDIR	GDSR	GDIR	GDSR	GDIR	GDSR	GDIR
Indonesia	21.6	19.3	31.8	30.4	36.8	35.2	38.7	35.5	40.4	36.6
Malaysia	29.1	24.9	33.0	34.7	34.5	33.9	39.4	34.5	38.7	35.0
Philippines	26.5	27.8	22.3	21.9	16.0	22.3	15.0	25.0	16.0	26.4
Singapore	30.0	41.2	42.6	42.2	46.6	40.1	45.0	41.5	45.0	42.0
Thailand	22.2	25.3	27.2	30.6	35.5	41.7	38.8	44.1	40.1	45.1

Source: Asian Development Outlook, various issues

It is also reported that the stock of foreign investment in developing countries (many of them in the region of Asia and Pacific), both direct and portfolio, rose from US$5.3 billion in 1870 to US$11.4 billion in 1900 and US$22.7 billion in 1914 (Maddison, 1989). Such foreign investment in the developing world was large in both relative and absolute terms. For one, it was probably equal to about one-fourth of the GDP of developing countries at the turn of the century. For another, it was substantial even by contemporary standards. The stock of foreign investment in developing countries in 1914, at 1980 prices, was US$179 billion. This amount almost doubled the stock of direct foreign investment in developing countries (US$96 billion) in 1980 (see Nayyar, 1995). Indeed, the empirical depiction of the evolution of the Southeast Asia economies remain incomplete unless one is able to appreciate how effectively these economies have penetrated international market and how they have recently forged closer regional linkages through trades, foreign investment etc.

Despite the fact that almost all countries in the region are latecomers in industrialisation, the acceleration of this process has shown that the time needed to catch up with those already industrialised is getting shorter; particularly when groups of nations in the region become more integrated in many forms: a faster spread of technology, ideas and capital across borders removing trade barriers and bilateral relationships between the governments of these countries. Statistics indicate that global economy and integration process reached a new significant level in the second half of the 1980s. Other than growing integration of economies with countries outside the region, many Southeast Asia economies show that both trade and foreign direct investment (FDI) are positive spin-offs of the growing economic interdependence between economies of the region. In this view, countries' trade links are intensifying with the share of intra-regional trade in the total trade of Asia-Pacific economies rising to 41 percent in 1990.

The remarkable economic growth in some countries in the region and the increasing global trade links in Southeast Asia are often attributed to the rapid market expansion. In this connection, Japan and NIEs are, it is noted, constantly faced with rising costs and have thus shifted their own industries to other Asia Pacific countries, further increasing the global trade in components and machinery (Dixon and Drakakis-Smith, 1993). Many regulatory controls in these countries have been relaxed, therefore allowing greater cross-border flows of goods, services and capital. Production networks in Asia-Pacific countries involve a wide range of economic interdependence, from history to proximity, comparative advantage, labour costs and intra-industry trade among similar economies. Free flows of product, capital, technology and labour are important in this process.

Table 5.6 Regional interdependence by two-way trade (%), 1955-1990

Absolute Measure (Intra-trade as a share of total world trade)

Region	1955	1969	1979	1985	1990
North America	6.7	6.9	4.2	6.4	5.3
Western Europe	19.6	28.7	29.3	27.1	33.8
East Asia	2.2	2.9	4.2	6.4	7.9
Pacific Region	13.5	16.9	15.6	24.8	24.6

Relative Measure (Intra-trade as a share of regional trade)

Region	1955	1969	1979	1985	1990
North America	33.4	37.9	28.7	33.0	31.3
Western Europe	49.1	64.7	66.4	65.4	71.2
East Asia	31.3	29.3	33.2	36.3	40.7
Pacific Region	45.0	56.6	54.5	64.3	64.9

Source: Memedovic, Kuyvenhoven and Molle, 1995

Furthermore, FDI from Japan, the United States and eventually the NIEs has provided the experience and know-how necessary for many other Asia countries to access world markets. Flows of FDI provide a strong example of a trend towards greater regional economic integration. It is well documented that the region has become one of the major recipients and major sources of FDI (UNCTAD, 1998). Countries in the region have also attracted significant investment flows especially Singapore and Malaysia, followed by Thailand, Indonesia and the Philippines (Table 5.7).

Table 5.7 Foreign direct investment receipts, 1975-1997 (US$ M)

	1975	1980	1985	1990	1995	1997
Indonesia	476	180	310	1,093	4,346	4,673
Philippines	97	106	49	530	1,361	1,113
Malaysia	351	934	695	2,333	4,178	5,106
Singapore	250	1,140	810	5,575	7,386	8,631
Thailand	22	187	162	2,444	2,068	3,733

Source: Lim, 2001, Table 6.3

One of the key features of the increasingly global Southeast Asia economies can be noticed through the development in the export trends. Indeed, the export-orientation of the Southeast Asia region has increased dramatically (Camilleri, 2000). It is noted that during the period from 1960 to 1997, the average growth rates in the value of mechanised exports in Thailand, Singapore, Malaysia, the Philippines and Indonesia are 9.8 percent, 9.2 percent, 8.8 percent, 5.0 percent and 4.5 percent respectively. In the period 1980 to 1992, the share of exports from Indonesia, Malaysia, the Philippines and Thailand has been increased from 2.0 percent to 3.1 percent (Kwan, 1993). According to the World Development Indicators, in 1997, Singapore, Malaysia and Thailand occupied the 13th, 19th and 23rd place in the world largest exporters (Tan, 2000, p.85).

Indeed, the openness and international orientation of Southeast Asia economies which has been described in terms of their share in the world's exports, their engagement in foreign trade as well as the share of the region in the world FDI inflows reveal another route of the emerging globalisation of the region's economies. Meanwhile, the figure also provides a substantive reflection of the emerging role that the countries in the region play and proves further evidence of the changing balance of the regions emerging position in the global economy. In addition, the issue of regional integration has also become the focus of considerable discussion along with the emerging globalisation in the Asia Pacific economies. Even though the emergence of an integrated Southeast Asia is far different to another regional bloc such as the European Union, there is a sense of regional integration through the process of market and political driven forces.

The scenario suggests the globalising trend is being accompanied by closer regional interdependence. Indeed the trend seems to be more pronounced in the later part of the 1980s as the overall part of the global world economy (Table 5.8). The total intra-ASEAN merchandise trade has been increased by almost 6 times from 1985 to 1997. This has been further encouraged through the establishment of the ASEAN Free Trade Area in 1992.

Table 5.8 Intra-ASEAN exports compared to country's total exports (%), 1985 and 1997

Countries	1985	1997
Brunei	20.9	12.7
Cambodia	n.a.	60.3
Indonesia	10.6	17.0
Laos	17.7	17.7
Malaysia	25.9	28.0
Myanmar	19.8	23.1
Philippines	11.4	12.0
Singapore	22.9	27.8
Thailand	14.9	21.5
Vietnam	22.3	14.0

Source: Lim, 2001, Table 7.9

Other than an increased engagement in international trade that provides ample evidence for intra regional linkages, other routes of integration such as FDI and labour migration within the region are also seen as highly paramount (Chan and Moha Asri, 1999). Labour migration, even though received little attention when compared to FDI and trade flows, shows an emerging global labour market within the region. A comprehensive survey conducted by Athukorala found that, 'in the last four decades new and complex patterns of international migration have been emerging, often with startling rapidity, in the Asian-Pacific region.... As the region becomes more economically integrated through the flow of capital and technology, pressure will grow in both the sending and receiving country for large international flows of labour' (1993, p.50).

Even though the macroeconomic linkages forged by labour migration in the region and the implications from such linkages are not yet fully documented, the realities embodied in the demand for, and supply of, migrant labour mean such forces will continue to mould regional linkages among the Southeast Asia countries and between it with the wider Asia-Pacific economies to varying degrees (Chan and Moha Asri, 1999). This is despite the fact that there has been restrictive immigration policies, and considerable social and political concerns pertaining to labour movement in both sending and receiving countries.

Table 5.9 Exports within ASEAN (US$ M), 1970-1999

Year	Exports
1970	1,456
1980	13,350
1985	14,343
1990	28,648
1995	81,911
1996	86,923
1997	88,770
1998	71,669
1999	81,929

Source: World Development Indicators, 2001, Table 6.5

Financial Crisis and Challenges in the Twenty-first Century

The emergence of global economy has brought about many implications on Asia Pacific countries. This trend will be more dominant and even greater in the twenty-first century. Many scholars and analysts remark that one of the most significant implications is that globalisation has widened the gap between the rich and the poor in the region, nations and within nations. Muller-Hofstede, for example, emphasises that,

> It is important to note that region as such less and less be conceived as winners and losers of globalisation process. Rather, we might have to deal with increasing polarised economies (and societies) in a growing number of countries: lean, rich and highly competitive globalized segments will contrast with conservative and poorly performing segments which are unable to cope with the new pace and productivity standards of the global market-place. Polarisation processes and long lasting structural 'social challenges' might become one of the features shared by East Asian and Western societies alike (1998, p.40).

The figures presented in earlier sections may reflect some of the facts that polarisation processes are taking place at a different pace in different countries in the region. Implications on the respective Southeast Asia economies are also expected to vary from country to country in the region. Meanwhile Rubbens Ricupero (1999), Secretary General of the UNCTAD, highlights that trade liberalisation is proceeding in a very unbalanced and biased way (in UNCTAD). According to him, it has been a constant that liberalisation took place mainly in areas of export interest of the industrial countries and much less in areas of export interest of developing countries over the years. Nonetheless, there are analysts who are more optimistic on the issues concerning uneven economic development. Sir Leon Britton (1997), for instance, asserts that it merely illustrates and reinforces the domination of the rich and the impoverishment of the poor. In this view, the distribution of global economic growth in recent times, with the spectacular emergence of the once underdeveloped Asia economies, demonstrated this.

Whatever the consequences might be, however, globalisation will not reproduce or replicate the United States everywhere. Data, statistics and evidence almost everywhere within the globe indicate that globalisation is closely associated with uneven economic growth rates and development, not only between countries but also within countries. The economic consequences of globalisation in the late nineteenth century were asymmetrical. History has proven that most of the gains from the international economic integration during the late nineteenth century and first half of the twentieth century were accrued by imperial countries which exported capital and imported commodities. During this period, there were a few countries such as the United States, Canada and Australia (so-called new lands with temperate climate and white settlers) that integrated economically with exported as well as received foreign investment and some benefits were derived from globalisation. In these new countries, the pre-conditions for industrialisation were already created and international economic integration strengthened the process of globalisation. Direct foreign investment in manufacturing activities stimulated by rising tariff barriers combined with technological and managerial flows, reinforced the process (Lewis, 1978; Panic, 1992). The outcome was industrialisation and development (Nayyar, 1995). While countries in Asia, Africa and Latin America, which were also part of this process of globalisation, were not so fortunate.

It is important to note that during the same early period of rapid international economic integration, some of the most open economies in this phase of globalisation such as Indonesia experienced de-industrialisation and under-development. Evidence shows that in the period 1870 to 1914, Indonesia practiced free trade as much as the United Kingdom and the Netherlands, where average tariff levels were only 3 to 5 percent. In contrast, tariff levels in Germany, Japan and France were significantly higher (12 to 14 percent), whereas tariff levels in the United States were very much higher (33 percent). Even though Indonesia was also among the largest recipients of foreign investment (Maddison, 1989), their globalisation did not lead to the much hoped for high growth rates and development (Nayyar, 1995). The outcome was almost similar elsewhere in

Asia, Africa and South America with a formation of so-called 'dualist economic structures' where benefits of globalisation accrued mostly to the outside world and in a small part to local elites. This was due to export-oriented production in mines, plantations and cash-crop agriculture that created enclaves in these economies that were integrated with the world economy in a vertical division of labour. There were no backward linkages; productivity levels outside the export enclaves stagnated at low levels.

Therefore, the processes of globalisation were uneven in view of economic development then and it is so even now. In the late twentieth century, even though almost all countries in Southeast Asia have been associated with the process of globalisation, only a few are noted once with a rapid industrialisation process such as Singapore, Malaysia, Thailand and Indonesia (Table 5.10).

The economic crisis in most Asian countries which began in 1997 recorded little effect on developed nations but devastated developing countries throughout 1998, with the exemption of certain countries which resisted speedy liberalisation of their financial system such as China and India. Indeed, there is no accurate data on the distribution of the portfolio investment. However, it is almost certain that the same countries, so-called 'emerging market', were the destination for an overwhelming proportion of portfolio investment flows to the developing world as shown in previous tables. Using Thailand as an example, the amount of portfolio investment had reached over USD 4,000 million in 1993 and 1995. By early 1990s, foreign portfolio investment has more than twice of foreign direct investment (Tan, 2000, pp.92-93). Although this financial flows accelerated economic growth, they are also considered as one of the factors contributing to the Asian financial crisis.

Table 5.10 Basic indicators for Asian countries

Countries	Population		GNP per capita (US$)		Average Annual Growth	
	1994	2000	1994	2000	1994	2000
Low-Income Economies						
Vietnam	72.0	80.3	200	320	--	4.0
Pakistan	126.3	138.6	430	492	1.3	5.3
Indonesia	190.4	209.4	880	617	6.0	3.2
Middle-Income Economies						
Philippines	67.0	75.8	950	1,046	1.7	4.6
Thailand	58.0	62.6	2,410	1,850	8.6	6.5
Upper Middle Economies						
Malaysia	19.7	23.0	3,480	3,248	5.6	11.7
High-Income Economies						
Singapore	2.9	3.9	22,500	22,710	6.1	9.1

Sources: World Development Report, 1996; Asiaweek, June 9, 2000, p.67

The economies of the countries have been affected but the processes of globalisation do not stop. The countries are upholding their policy in free trade and participating in regional and global organisations. FDI has been reduced in Indonesia, the Philippines, Malaysia, and Singapore, but increased dramatically in Thailand. However, exports of these countries may have been boosted by devaluation of their currencies (Table 5.11).

Table 5.11 Export and foreign direct investment (FDI) (US$ M), 1996-2000

	Indonesia	Malaysia	Philippines	Singapore	Thailand
Export					
1996	49,815	78,311	20,543	125,012	55,721
1997	53,444	78,519	25,228	125,008	57,604
1998	48,848	73,021	29,496	109,801	54,340
1999	48,665	84,621	35,037	114,628	58,549
2000	62,124	98,239	38,078	137,953	69,250
FDI					
1996	6,194.0	5,078.0	1,517.0	8,984.1	2,335.9
1997	4,677.0	5,136.5	1,222.0	8,085.2	3,894.7
1998	-356.0	2,163.4	2,287.0	5,492.9	7,315.0
1999	-2745.0	1,552.9	573.0	6,984.3	6,213.0

Source: ADB, 2001, Table 27 and 33

The result of the Asian financial crisis is a growing income gap between classes within a nation, as well as among nations, which reverse the trend of reducing income disparity as measured by Gini Index (Campos and Root, 1996, Table 1.1). This impact is similar to the process of globalisation over two centuries or more which has divided the region into the rich and the poor. This picture is clearly illustrated in the annual World Development Report that provides comprehensive and substantial data and figures on main economic and social indicators. It shows that Southeast Asia economic development falls into all four main categories i.e. low-income economies; middle-income economies; upper-middle income economies and high-income economies. Table 5.10 illustrates that countries such as Vietnam and Indonesia are grouped in the low-income economies with GNP per capita ranging from US$320 to US$617 in the year 2000, as compared to the Philippines and Thailand which are grouped in middle-income economies with GNP ranging from US$1,046 to US$1850. Malaysia is grouped into upper-middle income economies with a per capita GNP of between US$3,248, but still far behind countries that are grouped as high-income economies such as Singapore with GNP per capita of between US$22,710 for the same year.

Perhaps, this is the reason that the annual Trade and Development Report 1999 acknowledges that globalisation and liberalisation have not only yet to deliver promised wealth and growth but instead also increased external trade deficits and instability in the developing countries. The report also points out that attempts by developing countries to close the payments gap through increased exports to developed countries are met with sluggish markets, adverse movements in trade terms and protectionism. Moreover, the report notes that in low-technology industries alone, developing countries are missing out on an additional US$700 billion of annual export earnings as a result of trade barriers (World Bank, 1999).

Observing the implications of globalisation on economic growth in Southeast Asia specifically, it clearly shows that the benefits of integration with the world global economy accrue only to those countries which have laid the requisite foundations for industrialisation and development. All these reflect that investing in the development of human resources, the creation of physical infrastructure, raising productivity in the agricultural sector, acquisition of technological and managerial capabilities are essential. Therefore, the global economy that every country is now facing is bound to produce uneven economic growth rates even more unless, with the creation of institutions that would regulate, govern, and facilitate the functioning markets. Indeed, in each of these pursuits, strategic forms of state intervention vis-à-vis regional integration and co-operation are increasingly becoming essential. To large extent, this is indeed one of the greatest challenges faced the economy in the Southeast Asia as well as the Asia-Pacific in this twenty-first century.

Conclusion

The purpose of the chapter has been to provide a brief scenario of the emergence of the Southeast Asia economies within a global market economy. There is no doubt that countries in this region are becoming increasingly integrated with the world global economy. This trend is especially so in the last three to four decades or so with the manufacturing export-led growth of the Southeast Asia economies (Lim, 2001, ch.6). During the first two decades after World War II, the importance of primary commodities such as rubber, palm oil, tin, crude oil, rice etc. as generators of export revenues was clearly significant. Although many countries in Southeast Asia are still the important producers and exporters of primary commodities, the material resources of the region have assumed greater importance as a basis for economic transformation. This had occurred in the 1970s well after the rapid decline in profitability in Europe induced a massive shift in investment into developing countries (Thrift, 1986). Obviously, the attraction for FDI was not only cheap labour and land cost, other determinants such as good infrastructure and communication, educated and skilled labour force, local governments policies and incentives, and the like also played their parts.

The chapter has presented that the world has witnessed the emerging role of the Southeast Asia countries, or the ASEAN in the world economy, not only with the dramatically increased FDI, but also their overall volume of trade, particularly export of manufactured goods. Some of these countries have progressed far beyond the toys and textile stages, but now encompass more sophisticated products such as electronics and electrical and semi-conductor products, and automobile, while only Singapore has been developing their finance and services sectors. It shows that the economic linkages between the Southeast Asia region and the rest of the world is not only confined to flows of goods and money. Besides, there has been an increasing flow of people entering the international labour market, other than within the region. All of the scenario outlined in the chapter illustrates the emergence of a region more economically integrated into the globalisation and world economy in the 1990s and perhaps beyond than ever before. Having all these, however, it would be mistake if one thinks that the region is in any way homogeneous. Indeed, there have been many disparities and heterogeneous in nature, socially, culturally, politically and more important economically. Heterogeneous in nature and partly caused by the process of globalisation, may present contrasts and cause conflicts to the region. Perhaps heterogeneity and disparities provide the greatest challenges for the Southeast Asia economy with respect to the global and world competitive environment right into the twenty-first century.

Notes

1. There have been a number of definitions given by various agencies and scholars as to what they refer to the Pacific Asia Region such as Chris Dixon and David Drakakis-Smith (1993, p.3) categoried Pacific Asia to mean 12 low and middle-income countries; The World Bank 1995, p.248) defines East Asia and the Pacific to entail a total of 34 low, middle and high income economies; The Asian Development Bank (ADB, 1994) includes South Asia as a sub-classification in a wider developing economies in the region; and *Asian-Pacific Economic Literature* which is a premier journal dedicated to a study of the region defines it to include the developing economies of East and South East Asia and the Pacific islands.
2. There are many indications of the diversity of the economies in this region. At one extreme are rather populous economies of Indonesia with a population of more than two billion and a size of almost 2 million sq. km. compared to the other extreme of the tiny country of Singapore. Most countries in the region are contiguous entities, with the exemption of Indonesia and Philippines which are archipelagos containing a total of over 20,000 islands with considerable diversity in many aspects. The economies of the region also comprise a wide range of cultures, religions, ethnic group and languages. It is paramount to note that the ASEAN-4 and Singapore are rather pluralistic and multi-cultural. Many of the countries in the region also bear the imprint of different historical circumstances. Except for Thailand that was never really colonised, Malaysia and Singapore were British colonies, while Indonesia was a Dutch colony. In terms of per

capita GNP (in US$ at 1990), Singapore represent the richest economies (with per capita well over US$15,000, while Malaysia and Thailand represent a lower tier (with GNP per capita ranging from US$2,000 to US$10,000). The lowest income economies of the region represented by Indonesia and the Philippines well below US$1,000.

References

Asian Development Bank, *Asia Development Outlook* (various issues), Oxford University Press and Asian Development Bank, Hong Kong.
Asian Development Bank (2001), *Key Indicators of Developing Asian and Pacific Countries 2001*, Asian Development Bank, Manila.
Athukorala, P. (1993), 'International migration in the Asian Pacific Region: Patterns, Policies and Economic implications', *Asian-Pacific Economic Literature*, vol.7 no.2, pp. 28-57.
Brittan, L. (1997), *Globalisation: Responding to new political and moral challenges*, address of the Vice President of the European Commission at the World Economic Forum, 30 January 1997, Davos.
Camilleri, J.A. (2000), *States, Markets and Civil Society in Asia Pacific – The Political Economy of the Asia-Pacific Region, Volume 1*, Edward Elgar, Cheltenham.
Campos, J.E. and Root, H.L. (1996), *The Key to the Asian Miracle – Making Shared Growth Credible*, Brookings Institution, Washington D.C.
Chan, R.K.H. (2001), *Sustainability of Asian Welfare Systems – Reflection on the Case of Hong Kong*, City University of Hong Kong Southeast Asia Research Centre Working Paper Series No. 7, Hong Kong.
Chan, R.K.H. and Moha Asri, A. (1999), *Foreign Labor in Asia: Issues and Challenges*, Nova Science, New York.
Department of Statistics (2001), *The Malaysian Economy in Brief*, Department of Statistics Kuala Lumpur.
Dixon, C. and Drakakis-Smith, D. (eds) (1993), *Economic and Social Development in Pacific Asia*, Routledge, London and New York.
Gibney, F. (1992), *The Pacific Century*, Macmillan, New York.
Islam, I. and Chowdhury, A. (1997), *Asia-Pacific Economies*, Routledge, London and New York.
Kwan, C.H. (1993), *Economic interdependence in the Asia-Pacific Region: Towards a Yen Bloc*, Routledge, London and New York.
Lewis, W.A. (1978), *Growth and Fluctuations: 1870 – 1913*, Allen and Unwin, London.
Lim, C.Y. (2001), *Southeast Asia: The Long Road Ahead*, World Scientific, Singapore.
Memedocic, Q., Kuyvenhoven, A. and Molle, W. (1995), *Globalisation of Labor Market*, Kluwer Academic Publisher, London and Boston.
Moha Asri, A. (1998), '*Economic Downturn in East Asian Countries and Human Resources Development Strategies*', paper presented in International Conference on Interdepencence in Asia Pacific, 30th November – 1st December, Stockholm University, Sweden.
Moha Asri, A. (2000), '*Globalised Economy and the Strategic Importance of SMEs in Malaysia's Industrial Structure*', paper presented in International Conference on SMEs in East Asia in the Aftermath of the Asian Financial and Economic Crisis, 15th – 17th June 2000, University of Wollongong, Australia.
Muller-Hofstede, C. (1998), 'Strategic changes in Asia-Pacific political, economic and technological dimensions-A European perspective', in Arbeitspapiere zur Internationalen

Politik 100, *Forschungsinstitut der Deustchen Gessellschaft fur Auswartige Politik*, e.V., September 1998.

Nayyar, D. (1995), '*Globalisation: The Past in Our Present*', paper presented in 74th Annual Conference Indian Economic Association, 28th – 30th December 1995, Chandigard, India.

Ohmae, K. (1995), *The End of the Nation State: The Rise of Regional Economics*, The Free Press, New York.

Panic, M. (1992), *European Monetary Union: Lessons from the Classical Gold Standard*, Macmillan, London.

Tan, G. (2000), *Asian Development: An Introduction to Economic, Social and Political Change in Asia*, Times Academic Press, Singapore.

Thrift, N. (1986). 'The geography of international disorder', in R.J. Johnson and P.J. Taylor (eds), *A World in Crisis: Geographical Perspectives*, Blackwell, London.

UNCTAD, *Trade and Development Report*, (various years), UNCTAD, New York and Geneva.

Wallerstein, I. (1974), *The Modern World-System: Capitalist Agriculture and the Origins of the European World Economy in the Sixteenth Century*, Academic Press, London.

Western, D.L. (2000), *The East Asia: Growth, Crisis and Recovery*, World Scientific, Singapore, New Jersey and London.

World Bank (1993), *The East Asian Miracle: Economic Growth and Public Policy*, Oxford University Press, New York.

World Bank, *World Development Report* (various years), Oxford University Press, Washington D.C.

6 Labour Standards in the Southeast Asian Region: Retreats and Advances

DUNCAN CAMPBELL
DOROTHEA SCHMIDT

One observation that garnered a certain consensus as the Asian financial crisis unfolded in the late 1990s was the perception that a cause, if not the chief cause of the crisis lay in the absence of transparency and accountability in the commercial sphere and in business-government dealings generally (Lee, 1999). Another is a corollary of the first: if at least part of the economic and social havoc that swept the region in the late 1990s can be attributed to the absence of openness and mechanisms for democratic accountability, then building and strengthening such mechanisms are important keys to greater economic and social stability. These observations have now acquired new moment as much of the Asian region has become mired in 2001's global economic downturn, hastened and deepened by September's terrorist attacks against the United States, and the first such downturn to have simultaneously affected all the world's major economies since the 1970s.

The thesis that more open, democratically based governance structures result in superior social and economic outcomes receives some empirical support (see Rodrik, 1999, for example). Surely there are examples of high-growth, autocratic regimes, but the broader picture reveals these as exceptions to the rule. The empirical record shows that democratic countries outperform non-democratic ones because they instill commitment to often difficult governance choices and facilitate adjustment to change, on the one hand, and provide greater security and protection to citizens on the other. As Amartya Sen observes: 'the security provided by democracy may not be sorely missed when a country is lucky enough to be facing no serious calamity, when everything is running along smoothly. But as a matter of fact, the danger of insecurity arising from changes in the economic or other circumstances, or from uncorrected mistakes of policy, can lurk solidly behind what looks like a healthy State...The protective role of democracy is strongly missed when it is most needed.'[1]

This chapter looks at two of the most fundamental rights that democratic societies enjoy, those of freedom from discrimination and freedom of association. It does so from the perspective of the evolution of the International Labour Organization's (ILO) approach to human rights over recent years, characterised as it has been by two distinct milestones. The first was the promulgation of the Declaration on Fundamental Principles and Rights at Work, endorsed by the International Labour Conference in 1998. The Declaration rephrases and, arguably, reorients the ILO's longstanding interest in the promotion of labour rights in at least three ways:

1. The Declaration reaffirms that certain rights are indeed fundamental, thereby distinguishing these rights from others that, by implication, are less fundamental (although by no means unimportant). The Declaration identifies rights in four areas as fundamental: freedom of association and collective bargaining; freedom from discrimination; freedom from forced labour; and the elimination of child labour. Fundamental rights are distinctive in that steps taken to ensure them need not be dependent on any country's level of economic development. Moreover, respect for such rights undergirds progress in the effort to attain greater rights. Freedom of association, for example, is described as an 'enabling' right, or one whose practice enables the attainment of other rights.
2. The Declaration reorients the normative work of the ILO, which had traditionally been characterised by the promotion of the ILO's corpus of international labour standards and their ratification by Member States. While the creation, ratification, and implementation of international labour standards remain and will remain central to the Organization's core mandate, the Declaration's emphasis is on the promotion of a narrower range of principles, rather than the adoption of legal instruments *per se*, and the offer of ILO technical assistance in that promotion.
3. With the adoption of the Declaration, ILO Member States now commit themselves to making progress in ensuring these four areas of basic human rights, irrespective of whether a Member State has ratified the relevant conventions to which the Declaration refers. Prior to the Declaration, the respect of freedom of association had been the only constitutional condition of ILO membership which was independent of whether a Member State had ratified the relevant conventions. The Declaration now commits Member States to strive to fulfil a broader

range of human rights as an obligation of membership in the Organization.

While the Declaration brings into clear focus those rights that are fundamental, the second major step in the recent evolution of the ILO's approach to labour rights, the concept of 'decent work', defines the principal objective to which the Organization and its constituents aspire. The concept of decent work implies that basic rights at work and freely chosen, productive employment must advance together. They are a package. Rights at work embody core values, but these obviously cannot be fulfilled without work itself. At the same time, however, labour markets are different from markets for goods and services; they are about people, their skills and competencies, their health and their need for security, their aspirations and their motivation. They are also about the way that the self-employed earn their living and decide whether to seek wage employment and the way that wage workers interact with enterprises. Basic to the concept of decent work is that respect for human rights is not only a moral imperative, but a productive factor in its own right. The latter is the subject of this paper: there are economic costs associated with the absence or underdevelopment of basic rights at work and in society, such as those relating to discrimination and freedom of association. We first review aspects of the economic context in which the challenge of decent work is now situated.

An Imperfect Labour Market Recovery for working Women and Men in Asia

Prior to the mid-year downturn in the global economy, evidence of the Asian recovery from the trough of the crisis years existed in a broad series of economic indicators. For the most affected countries, for example – Thailand, South Korea, Malaysia, and Indonesia – the growth rate of 7.1 percent in 2000 had been an improvement over the 6.9 percent of 1999. Poverty rates exacerbated by the crisis had also begun to fall. Export growth led the recovery and was improving trade balances in the region before the slump in the technology sector. Steady, if often slow progress had been made in the reduction of non-performing loans and the restructuring of the banking and corporate sectors. Indeed, it had been anticipated that 2001 would see the return of positive net inflows of private capital to the region.

The signs of recovery, however, are no longer uniformly favourable in two regards. International financial institutions, such as the World Bank and the International Monetary Fund, as well as the OECD, revised downward their growth forecasts for 2001. Economic weakness arose not only in the puncture of the 'dot-com' bubble and deflation of equity values in technology shares, but in the over-capacity and mounting layoffs in major technology companies themselves. East Asia could not remain unaffected, not only by the slowdown in global growth, but by the region's great reliance on export markets in the electronics sector. As the Asian Development Bank's Asia Recovery Report observed even prior to the terrorist attacks:

> the downside risks to recovery in the affected countries have increased. External risks have heightened because of the faster than expected slowdown in the US and global economies, accompanied by a rapid fall-off in the growth of electronics demand. Exports, which had driven recovery in the affected countries, started to slow in September/October 2000. The slowdown is expected to be quite sharp this year (retrieved on June 25, 2001 from World Wide Web: www.aric.adb.org).

Since the terrorist attacks, global growth forecasts have been revised downward still further, as shown in Table 6.1, and this is also true for the Southeast Asian countries (Table 6.2). The slowdown in the region is all the more worrisome as, despite progress in many macroeconomic indicators, the recovery had been incomplete in the labour market. Table 6.3 shows that, with the exception of the Philippines, where the growth of labour supply has outpaced employment growth, unemployment rates had indeed come down in the affected countries. In no case, however, had they returned to their pre-crisis levels. Continued progress in the reduction of unemployment is now menaced by global economic conditions.

Table 6.1 2001 revisions in global output growth estimates

	Before the Sept 11th Attack		After the Sept 11th Attack	
	2001	2002	2001	2002
High-Income Countries	1.1%	2.2%	0.9%	1 – 1.5%
Developing Countries	2.9 %	4.3%	2.8%	3.5 – 3.8%
Global Growth	1.7%	2.7%	1.5%	2.6%

Sources: World Bank estimates, News Release No. 2002/093/S; Economist Intelligence Unit, 2001

Table 6.2 Revision in official growth projections for 2001 (%)

Countries	June 1, 2001	June 1, 2002	Sept 1, 2001	Sept 1, 2002
Cambodia	5.0	6.0	6.1	6.3
Indonesia	2.9	3.9	3.0	3.9
Laos	6.0	6.5	5.7	6.5
Malaysia	3.2	5.5	0.7	4.5
Philippines	2.6	3.5	2.5	3.4
Singapore	3.7	5.9	-0.6	4.7
Thailand	2.8	4.3	1.9	3.4
Vietnam	5.8	6.1	5.9	6.1

Sources: Consensus Economics, Inc., Asia Pacific Consensus Forecasts, for all countries expect for Cambodia and Lao PDR, which are from ADB, Asian Development Outlook and official sources; cited from Asia Recovery Report 2001, September 2001 Update

Table 6.3 Evolution of unemployment since the crisis (%)

	1996	1997	1998	1999	2000
Indonesia	4.9	4.7	5.5	6.4	6.1
Malaysia	2.5	2.6	3.2	3.4	3.1
Philippines	7.4	7.9	9.6	9.4	10.1
Thailand	1.1	0.9	4.4	4.2	3.6

Source: ADB, 2001

The Different Labour Market Experience of Women and Men

Nor is unemployment the sole indicator of lagging recovery in the labour market. The most affected countries have also seen changes in patterns of labour force participation (Table 6.4). These are quite marked in the case of the Indonesia, Malaysia, and Thailand, where the crisis appears to have resulted in a substantial decline in female labour force participation rates (LFPR). Of course, reductions in labour force participation result from a variety of factors which are neither all negative (increased schooling, improved family income) nor necessarily related to the crisis. Nevertheless, it is plausible to assume that at least some of the changes may result from discouraged workers withdrawing from the labour force altogether. This supposition can be entertained for two reasons: first, in most countries, the LFPR of women had been increasing over time; second, the declines, particularly for women, in the LFPR have occurred only in the most-affected countries of the crisis.

Table 6.4   Labour force participation of women, aged 15-64, before and after Asian financial crisis (%)

Countries	Pre-crisis	Post-crisis
Cambodia	80.0 (1996)	76.2 (1998)
Indonesia	54.9 (1995)	53.2 (1999)
Malaysia	48.9 (1995)	44.7 (1998)
Philippines	50.6 (1997)	51.8 (1999)
Singapore	55.8 (1997)	56.3 (1998)
Thailand	72.4 (1997)	69.2 (1999)

Source: Key Indicators of the Labour Market, 2001, ILO

For the sake of argument, consider the combination of increased unemployment and declining labour force participation for women in Thailand. Compared with the pre-crisis period, the current female unemployment rate is 1.9 percent above what it was and female labour force participation is 8.9 percent less than what it was.[2] While it would require more empirical work to verify, in summing these figures, it is possible that over 10 percent of women workers in the 15 to 64 years of age group continued to remain affected by the crisis prior to the late 1990s recovery having been derailed in 2001. Indonesia had seen a post-crisis increase in men's LFPR, whereas women's LFPR had declined by 1.6 percentage points. In Malaysia, men's LFPR declined by 0.4 percent, whereas the rate for women declined by 4.2 percent. In almost every case, women's unemployment rates remain lower than those for men. When LFPR changes are considered, however, the labour market and livelihood consequences for women in crisis-affected countries have arguably increased or even surpassed those of men.[3]

An additional indication of labour market disparities between men and women is worthy of note. In Table 6.5, men's real wages are seen to have increased less greatly than women's. But there are two reasons why one should not be too optimistic about this fact: first, there remains a gap between male and female wages; second, the rate at which the gap is narrowing is decreasing, and in some years real wage increases for men have been greater than those for women. Perhaps the declining rate of convergence is a reflection that the gender wage gap is closing. Even if true, however, it would take an additional 15 years for gender wage parity if convergence occurs at the same average rate as in the 1990s.

Inequality and Growth: the New Consensus

For years, the mainstream view of economists was not only that growth in developing countries was accompanied by rising income inequality, but that such inequality was in fact good for growth. The wealthier segments of the population had higher savings rates which, in turn, would lead to higher rates of investment the advantages of which would trickle down the income hierarchy. Several recent studies challenge and, indeed, reverse these earlier conclusions.[4] There is now substantial support for the proposition that lower initial levels of inequality result in greater long-term growth. The most common measures of inequality are income and land distribution. Of the two, it is the latter that appears to be the most important factor in relation to long-term growth.

Table 6.5 Male and female real manufacturing wage index

Year	Malaysia		Singapore		Thailand	
	Male	Female	Male	Female	Male	Female
1990	100.0	100.0	100.0	100.0	--	--
1991	103.0	107.0	105.9	107.8	100.0	100.0
1992	107.2	115.2	111.9	114.5	104.9	106.1
1993	108.0	122.0	116.5	121.7	101.2	109.7
1994	111.7	130.2	123.4	129.1	97.4	109.0
1995	115.6	133.7	129.6	138.1	110.3	117.8
1996	120.8	151.3	136.1	147.9	--	--
1997	126.9	159.6	142.3	157.0	--	--
1998	--	--	157.4	166.5	--	--
1999	--	--	160.8	174.3	--	--

Source: Key Indicators of Labour Market, 2001, ILO

Competing reasons have been proposed to explain the positive and causal relation between equality and growth.[5] Two, however, have mustered substantial consensus. First, in unequal societies, credit and insurance markets are often under-developed and constrain growth. It has also been found that in countries with unequal land distribution school attendance is lower, a constraint in human capital formation which, too, is an obstacle to growth. Second, in countries with high levels of inequality there is greater social instability, as reflected in strikes and protests, and in political instability. Social instability is a deterrent to growth.

In the context of East Asia, the global findings on the relationship of equality and growth are perhaps best demonstrated. Indeed, among other studies, the World Bank's influential account of the Asian 'miracle' economies highlights the relatively equal land distribution of many of the most successful countries in the region as a factor in rapid economic growth.

Gender-Based Inequality

Inequality, of course, has an important gender dimension beyond measures of income inequality for the population as a whole. One such measure is access to education: worldwide, boys are more likely to receive formal schooling than girls. In many Asian countries, boys' and girls' access to education is relatively more equal than elsewhere in the developing world. Thus, as Table 6.6 shows, girls' secondary school enrolment as a percentage of boys' is in many countries quite high, particularly relative to the girl / boy enrollment ratio for the UNDP's middle human development countries as a whole (i.e. 79%).

Table 6.6 Female to male ratio of secondary school enrolment, 1997

Countries	Female to Male Ratio of Secondary School Enrolment
Myanmar	96
Cambodia	66
Indonesia	91
Malaysia	95
Philippines	102
Thailand	97
Vietnam	97

Source: Human Development Report, 2000, Table 28

Relative, gender-based equality in access to education in the Asian region, however, would seem to contrast with the observations made above. Indeed, what is remarkable about Southeast Asia is the contrast between the relatively low inequality in access to education and the existing inequality in earnings between men and women. This surely suggests that there are other factors than educational attainment that explain gender-based discrimination in labour markets, or in society as a whole. For example,

Singapore is a country that ranks high in terms of per capita income. It is also among the UNDP's high human development countries. Nevertheless, when countries in the high human development index classification are ranked on the basis of how closely their overall rank in human development compares with their ranking for 'gender empowerment',[6] it is the countries in the Asian region where the disparity is greatest.

For example, the three Asian countries included in the high development category show the greatest disparity of all high development countries between their Human Development Ranking and their Gender Empowerment Ranking (UNDP, 2000, Table 1 and 3). In short, one would expect to see a higher level of gender empowerment in these countries, commensurate with both their wealth and their level of human development, as measured by the UNDP index.

Other, societal factors may therefore account for gender-based labour market discrimination, factors unrelated to the otherwise relatively equal levels of educational attainment between boys and girls. One study finds, for example, that unequal earnings between women and men reflect a predominant industrial strategy in which the workforce in relatively low-paying and low-skilled export-oriented industries is for the most part female. Furthermore, counter to the studies that find an inverse relationship between income inequality and economic growth, this study finds that the low pay of unorganised women in export-oriented industries has in fact increased the rate of economic growth:

> Inequality borne by women appears to have a positive effect because this condition stimulates exports and raises profit expectations. These together stimulate investment and productivity growth, without apparently generating the negative political repercussions that would undermine gains in measured GDP growth. Why then so little growth-retarding conflict in response to gender-based inequality? The key seems to lie in the socialization of women who are less inclined than men, at least in the sample of countries used in this study, to protest income inequality sufficiently to slow investment and growth (Seguino, 2000, p.1222).

It is clear that a variety of factors are at play in explaining gender-based discrimination. But it remains the case, even for Asian countries, that access to education may be an important factor in explaining growth, and that unequal access is a constraint on growth.

An Empirical Analysis of Gender Inequality in the Asian Region

For the purpose of understanding how labour standards can contribute positively to economic outcomes, we undertook an empirical investigation of the implications of gender equality for economic growth in the Asian region. The results are reported below.

Education indicators are one of the best measures of gender inequality (in primary education for low-income countries, and in secondary education for middle income countries as higher education becomes relevant in the development process), and GNP per capita is a reliable indicator for the economic development of a country. Regressing these two leads to the following results:

1. there is a correlation between the two;
2. there is a stronger correlation between women's education and per capita income than between men's education and per capita income and;
3. the smaller the difference between the male and female education level, the better the economic performance.

The correlations are not very strong – which does not surprise, considering all the other influences on economic development – but they are relatively stable over time. The regression results are presented in Annex A. The findings suggest for all developing countries that it pays to invest in women's education and to reduce differences in educational attainment levels between boys and girls.

As the Asian countries we reviewed are not at the top end of education equality in their income groups, it follows that they could have done even better before the crisis years had they had more gender equality. In the period after the crisis, indicators presented in Table 6.4 show that equality with respect to labour market participation of women has worsened. For some countries this is also reflected in the Gender Related Development Index of UNDP[7] as shown in the Table 6.7 below.

As a consequence, Southeast Asian countries risk growing more slowly in years to come than might have otherwise been possible. This is particularly true as the regressions show a time lag between the moment of improving gender equality and the time when it impacts on economic development. After the first and preliminary investigation, it takes from 20 to 30 years – an entire generation – until the effects are fully realised. This in turn means for Southeast Asian as well as other Asian economies that, if momentum is lost in improving gender equality now, it might not just influence current economic performance but also the performance for the next few decades.

Table 6.7   Changes in position of gender development index (GDI) relative to human development index (HDI) rankings

Country	GDI 1995	GDI 1998	Change	HDI 1995	HDI 1998	Change
Singapore	29	24	+ 5	28	24	+ 4
Malaysia	45	57	- 12	60	61	- 1
Thailand	40	62	- 22	98	77	+ 21
Philippines	82	64	+ 18	98	77	+ 21
Vietnam	108	89	+ 19	122	108	+ 14
Indonesia	88	90	- 2	96	109	- 13

Sources: Human Development Report 1995, Table 1 and 2; Human Development Report 2000, Table 1 and 2

This time lag can be explained by analysing some relations between gender equality and economic growth. By the time a child finishes primary education, she has reached the age of about eleven, an age where the impacts on human capital cannot yet work as the child is not part of the labour force. Once this child starts working, she still needs some on the job training until skill formation can really lead to higher productivity and thereby influence the growth rate. As a consequence, investments in a higher level of human capital will not have a return at the time that educational access is improving, but at a point when the generation with the higher education turns into the productive labour force.

An obvious effect of gender equality is the decline of fertility, which in developing countries is very important for economic development. But again, this needs some time before lower fertility rates are achieved. For example, women will only have fewer children when they notice that the child mortality rate drops. This does not happen from one day to the next. Another argument is that families need time to realise that investing in children's education pays; they can only afford these investments, moreover, if they do not have too many children. Finally, from the moment that mothers acquire a better education until their children are healthier and have become part of the labour force also takes some time.

A final argument is worthy of note: better educated women with more rights in the family improve the level of knowledge of the whole family in two ways. First, it is mainly women who pass on their knowledge to their children, which results in a higher level of human capital. Second, having partnerships based on equality raises the possibility of finding solutions to problems in a cooperative manner. In addition, it is the pre-condition for 'living democracy' in the family, and this in turn then reinforces democracy in the society as a whole. All these factors impact on growth via a higher level of human and social capital, but again, these processes take time.

The reduction in female labour market participation after the crisis may influence Southeast Asian growth perspectives negatively. Lower participation rates will lead to lower income for women, which may weaken their position in the family. This will lower the chances of girls to get an education with all the negative spillover effects on growth. It will also lower the chances of 'living democracy' in the family, with negative results for the society as a whole. Southeast Asian economies would thereby give away some of their growth potential, which they had already achieved.

While democracy is an applicable concept to the family, in labour markets, democracy is best understood as the development of freedom of association and the ability of workers to participate in choices on the job and in economic and social policy formulation as a whole. As with discrimination, economic costs can attach to societies that constrain freedom of association. It is to this discussion that we now turn.

Social Dialogue and Economic Outcomes

The frequent reluctance of both governments and employers, in the Southeast Asian region and elsewhere, to endorse full freedom of association is typically predicated on two grounds in the main. The first is broadly political: the cession of unilateral decision-making authority implied by the unencumbered participation of workers through their organisations is threatening to those who hold power. Obvious instances of this exist in Vietnam, where the repression of independent trade unionism remains the norm. The implicit assumption is that political stability is enhanced by the repression of dissent when, in fact, the opposite is more likely to be the case, as noted at the outset.

The second reason why freedom of association arouses the suspicion of some is economic: even those governments and employers who might acknowledge the right to freedom of association as defensible on moral grounds are nevertheless wary of its costs. Thus, for example, existing constraints on the right to organise and the scope of collective bargaining in Malaysia and Singapore are sponsored in part on the belief that such constraints are part of an 'investment-friendly' environment. Some evidence supports the thesis that investment flows toward weaker institutional environments where trade unionism is less developed:[8] the relocation of foreign direct investment (FDI) toward the southern region of the United States is a case in point.

Yet contrary evidence is not difficult to come by. Overall, FDI is concentrated in those countries in which mechanisms for social dialogue are particularly well established. A recent, broad-based econometric study undertaken by the ILO finds that trade unions do indeed increase workers' wages, and freedom of association is negatively correlated with inward FDI at a certain level of earnings. But the study finds that this effect is overwhelmed by the positive correlation between FDI, trade unionism and wages at higher levels of earnings. One reason may be that foreign investors are segmented into those for whom labour costs are a significant factor in investment location decision-making, and those, at higher levels of value-added, for whom labour costs are less significant. Another reason could be that foreign investors are as a whole less concerned about labour costs than they are about social stability, the latter being more likely to pertain in countries with well-established systems of industrial relations (Kucera, 2001). These findings are quite consistent with earlier empirical work showing that trade unions do indeed raise wages (a 'monopoly effect'), but that this cost is more than offset by the greater stability and lower turnover of the unionised workforce (a 'voice effect') (Freeman and Medoff, 1984).

Institutional adjustment in the course of the Asian financial crisis suggests two principal channels through which the beneficial economic effects of freedom of association and social dialogue occur. One is through greater access to information: representative parties to social dialogue increase the amount of information bearing upon a particular decision, which can in turn improve the quality of that decision. In Malaysia, for example, the Malaysian Trade Union Congress (MTUC) was able to convince the Government and the employers that an across-the-board wage freeze was unnecessary, and that negotiated wage adjustments at the enterprise level would be disciplined by the economic climate and capacity to pay (Campbell, 2001). Since experience shows that wage freezes, when lifted, can often result in a damaging inflationary spiral, this particular joint decision was superior to the one that would have been taken unilaterally.

The second advantage of social dialogue – again, when engaged in by parties that are truly representative of constituencies – is the greater likelihood by those involved by the decision to commit to its consequences, and thus facilitate more rapid adjustment. When, in 1998, Singapore's social partners sought to relieve cost pressures on enterprises by reducing non-wage labour costs instead of earnings, enterprises were able to avoid retrenchments and workers, their earnings intact, were able to stem the decline in aggregate demand. The Singaporean economy – even if now gravely affected by the global recession in electronics exports – was considerably less affected than its neighbours by the financial crisis, in part because of the existence of machinery of social dialogue through which an adjustment could be quickly made. A number of small European economies have also outperformed other countries in Europe in both employment and economic growth by the same skillful management of difficult tradeoffs through social dialogue (Auer, 2000).

Constraints on Freedom of Association in the Asian Region Remain Serious

Despite the economic advantages of social dialogue which can repose in greater information symmetry and the commitment to more rapid adjustment, constraints on freedom of association in the Asian region continue to be widespread. The economic advantages of social dialogue are foregone in consequence. Only few Asian countries have ratified the ILO's Convention on Freedom of Association (No. 87), as noted in Table 6.8.

Departures from full freedom of association and the right to collective bargaining in the Asian region take many forms. The most egregious include the following.

The Right to Organise

The basic labour laws of Vietnam provide for union recognition and collective bargaining, and ban anti-union discrimination. Indeed, by international standards, it could be argued that these laws encourage workers' organisation to an unusual degree. The problem in this country is that trade unions must by law be affiliated to the state-sanctioned monopoly trade union federations, the Vietnam Confederation of Labour (VGCL). Independent trade unions have no right to exist.[9]

While the foregoing are, with the exception of Myanmar, undoubtedly the most overt examples of the absence of freedom of association, many other countries also impose a variety of constraints on the right to organise. In Thailand, for example, the law governing private-sector labour relations protects workers from anti-union discrimination in existing organised workplaces. Workers, however, that would organise a new, as yet unregistered union have no such protection. The Philippines has ratified ILO Convention No. 87, no doubt one reason why trade union density of approximately 28 percent in the Philippines is relatively high among the Asian democracies. Still, the right to organise is commonly obstructed in the country's export processing zones. As the former Secretary-General of the International Confederation of Free Trade Union's Asia and Pacific Regional Organization (ICFTU-APRO) described: 'although the labour law applies, in practice 'no union, no strike' policies usually exist and are enforced by foreign investors, local government officials, and zone administrators' (Izumi, 1999, p.25).

Table 6.8 Date of ratification of ILO fundamental conventions in the areas of freedom of association and freedom from discrimination

Countries	No. 87 Freedom of Association and Right to Organize	No. 98 Right to Organize and Collective Bargaining	No. 100 Discrimination (Employment and Occupation)	No. 111 Equal Remuneration
Cambodia	1999	1999	1999	1999
Indonesia	1997	1958	1958	1999
Malaysia	--	1961	1997	--
Philippines	1953	1953	1953	1960
Singapore	--	1965	--	--
Thailand	--	--	1999	--
Vietnam	--	--	1997	1997

Source: ILO Website

The principle of freedom of association allows great latitude to workers to form organisations – to associate – with those of their own choosing. In Malaysia, the labour law restricts trade unions to representing only workers within: 'any particular trade, occupation, or industry, or within any similar trades, occupations, or industries, or within a single enterprise or establishment. These provisions have been invoked to direct industrial unions to remove several thousand members from their membership' (Izumi, 1999, p.23). State encouragement of the formation of in-house unions, and, in the electronics sector, restricting the right to organise only to the formation of in-house unions, reduce the strength of trade unions and render organisation difficult.

The Right to Bargain

More often than not in the Southeast Asian region, trade union membership, which, in any case, is usually meagre, nevertheless greatly exceeds the level of collective bargaining coverage. Thus, in the Philippines, for example, despite the level of 28 percent trade union density in the formal sector, perhaps only one-seventh of trade union members are covered by a collective bargaining agreement. In Thailand, little over one percent of the formal-sector workforce is covered by collective bargaining, perhaps one third of total union membership in the private formal sector (Campbell, 1999).

While there are many reasons for this disparity, weak legal support for collective bargaining is clearly a factor. Frequently, constraints on the right to organise and to bargain collectively are applied with particular vigour to the public sector. Thus, in Thailand, trade union membership and the right to collective bargaining in the state-owned sector were removed with the military coup in 1991. The then trade unions were legally transformed into 'associations' overnight. Only in 2000 did amendments to the State Enterprise Labour Relations Act (SELRA) restore union membership and bargaining rights.

Restrictions on collective bargaining also occur governing its scope. Countries in the region that have rather narrowly defined the scope of collective bargaining include Malaysia and Singapore. Moreover, the state has discretion in whether to approve the contents of a collective bargaining agreement or not. In Malaysia, collective bargaining in the 'pioneer' industries – industries that are heavily foreign-invested and export-oriented – is more restricted in scope than elsewhere in the economy. In Singapore, any collective agreements in newly established enterprises cannot include terms that exceed the legally prescribed minima in the Employment Act, although, in practice, exceptions can be made.

The Right to Strike

In many countries of the region, the machinery for dispute resolution remains weakly developed. Two characteristics apply to many countries. First, the procedures for engaging in a legal strike are unusually drawn out and intricate. Often, many mandatory steps of conciliation, mediation, or, indeed, even arbitration must occur before a strike is considered legal. A second characteristic is closely related: the involvement of the state in industrial disputes is unusually great, a situation that often leads to the assumption by workers and employers that it is the role of the labour ministry to resolve disputes, whether individual or collective. Over-reliance on the state's dispute settlement machinery, in turn, both clogs that machinery, resulting in substantial delays, as it has done in the Philippines, and weakens the reliance on negotiation and compromise as the primary means of dispute settlement.

In Vietnam, the Labour Code, which dates from 1995, provides for legal strikes to occur, but only following a series of mandatory steps at dispute settlement. As experience with the governance of the labour-management relationship in a market economy remains relatively new, and also because knowledge of the Labour Code and its procedures is not very widespread, the vast majority of strikes that occur are illegal. Indeed, the irony is that a major cause of strikes are workers' efforts to force employers to comply with the Labour Code as it relates to hours of work or pay, for example, while most such strikes are in violation of procedures stipulated in the Labour Code. States can also constrain the freedom to engage in a peaceful strike by evoking 'essential service' restrictions on industrial action in particular enterprises and industries. The list of essential services included in some countries' labour laws, such as in Thailand, is particularly long, extending well beyond industries that are truly essential.

A Change in the Climate for Freedom of Association?

The foregoing, brief review of the status of a fundamental labour standard in many parts of Southeast Asia gives legitimate grounds for concern. Such a static review, however, ignores the more dynamic issue of the direction of change. Is progress toward greater freedom of association being made, or is the context such that the situation is either stagnating or deteriorating? There would appear to be no easy answer to the question, even less one that applies to the region as a whole. Substantial uncertainty also clouds the current economic conjuncture: employment will suffer, the question is whether this will weaken or strengthen institutions of participation.

In the past few years, there have been at least some signs of an improvement in the climate for freedom of association. These signs have emerged in the political, legal, and, for want of a better term, behavioural spheres. Some examples are shown in Table 6.9.

As is apparent from Table 6.9, many countries in the region have made steps, however tentative at times, toward the direction of greater respect for freedom of association over the past few years. The continuing effort will need to be to ensure that the tendency toward democratisation, which undergirds measures to ensure the development, openness, and transparency of labour market institutions, continues, even as the economic climate remains turbulent.

Conclusion

Freedom from discrimination and freedom of association give evidence of setbacks and steps forward, advances and retreats in the Southeast Asian region. The original evidence presented in the foregoing pages showed a deterioration in the labour market conditions of women workers in several Southeast Asian countries since the late 1990s crisis. Declining labour force participation rates for women, and narrowing but still existing income inequality between men and women do not augur well for future economic growth if girls and women are deprived in the present of making choices that determine future outcomes. As observed, the negative effects of discrimination against women in access to education show up years in the future, transmitted from one generation to the next. A continued policy effort to promote gender-based equality makes as much economic as it does moral sense. It is equally clear that, when tough times emerged in the late 1990s in many parts of the region, countries found themselves with weak mechanisms for social dialogue for forging consensus and minimise social costs. At the same time, a new consciousness of the value of these missing or weak institutions arose in several countries. A renewed bout with economic adversity has characterised the present. Has the lesson that the right to a voice makes good economic sense been fully learned?

Table 6.9 Examples of improvements in climate of freedom of association

Cambodia

Political Climate	Toward greater democratic openness, despite uncertainties.
Legislative Changes	Ratification of all of the ILO's core human rights standards, including Convention Nos. 87 and 98 on freedom of association and the right to bargain.
Behavioural Changes	Employer opposition to trade unions continues, although institutional changes toward greater acceptance are evident in the garment industry, where sound industrial relations are now directly linked to the industry's export quota entitlements to the US market.

Indonesia

Political Climate	Toward greater political openness, despite uncertainties, (e.g. relatively peaceful transition of power in 2001).
Legislative Changes	Revisions to Manpower Act; ratification of all of the ILO's core human rights standards, including Convention Nos. 87 and 98 on freedom of association and the right to bargain.
Behavioural Changes	Proliferation of new trade union federations in climate of greater tolerance for freedom of association.

Thailand

Political Climate	Constitutional reforms of 1997, with explicit support to freedom of association and democratic participation
Legislative Changes	Revision of State Enterprise Labour Relations Act (SELRA), restoring trade union and collective bargaining rights in the state-owned sector in 2000. Ongoing reform at parliamentary level of the law governing labour relations in the private sector – reforms would strengthen freedom of association and worker participation.

Philippines

Political Climate	Relatively peaceful removal from power of previous president in 2000.

Legislative Changes	Reforms slated for basic labour law toward aim of minimising its legalistic and adversarial framework.
Behavioural Changes	Labour-management cooperation pacts initiated in the course of the financial crisis between employers and main trade union federations.

Annex A Regressions of all Low Income Countries

Regression with	*GNP/Capita ($) / 1998*
Primary Gross Enrollment Ratio, Male / 1970	$y = 0.0718x + 41.357$ $R^2 = 0.1615$
Primary Gross Enrollment Ratio, Male / 1990	$y = 0.0576x + 65.472$ $R^2 = 0.1503$
Primary Gross Enrollment Ratio, Female / 1970	$y = 0.1027x + 13.58$ $R^2 = 0.2421$
Primary Gross Enrollment Ratio, Female / 1990	$y = 0.0833x + 41.497$ $R^2 = 0.2226$
Primary Gross Enrollment Ratio / 1970	$y = 0.0976x + 23.091$ $R^2 = 0.26$
Primary Gross Enrollment Ratio / 1990	$y = 0.0707x + 53.771$ $R^2 = 0.1922$

Regression with	*GNP/Capita ($) / 1996*
Literates as % of Adult Population, Estimated, Female / 1970 (1)	$y = 0.0584x + 1.3267$ $R^2 = 0.1691$
Literates as % of Adult Population, Estimated, Male / 1970 (2)	$y = 0.036x + 28.17$ $R^2 = 0.0763$
Gender Gap in Education (1)-(2)	$y = -0.0225x + 26.843$ $R^2 = 0.1058$
Literates as % of Adult Population, Estimated, Female / 1980 (3)	$y = 0.0661x + 6.4693$ $R^2 = 0.197$
Literates as % of Adult Population, Estimated, Male / 1980 (4)	$y = 0.037x + 36.541$ $R^2 = 0.0875$
Gender Gap in Education (3)-(4)	$y = -0.0291x + 30.072$ $R^2 = 0.1695$

Note: Include all low income countries where data available

Source: Global Education Database, UNESCO 2001

Notes

1. Amartya S. (1999), *Development as Freedom*, Knopf, New York.
2. Figures from *Key Indicators of the Labour Market* 2001, ILO, Geneva, Indicators 1 and 8.

3. ILO, Regional Office for Asia and the Pacific (1999), *Towards Gender Equality in the World of Work in Asia and the Pacific*, ILO, Bangkok, p.5.
4. See, for example: *Engendering Development - Through Gender Equality in Rights, Resources, and Voice*, Oxford University Press and World Bank, New York (2001); Dollar, D. and Gatti, R. (1999) 'Gender Inequality, Income and Growth: Are Good Times Good for Women?,' in *Policy Research Report on Gender and Development*, The World Bank Development Research Group/ Poverty Reduction and Economic Management Network Working Paper Series, No. 1; Klasen, S. (1999), 'Does Gender Inequality Reduce Growth and Development? Evidence from Cross-Country Regressions,' in *Policy Research Report on Gender and Development*, The World Bank Development Research Group / Poverty Reduction and Economic Management Network Working Paper Series, No. 7.
5. This literature is surveyed in Galli, R. and Kucera, D. '*The Economic Impacts of Fundamental Rights at Work*', an unpublished ILO International Institute for Labour Studies working paper, May 2001.
6. The UNDP's 'gender empowerment' index comprises the number of seats held in parliament by women, women's share of administrators and managers in the workforce, women's share of professional and technical jobs in the workforce, and women's GDP per capita.
7. The UNDP's gender-related development index comprises women's life expectancy, literacy, school enrolment, and GDP per capita, all relative to men's.
8. *World Labour Report 1997-1998: Industrial Relations, Democracy, Social Stability*, ILO, Geneva (1998), reviews some of this literature in Chapter 4.
9. One source of information on the status of human rights in Asia and elsewhere is the US State Department's annual survey of human rights, the latest edition of which can be accessed at website: www.state.gov

References

Auer, P. (2000), *Employment Revival in Europe: Labour Market Success in Austria, Denmark, Ireland, and the Netherlands*, ILO, Geneva.

Campbell, D. (1999), Industrial Relations: Notes from the Field, *Labour Education*, vol. 4, no. 117.

Campbell, D. (2001), 'Social Dialogue and Labour Market Adjustment in East Asia after the Crisis', in G. Betcherman and R. Islam, *East Asian Labor Markets and the Economic Crisis*, World Bank, Washington, D.C.

Economist Intelligence Unit (2001), *Terror in America: the Impact on Business*, Economist Intelligence Unit Limited, London.

Freeman, R. and Medoff, J. (1984), *What do Unions do?*, Basic Books, New York.

ILO (1999), *Towards Gender Equality in the World of Work in Asia and the Pacific*, ILO, Bangkok.

ILO (2001), *Key Indicators of the Labour Market*, ILO, Geneva.

Kucera, D. (2001), *Fundamental Rights at Work' as Determinants of Manufacturing Wages and FDI Inflows*, unpublished working paper, ILO International Institute for Labour Studies, May 2001.

Lee, E. (1999), *The Asian Financial Crisis: The Challenge for Social Policy*, International Labour Office, Geneva.

Rodrik, D. (1999), *The New Global Economy and Developing Countries: Making Openness Work*, Overseas Development Council, Washington, D.C.

Seguino, S. (2000), 'Gender Inequality and Economic Growth: A Cross-Country Analysis',

World Development, vol. 28, no. 7.
Sen, A. (1999), *Development as Freedom*, Knopf, New York.
UNDP (1995), *Human Development Report 1995*, United Nations Development Programme, New York.

PART 3
SOCIAL POLICY

7 The Welfare System in Southeast Asia: Development and Challenges
RAYMOND K H CHAN

Since the Second World War, Asian countries have experienced unprecedented economic growth. The development of Southeast Asian countries, with the exception of Singapore, began later than that of the countries in East Asia. However, in recent decades, Southeast Asian countries have invested in the development of their own welfare regimes, and have built up a system, with mixture of public (formal) and private (informal) contributions, that offers support to individuals, even though public funding is limited. The system is based on individual work and intra-family assistance, which are based on their traditional norms and values, in a liberal capitalistic economy. Mutual assistance in local community is still important, but it is gradually being replaced by institutionalised non-governmental organisations. The development of a welfare system, however unstable, has received growing attention in Asia.

The financial crisis that began in 1997 signified a drastic change in the policy context. The future of the economy is bleak and unemployment is increasingly widespread and prolonged, and has had a significant impact on individual's (and household's) self-reliance. Economic growth is no longer taken for granted in national and individual planning, and governments are faced with the long-term prospect of shrinking public resources and increasing social demands. The sustainability of the traditional welfare system is in doubt. This paper will describe and compare the characteristics, achievements, and problems of the welfare systems of Indonesia, Malaysia, the Philippines, Singapore, and Thailand. It will also examine the risks to the welfare system that emerged after the Asian financial crisis.

The Asian Welfare System

During recent decades, various social protection and welfare systems have been established in Asian countries. Comparative studies of the welfare systems in this region, particularly those in East Asian countries, have been undertaken by outside scholars. They have identified distinctive features of the Asian system which distinguish it from Western welfare models. Since there are very few studies of Southeast Asia's welfare systems, we have to rely on the findings of studies of the East Asian welfare models.

Although some time-honoured terms were retained, such as 'institutional' and 'residual', new terms emerged in the course of these studies. Jones employs the terms 'Oikonomic Welfare State' (1990) and 'Confucian Welfare State' (1993) to describe the systems in Asia. Esping-Andersen's notion of 'Three Worlds of Welfare Capitalism' was popular, but only Japan was considered in Esping-Andersen's study and it has been described as highly liberal (1990). Hong Kong has also been viewed as adopting a liberal welfare capitalism (Chan, 1996; McLaughlin, 1993).

However, the liberal attitude does not adequately characterise the Asian system. The social arrangement, arising from the unique cultural context in this region, has been characterised as 'conservative corporatism without worker participation', 'solidarity without equality; laissez-faire without libertarianism' and a 'household economy' (Jones, 1993, p.214). Doling and Kling argue that there are strong and pervasive cultural-religious forces underlying the notions of welfare, such as Confucianism for the Chinese and Islam for the Muslims (2000, p.11). The World Bank, in a discussion of care for elderly, describe the Asian system as 'family-solidarity based' (1994).

The term, 'East Asian welfare model' was used by Kwon (1997) to differentiate the systems in Japan and South Korea. In his analysis, he shows this model to be characterised by low public expenditure, a strong regulatory mechanism, and limited income redistribution. Holliday (2000) derives the 'productivist welfare capitalism' in which social policy is subordinated to economic policy. He suggests that there is no uniform model of Asian welfare system, it can, however, be broadly divided into three sub-types: 'facilitative' in which the state only plays a facilitative and regulatory role (e.g., Hong Kong); 'developmental-universalist' which emphasises the principle of universalism in provision (e.g., Japan, South Korea, and Taiwan); and 'productivist-particularist' in which the state directs individual welfare provision, with minimal rights and forced individual provisions (e.g., Singapore). White and Goodman (1998) and Ramesh (1995) also argue that there is no single and unified model in this region. Similar observations on the differences in state intervention, scale, and the principles of provision are also supplied by Flynn (1999, ch.6).

At the same time, scholars have argued that, despite marked differences, Asian welfare systems do have some common characteristics. Wilding (1997) identifies several similarities: low public expenditure on welfare and the adoption of a facilitative, regulatory, and enabling role by the state; productivist social policy focused on economic growth; a general dislike of the notion of the 'welfare state', strong residualist elements; limited commitment to social citizenship; and the central role of the family.

Gough also observes that welfare in this region is increasingly in the hands of growing private markets and community-based organisations (2000a, p.4). However, with decreasing government investment and small market shares, the region can only achieve poverty reduction and high standards of health and education if there are substantial family provision and private market consumption (2000a, p.11). State provision focuses on items of social investments, such as education and health. Welfare arrangements in these countries are the product of specific socio-economic-political factors in each country and historical legacy (Gough, 2000b). Social citizenship is still a new concept in some Asian countries.

Analysis of the welfare system involves a consideration of the welfare mix and welfare outcomes. 'Welfare mix' refers to the pattern of state provisions and the wider provisions of welfare in society by the market, family/household, and community. According to Gough's analysis, family and market provisions are the dominant mode of delivery and consumption of education, health, pensions and safety nets in East Asia (2000a, Figure 2). The outcome of this situation in Asia is a low level of de-commodification and de-familiarisation, and high degree of social stratification. It is generally believed that such an arrangement supports the welfare system and protects people's welfare. Individuals must work to receive monetary reward and must redistribute these resources to their family member in accordance with a strong sense of mutual obligation within the family. The family deploys these resources to purchase services in the private market. The community provide support to those in need on a moral basis. For those who have to rely on public services, the state will strategically intervene. Employment and income derived from employment are of utmost importance in this welfare arrangement.

The Development and Characteristics of Welfare Regimes in Southeast Asia

There is a general assumption that welfare systems in Southeast Asia have lagged behind the systems developed in the West. According to the

Human Development Index (HDI) compiled by the United Nations Development Programme, the scores for Southeast Asian countries are below the OECD average. Only Singapore and Brunei achieved the status of high human development. Nevertheless, five countries in Southeast Asia (Brunei, Malaysia, the Philippines, Singapore and Thailand) achieved higher scores than the world average. Moreover, according to the same index, the progress of the Southeast Asian countries has been stable and observable in the past decades (Table 7.1).

From these figures, it is clear that the progress of human development in Southeast Asian countries is commendable. Various social services were initiated and established in many of these countries during the colonial period. However, real development did not take place until the 1960s when these countries gained autonomy from their former sovereigns and experienced industrialisation.

Different policies were developed in different countries for different reasons. However, there are two commonly accepted reasons given for this development. The first is a political concern for legitimacy, and the second is a response to the needs arising from economic and national development. According to Ramesh (2000, p.175), the policies adopted should be one that promote economic development, and are a credit to the state. The development of social services in these Southeast Asian societies is connected to the development of their economies. The primary objective of the governments of these countries is to promote economic development by various strategies, and, according to the logic of 'productivist', social services are measured by their contribution to economic development. On the other hand, social services and other policies are used to address the problems that arise in the process of economic and social development.

Table 7.1 Human development index (HDI), selected countries, 1975-1999

	1975	1980	1985	1990	1995	1999
Singapore	0.719	0.753	0.779	0.816	0.885	0.876
Brunei	--	0.806	0.811	0.825	0.889	0.857
Malaysia	0.614	0.657	0.691	0.720	0.758	0.774
Thailand	0.603	0.645	0.675	0.713	0.749	0.757
Philippines	0.649	0.683	0.687	0.716	0.733	0.749
Vietnam	--	--	0.581	0.604	0.647	0.682
Indonesia	0.467	0.529	0.581	0.622	0.662	0.677
Myanmar	--	--	--	--	--	0.551
Cambodia	--	--	--	--	--	0.541
Laos	--	--	0.372	0.402	0.443	0.476
East Asia and Pacific						0.719
South Asia						0.564
OECD						0.900
World						0.716

Note: Figures for Brunei from 1980 to 1995 are from Human Development Report. As these are based on different calculations, they are not strictly comparable to the figure given for 1999.

Source: Human Development Report, various years

Using social expenditure as an indicator, we can observe a continuous increase in social expenditure (Table 7.2). The percentage of the GDP allocated to social expenditure has increased from 1972 to 1995, though at different paces in different countries. The percentage of total government expenditure allocated to social expenditure has remained stable, at approximately 33 percent in Malaysia, Singapore, and Thailand. The Philippines records a stable figure of approximately 25 percent of total government expenditure in the past decades. Although Indonesia has the lowest percentage among the five countries, it has doubled in recent years. Among the four categories of social expenditure, education consistently claimed the greatest share, while social security invariably claimed the least.

Table 7.2 Percentage of government spending on social policies, annual average

	% of GDP			% of Total Govt. Expenditure		
	1972-79	1980-89	1990-95	1972-79	1980-89	1990-95
Indonesia						
Education	1.93	2.01	1.68	8.77	9.15	9.57
Housing	0.31	0.32	1.21	1.40	1.48	7.62
Health	0.51	0.48	0.47	2.28	2.18	2.69
Soc Security	--	--	0.88	--	--	5.75
Total	2.75	2.81	4.24	12.45	12.81	25.63
Malaysia						
Education	5.63	5.88	5.39	22.45	19.20	20.03
Housing	0.17	1.79	1.55	0.69	5.97	5.79
Health	1.68	1.52	1.46	6.71	4.82	5.49
Soc Security	0.77	1.25	1.47	3.11	3.99	5.51
Total	8.25	10.44	9.87	32.96	33.98	36.82
Philippines						
Education	1.89	2.29	3.03	14.53	17.24	16.08
Housing	0.24	0.30	0.23	1.95	2.42	1.20
Health	0.58	0.66	0.65	4.42	5.01	3.42
Soc Security	0.34	0.21	0.43	2.60	1.61	2.25
Total	3.05	3.46	4.34	23.50	26.28	22.95
Singapore						
Education	3.00	4.73	4.08	16.63	18.62	21.89
Housing	1.27	2.09	1.18	6.86	7.99	6.59
Health	1.45	1.42	1.12	8.05	5.72	6.30
Soc Security	0.28	0.37	0.53	1.56	1.47	3.04
Total	6.00	8.61	6.91	33.10	33.80	37.82
Thailand						
Education	3.28	3.66	3.22	20.72	19.62	21.04
Housing	0.48	0.35	0.49	2.95	1.85	3.18
Health	0.66	1.00	1.15	4.24	5.57	7.56
Soc Security	0.61	0.57	0.55	3.68	3.13	3.61
Total	5.03	5.58	5.41	31.59	30.17	35.39

Source: Ramesh, 2000, Table 2.8

Education

Education received the greatest input from the state in all five countries. With the exception of Thailand, close to full enrollment to primary education has almost been achieved (Table 7.7) through the implementation of heavily subsidised (or free) and often compulsory education service. Among the five countries, the Philippines was the first to implement six-year free education policy in 1935. Thailand adopted the policy in 1939 but could not achieve the goal at that time; the policy was restated in 1978. Malaysia adopted the policy in 1961, and Indonesia, in 1994. Singapore had no policy of compulsory or totally free primary education, though the government has heavily subsidised primary education since the 1960s, and students pay only a token fee. It was not until 2000 that the Singapore government decided to adopt and implement compulsory education for six years (Ministry of Education, Singapore, 2000). The aim of these countries is to secure primary education for all as the initial priority, and then followed with an expansion of secondary and higher education. In 1995, Singapore recorded the highest gross enrollment rate to tertiary education (33.7 percent) among the five countries, followed by the Philippines (29.0 percent), Thailand (20.1 percent), Malaysia (11.7 percent), and Indonesia (11.3 percent). Higher education remains restricted to a relatively small sector of the population. Educational facilities in these countries receive large subsidies from the state, as investment in human capital through education is considered as one of the major forces in economic miracle.

Private consumption of education is significant in these countries; parents are willing to invest in their children's future. While public primary and secondary education still heavily subsidised by the state, the private sector can have relatively more responsibility for higher education and specialised technical and skills training programmes. The private sector in the Philippines is responsible for a large number of educational institutes at every level, particularly the higher level. In the rest of countries, education is heavily subsidised by the state and, therefore, regulated by it. Due to the regulations and restrictions, especially those pertaining to higher education (in, for example, Malaysia and Singapore), the private sector has had difficulty establishing centres for education. However, in recent years, private participation has increased, particularly in creating opportunities for higher education in Malaysia, Indonesia, and Thailand (Ramesh, 2000, ch.5).

Table 7.3 Private enrolment as a percentage of total enrolment

Countries	Primary			Secondary			Higher
	1980	1990	1996	1980	1990	1996	Mid-1980s
Indonesia	21	18	17	49	48	42	57.7
Malaysia	n.a.	0	1	n.a.	4	3	7.6
Philippines	5	7	7	48	36	29	83.0
Singapore	26	24	27	28	28	33	n.a.
Thailand	8	10	13	13	10	6	6.3

Sources: UNESCO, 1993, 2000

Housing

The main housing issues in these countries are housing shortages and the creation of slums in urban areas, which are the result of rapid urbanisation, massive rural-urban migration (with the exception of Singapore), and population increases in recent decades. Public housing remains a relatively minor public policy issue in all the countries except Singapore. Generally speaking, housing policy consists of strategies for slum clearance and improvement in urban areas (to achieve better urban land use and development) and for the provision of affordable housing for low-income residents. Except in Singapore, the private sector has a relatively major role in public projects, and the government's role is to facilitate their participation. Self-built housing is quite common, especially in rural areas and in lots that are the focus of site and services improvement initiatives.

In Singapore, public housing not only addresses the housing needs of low-income groups who cannot afford housing in the private market but is used as a political tool to achieve the long-term objectives of national development and the stabilisation of society. Singapore's public housing policy was initiated in 1960 and promoted home ownership as the dominant tenure form from 1964. Almost 90 percent of their residents are now living in owned flats constructed by Housing and Development Board. The housing construction scheme, housing grant scheme, and housing upgrade and urban redevelopment projects are primarily funded by public sources. To register to purchase a public housing flat is a social right of citizenship. The private sector plays a relatively minor role in Singapore; it focuses on providing more expensive housing for the higher-income groups. Since 1968, homebuyers have been able to withdraw money from their Central Provident Fund (CPF) account to purchase a flat.

In other Southeast Asian countries, low-cost public housing has been initiated to promote the welfare of low-income groups and to deal with the increasing problem of slums in urban areas. The public housing sector is smaller than that of in Singapore. Thailand developed its public housing policy in the 1950s and adopted the National Housing Policy in 1983. The National Housing Authority, which concentrated on housing construction, was established in the same year. The government and private banks provide the funding for various housing programmes. To generate adequate funding for low-cost housing construction, the National Housing Authority sometimes builds and sells expensive housing and applies the profit gained to low-income housing projects. The basic strategy of National Housing Authority is to develop housing for those who have the desire and means to be home owners and to assist those who without sufficient means through other programmes, such as site and service improvements and slum upgrading projects. The government also provides funding to private developers in joint ventures to provide low-cost housing (Buracom, 1987; Goh, 1997; Pongprayoon, 1997; Porananond, 1997).

In Indonesia, several groups participate in the provision of low-cost housing. The National Housing Development Corporation (*Perum Perumnas*) was established in 1974; its initial aim was to provide 24,000 units in urban areas for civil servants and the military. Since the mid-1980s, it has built small, affordable houses for low, and middle-income groups, usually in the demolished slums (the 'kampungs') of urban areas. The public sector has joined the private sector in efforts to increase the quantity and quality of housing. Financial services, such as mortgage financing, can be obtained through the State Saving Bank (Bank Tabungan Negara). Improvement of the kampungs is another major focus of the housing policy. In 1969, the government initiated the Kampung Improvement Programme (KIP) in Jakarta and gradually extended the programme to 220 cities around the country. The government provided initial funding but in the 1970s, the World Bank continued the programme by providing loans. The focus of the programmes is to improve the standard of living by creating better public facilities. In 1985, the KIP built some rental units for low-income households as a demonstration project for the private sector (Koswara, 1997).[1]

Similarly, in the Philippines, the housing policy focuses on tackling the issue of slums and providing affordable housing to low-income groups. The slum upgrading programme, initiated in the 1960s, focused on slum clearance and resettlement. Since the 1980s, the government's official human settlements policy has addressed the issue of slums. The National Housing Authority is the sole authority for shelter development. The Authority has developed site and service programmes for households with incomes between the 15th and 65th percentile. Lots are made available to the lowest-income households in the target group through cross subsidisation from the sale of commercial plots. Under the relocation and resettlement program, serviced lots were sold to the squatters who were made homeless when they were displaced. This was to discourage them from moving back to the urban centre. It also provided a small amount of conventional housing for the middle-income group. The National Home Mortgage Finance Corporation established in 1977, operates a secondary mortgage market system to increase the flow of funds into housing. The Home Mutual Fund was established in 1978 as a saving system for government employees.[2]

In Malaysia, the major objectives of the housing policy are to provide cheap housing meeting basic social needs (based on concept of democratic home owning) and to improve the living condition of urban squatters (Agus, 2000, p.158). Under the New Economic Policy, more resources have been devoted to the low-income sector, accounting for 42.5 percent in the Second Malaysia Plan (1971-1975) and 54.5 percent in the Seventh Malaysia Plan (1996-2000) of the total housing budget. Sixty-eight percent of the housing units funded by the federal government, in accordance with the Sixth and Seventh Malaysia Plan, are low- and low/moderate-cost. Squatter improvement is addressed by two strategies: the provision and improvement of public facilities, such as sanitation, water and electricity supply, and squatter clearance. Squatter clearance involves the demolition and redevelopment of squatter areas and the relocation of residents to low-cost housing blocks with better facilities. In the 1990s, the involvement of the private sector in the provision of housing units, including low-cost housing, has been encouraged by the government. The government is willing to provide low-premium land for the private sector to build low-income housing. The private sector is also actively involved in programmes in which relocated squatters are sold housing units at a price that is guaranteed to be comparable to that of government low-income housing (Agus, 2000). Like the CPF scheme in Singapore, the Employees Provident Fund (EPF) allows account holders to withdraw money from their account for purchasing a flat, purchasing and/or building a village house, or reducing or redeeming a mortgage loan.

Health

In all countries, except the Philippines, the public sector has played a dominant role in in-patient and primary health-care services. Free or low-cost public health services are provided, especially for low-income groups, the rural population, and, in the case of the indigent in the Philippines. Social insurance schemes are not a popular strategy in these countries, although there are some employee insurance schemes covering sickness and accidents. There are government-funded insurance policies for civil servants in Indonesia and Thailand. In other countries, health expenses are partially covered by employee and employer contributions to social security programmes, such as EPF in Malaysia and CPF in Singapore. Out-of-pocket expense is a primary source of funding for health services in these countries, accounting for between 42.4 percent of the funding (in Malaysia) and 65.4 percent of the funding (in Thailand).

A relatively small share of these countries' resources is used to finance the public provision of health services. In 1997, the private sector contributed more to total health expenditure (between 51.5 percent and 63.2 percent) than the public sector in all countries, except Malaysia (Table 7.4). It is common knowledge that the public sector has limited manpower and resources. For example, in Malaysia, the public sector hired 45 percent of all doctors but was responsible for 75 percent of all hospital beds (Ramesh, 2000, p.117). In Singapore and Malaysia, CPF and EPF contributors are allowed to use their savings to purchase additional health insurance from approved private insurance companies.

Table 7.4 Public and private health expenditure

Countries	% of total health expenditure, 1997			% of GDP, 1998	
	Public	Private	Out-of-pocket	Public	Private
Indonesia	36.8	63.2	47.4	0.7	0.8
Malaysia	57.6	42.4	42.2	1.4	1.0
Philippines	48.5	51.5	49.1	1.7	2.0
Singapore	35.8	64.2	64.2	1.2	2.1
Thailand	33.0	67.0	65.4	1.9	4.1

Sources: WHO, 2000; UNDP, 2001

In recent years, Singapore and Malaysia have experienced an increasing trend of privatisation. In Singapore, the trend is to achieve higher efficiency and better quality of service through corporatisation of the former public health facilities. In Malaysia, the changes have occurred in the public health support services and the monitoring of health services rather than in the actual provision of health care and clinical services (Barraclough, 2000; Ramesh, 2000).

Social Security

Social insurance schemes are not extensive in the five countries under review; people must rely instead on compulsory personal saving programmes. In all five countries, governments play a minor role, mainly restricted to monitoring and managing compulsory saving programmes for private sector employees. However, they shoulder the major responsibility for financing the programmes for public sector employees. Under the compulsory saving programmes, employees and employers are required to contribute a percentage of the employees' income. In recent years, employees have been encouraged to purchase additional insurance schemes from the private sector to supplement their protection, such as in Singapore.

All the major retirement protection programmes, except the Government Services Insurance System (GSIS) of the Philippines, were created after the Second World War. In the 1950s, the EPF in Malaysia, the CPF in Singapore, the pension fund for public sector employees in Thailand, and the Social Security System (SSS) in the Philippines were established. The *Asuransi Sosial Tenaga Kerja* (ASTEK), which was replaced by the *Jaminan Sosial Tenaga Kerja* (JAMSOTEK) in 1982, was set up in 1977 in Indonesia (similar schemes, *Tabungan dan Asuransi Pegawai Negeri* (TASPEN), *Asuransi Social ABRI* (ASABRI), and the pension schemes for public sector employees, had already been established in the 1960s). Private sector employees in Thailand are required to participate in the provident fund scheme established in 1983.

As Asher (Ramesh, 2000) observes, the system follows a provident fund model, which is a compulsory individual saving model, relying on employee and employer contributions. This is a system based on work, and benefits are tied up with contributions, which are determined by income level. Inter-account transfer, except in approved circumstances (such as between family members in Singapore), is not allowed. The level of benefit obtained when the policy matures varies among employees and between private and public sector employees. The schemes reflect the ideology of status differentiation, and the result is to reinforce the stratified society. The coverage of these schemes is rather limited (Table 7.5).

In addition to retirement protection, social security insurance offers protection in cases of sickness, accidents, pregnancy, disability, and death. These programmes include the Social Security Act in Thailand, the SSS in the Philippines, JAMSOTEK in Indonesia, the Employee's Social Security Act (SOCSO) in Malaysia, and employee insurance programmes in Singapore.

Table 7.5 Coverage of social security programme, 1992-1995

Countries	% of population	% of labour force
Indonesia	9	20
Malaysia[1]	20	50
Philippines	29	73
Singapore[2]	39	81
Thailand[3]	18	32

Notes:
a. Figures for Malaysia include active contributors to EPF only
b. Figures for Singapore include active contributors to CPF only
c. Figures for Thailand exclude public sector employees

Source: Ramesh, 2000, Table 3.8

Personal Social Services

Personal social services provided to persons with special needs are diversified in this region. The services are very much determined by their specific socio-demographic characteristics. All the countries provide services to children and youth (particularly those who suffer from abuse, poverty, or homelessness), the elderly, women and families at risk; and the disabled. Generally speaking, most funding is invested in remedial services.

At a very general level, we can identify some similarities across the countries. Informal care (provided by family and community), as opposed to formal care (provided by the state), is a very important source of care in this welfare system. People in difficulty rely first on themselves, then on their family, and then on their community. This is reflected in policy documents. For example, the 'Family Values' of Singapore depicts the family as the core of the society, which provides care and support to individuals. Familial responsibility was furthered strengthened by the Parents Maintenance Act in 1996 and the establishment of the Public Education Committee on Family in 2001. This is a measure to avoid the pitfalls of welfare state in the West, such as high taxes and social security contributions (Lim, 1994).

The Eighth National Economic and Social Development (1997-2001) of Thailand describes the government's policy as an attempt to boost the capabilities of families and communities in order to help them achieve greater self-reliance and to support individual development (NESDB, 1996). The Seventh Economic and Social Development Plan (1992-1996) and long-term policies and plans for elderly care covering the period from 1992 to 2011 also call for greater reliance on the family to provide for its elderly members (Knodel et al., 1992).

In the Philippines, the Comprehensive and Integrated Delivery of Social Services (CIDSS) established to help families cope with poverty, is very much family- and community-based. The National Social Welfare Policy of Malaysia, completed in 1990, states that in order to achieve the goals to secure and stabilise society to facilitate continuous national progress, it is necessary to 'inculcate the values of community living', and 'to nurture the spirit of mutual assistance and altruism at all levels of society'. As well as governmental bodies, religious and charitable organisations provide social services, based on their own social networks, and systems to help their local communities (Yunus and Bakar, 2000, p.103).

Malaysia, like other countries, is dependent on informal community assistance but has also witnessed the establishment of an increasing number of non-governmental organisations (NGOs). They represent the institutionalisation and, to a certain extent, the professionalisation of the former amateur, charity and philanthropic activities. NGOs have already evolved as partners in national social welfare strategies, with or without subsidy from the public sector. A recent development in the region is the growth of the self-help organisation, for example the disabled, as another alternative means for assistance and services (Kwok, Chan and Chan, 2002).

Characteristics, Achievements and Problems

As the above descriptions reveal, the systems in these countries vary but contain important similarities which reflect the general assumptions of the Asian welfare system. It is clear from the amount of public expenditure that the state's intervention in social provision is not as high as that in the West; however, these countries have, in fact, increased their investment in their welfare systems. Of the five policy sectors, education and health receive the most attention and, perhaps, the widest coverage. This may reflect the need of improve human resource in order to support economic development in these countries.

The social security programmes cover only a limited percentage of population, primarily those who work, and their benefits are commensurate to their income level and their status as private or public sector employees. It is not surprising, then, that the outcome of this arrangement is a highly stratified society. There is little, if any, opportunity to transfer money across accounts, which means there is no effort to redistribute the benefits among other income groups. The outcome reinforces the existing inequalities created by the market and social structures. It is not surprising that income inequality in these countries is relatively high (Table 7.6). The issue of attaining equity is not a primary concern (Schmidt, 1997, p.40).

Table 7.6 Income inequality

Countries	Gini index	Share of income / consumption	
		Poorest 20%	Richest 20%
Indonesia	31.7 (1999)	9.0% [a]	41.4%
Malaysia	49.2 (1997)	4.4% [b]	54.3%
Philippines	46.2 (1997)	5.4% [a]	52.3%
Singapore	46.7 (1999)	2.8% [b]	49.9%
Thailand	41.4 (1998)	6.4% [a]	48.4%

Notes:
a. consumption based
b. income based

Sources: UNDP, 2001; Department of Statistics, Singapore, 2000

There is not a strong sense of social citizenship in these countries, though citizens may consider themselves entitled to certain public services. This sense of entitlement has gradually evolved during the process of welfare development through expanded provision and legislation. It is a by-product rather than the intended policy outcome of continuous political struggle. Policy development is seldom the result of competition among political parties and classes. In fact, the ruling parties in these countries have enjoyed a relatively long and stable period of governing, unchallenged by any equal political force. The policies are more the result of calculation and design, which reflect the ruling elite's interpretation of the changing environment. Working class mobilisation, which is popular in the West, is not a significant political force in this part of the world.

In Southeast Asia, work is the primary source of income for individuals and families. Income from employment is used to pay for various social security programmes, and to support private consumption of social services, such as education and health. The ability of individual to get a paid work is important; the wage-earning sector is growing in the process of modernisation and industrialisation. In 1997, Thailand had the highest percentage among the five countries of its labour force (57.4 percent) engaged in the agricultural sector (the percentage declined from 82 percent in 1965). In Indonesia, the Philippines, Malaysia, and Singapore, 60.6 percent, 62.7 percent, 72.7 percent and 100 percent, respectively, of their labour force worked in

1997 (Lim, 2001, p.43). Schmidt argues that these countries encourage economic competition by adopting a strategy of coercive incentives to work and save, and providing less welfare-state-inspired intervention (1997, p.40).

Family and community also play a significant role in providing assistance and support to members in need. Their contributions are particularly important for those who are not formally employed such as homemakers and the long-term unemployed. The social assistance programmes in these countries, with the exception of Singapore, have not been systematised and properly installed. Instead, economic development and employment are considered the best solutions to the problem of poverty, followed by community- and household-based support, and training programmes. This response reflects, in sequence, the work-family-community-based ideology within the system.

On the whole, Southeast Asian society emphasises the merits of individual self-reliance, family and community mutual care, voluntary charity, and philanthropic initiatives. These elements have been strongly supported by the governments and have been cherished by certain sectors of the society. These cultural traits also partially explain the weak sense of social citizenship and the continuous dominant role of family, community, and NGOs in this welfare arrangement. On the whole, the governments in this region regard the Western style of welfare state with scepticism for two reasons: they believe it destroys entrepreneurial initiative and creates a culture of welfare dependency, which is contrary to the ideals of their culture (Booth, 2000, p.160).

The private sector has always had an important role, either through its own initiative or through joint ventures with the government. There have been joint ventures in housing, education, and health services. In recent decades, private sector participation in the provision of education and health services, and in private insurance policies has increased. People are becoming more affluent, so they are more willing and able to invest in higher quality services.

As the human development indicators reveal, Southeast Asian countries are on a course of continuous improvement. Their achievements are reflected by various social indicators: higher levels of education, improved health, and a reduction of poverty (Table 7.7). However the figures also indicate that there is still ample room for improvement. Apart from income inequality, there are problems in the eradication of poverty, as well as regional disparities, and gender inequalities.

Regional disparities, especially between rural and urban areas, present a problem. Studies have shown that the people living in rural areas are poorer and more vulnerable to health problems and long-term poverty. The poverty rate in Indonesia varies between urban and rural areas and across provinces (Booth, 2000, p.151). For example, in Jakarta, the poverty rate was 4.13 percent in 2000, while in East Nusa Tenggara and Irian Jaya, they reached 44.7 percent and 55.2 percent respectively (Tarmidi, 2001, Table 2). In Malaysia, there are concentrations of poverty in the states of Terengganu (33 percent), Kelentan (27 percent), and Sabah (18.5 percent). In the Philippines, the completion rate for primary education is 100 percent in Manila and barely 30 percent in the poorest provinces.[3] In Thailand, the provinces in the north, northeast and south are poorer than Bangkok and the central provinces (Booth, 1997). The probability of dying is much higher among the poor. For example, for persons between 15 to 59, the probability of death is 2.3, 3.1 and 2.9 times higher for poor men than for those with higher incomes in Indonesia, Malaysia, and the Philippines respectively. For females, the ratios are 3.1, 5.1 and 6.1 in these three countries respectively (WHO, 1999).

Table 7.7 Social indicators

	Indonesia	Malaysia	Philippines	Singapore	Thailand
Education					
Net primary enrollment rate					
1980	89	92	95	100	92
1997	99	100	100	91	88
Net secondary enrollment rate					
1980	42	48	72	66	25
1997	56	64	78	76	48
Adult literacy rate					
1985	100	100	100	100	100
1999	115	114	105	107	105
Health					
Life expectancy					
1970-1975	49.2	63.0	58.1	69.5	59.5
1995-2000	65.1	71.9	68.6	77.1	69.6
Infant mortality rate					
1970	104	46	60	22	74
1999	38	8	31	4	26
Poverty % of population*					
1975	64.3	17.4	35.7	--	8.1
1995	11.4	<1.0	25.5	--	<1.0

* Define as income level of less than USD 1 a day per capita using 1985 prices

Sources: Bidani, 1997; Department of Statistics, 2000; UNDP, 2001; World Bank, 2001

Women have enjoyed a more favourable social environment in recent decades. They have achieved standards comparable to those of men in, for example, enrollment rate. Increasing numbers of women have joined the workforce; they have more opportunities. However, they still suffer from hidden sexual discrimination and stereotyping. There are still discrepancies between men and women in literacy rates, participation in public affairs, and income. These factors limit the ability of women to attain a better standard of living and to achieve greater security through work and income (Table 7.8).

Table 7.8 Gender social indicators, 1999

Countries	Adult literacy rate (% of those aged 15 and above)		Combined enrollment rate (%)		Estimated earnings per capita (PPP USD)	
	Female	Male	Female	Male	Female	Male
Indonesia	81.3	91.5	61	68	1,929	3,780
Malaysia	82.8	91.1	67	64	5,153	11,183
Philippines	94.9	95.3	84	80	2,684	4,910
Singapore	88.0	96.2	75	76	13,693	27,739
Thailand	93.5	97.0	61	60	4,634	7,660

Source: UNDP, 2001

There are loopholes and limitations in the existing welfare system, and the gaps are largely filled by private services, informal care from families and communities, or NGOs. This arrangement was possible when individuals and the state enjoyed stable and almost full employment, growing incomes and increasing revenue. Individuals had generated sufficient income to support themselves and their families, and able to contribute to personal saving plans, public social security programmes, and private insurance policies. However, the weaknesses of such arrangement have been shown in the past and resurfaced, on a large scale, during the recent Asian financial crisis. The current arrangement of the public welfare system, the individual, the family, and the community has limitations and is incapable of dealing with emerging challenges.

The Asian Financial Crisis and its Social Impacts in Southeast Asia

The crisis in 1997 had a significant impact on the Southeast Asian welfare system. All the major economies in the region recorded a sharp decrease in their GDP growth rate from 1997 to 1998. As Table 7.9 indicates, economic problems and subsequent reforms led to rising unemployment during the period from 1997 to 1999. The latest figures show that unemployment is still higher than it was before the financial crisis in most countries.

In the countries under review, rising unemployment has been accompanied by a reduction in workers' incomes. The situation is worse in countries that had experienced a high rate of inflation: Indonesia, the Philippines, Malaysia and Thailand. A comparison of 1998 and 1997 data shows that the real earnings of workers in Thailand, Indonesia, and Malaysia were reduced by 21 percent, 27 percent, and 1 percent, respectively (Knowles et al., 1999, p.2). The real per capita household income was reduced by 12 percent in the Philippines during the same period (Knowles et al, 1999, p.3).

All the countries except Indonesia, have experienced a slight increase in income inequality (Knowles et al., 1999, p.4).[4] From 1997 to 2000, the Gini coefficient of Singapore climbed steadily from 0.444 to 0.481 (Department of Statistics, Singapore, 2001). Similarly, the number of Southeast Asian people living in poverty increased dramatically in the early phase of the financial crisis, particularly in Indonesia, and then gradually declined (World Bank, 2000b). The poverty rate in Indonesia increased from 17.7 percent in 1996 to 24.2 percent in 1998, and then declined to 15.8 percent in 2000 (Tarmidi, 2001). Thailand also recorded a 14 percent increase in the incidence of poverty in the same period (World Bank, 2000a, Table 6.1). In the Philippines, more than 90 percent of families reported that they were adversely affected by higher prices for food and other commodities (World Bank, 2000a, p.114).

The impact of rising unemployment and decreasing income was counteracted by various strategies on the part of individuals, households, communities, and governments. Individuals searched for alternative jobs. In Thailand, more people responded to unemployment by relocating in rural areas and engaging in agricultural labour as a temporary measure in the early phase of the crisis. The poor people in Indonesia responded by doing extra jobs and working for longer periods of time (Tarmidi, 2001, Table 9). Some countries, such as Indonesia and the Philippines, continued and even increased the export of migrant workers to reduce local unemployment. At the same time, Malaysia and Singapore tried to reduce the influx of migrant workers in order to restrict job opportunities to the local workforce (Chan & Moha Asri, 1999). Households across Asia have adopted various strategies to cope with the crisis, such as altering their consumption and saving patterns,[5] borrowing and selling assets, and redistributing their assets among family members (Atinc, 2000; Tarmidi, 2001, Table 10; World Bank, 2000a, pp.121-123).

Table 7.9 Economic change, inflation and unemployment in Southeast Asia

	Indonesia	Malaysia	Philippines	Singapore	Thailand
GDP Growth Rate					
1995	8.22	9.46	4.68	8.07	8.9
1996	7.84	8.58	5.85	7.56	5.93
1997	4.69	7.5	5.17	8.23	-1.68
1998	-13.2	-7.5	-0.48	0.4	-10.17
1999	0.23	-1.7	2.9	5.35	4.16
GNP per capita (US$)					
1997	1,110	4,680	1,220	32,940	2,800
1998	680	3,600	1,050	30,060	2,200
1999	580	3,400	1,020	29,610	1,960
Inflation Rate					
1997	12.58	3.35	6.00	0.59	4.33
1998	73.07	9.10	10.49	-1.77	9.17
1999	17.17	1.42	7.51	-1.34	0.3
2000	3.80	1.5	4.4	1.3	1.6
Unemployment Rate					
1995	7.2	2.8	8.4	2.0	1.1
1996	4.86	2.5	7.4	2.0	1.1
1997	4.68	2.5	7.9	1.8	0.9
1998	5.46	3.2	9.6	3.2	3.4
1999	6.36	3.4	9.4	3.5	3.0
2000	6.14	3.1	10.1	3.5	2.4

Sources: Asian Development Bank (monthly reports); Chan, 2001

One of the primary areas that has received less funding after the financial crisis is education. For example, Indonesia recorded a drop of 7 percent in the enrollment rate, while the Philippines also reported that 7 percent of families took their children out of school in 1998 (World Bank, 2000a, p.123). In Malaysia, private hospitals and clinics have reported a 50 percent decline in the number of patients seeking treatment. In Indonesia, people have resorted to traditional healers and self-treatment to reduce their medical expenses (Asian Development Bank, 1999; World Bank, 2000a, p.121).

In Thailand, the strategies adopted emphasise the importance of people's organisations, such as saving groups, cooperative groups, community welfare groups, village banks, and village industrial groups in tackling individual and community problems. The government contributed to the village funds and worked with various local communities to foster social cohesion and raise awareness of the importance of mutual support

(Na Ranong, 2001). Indonesia has also witnessed an increase in community aid to its poorest citizens. Several communities in Java, for example, formed a rice aid campaign known as *Perelek* or *Jimpitan* in which participating households contribute rice to families in need. However, these services gradually declined as the crisis developed (World Bank, 2000a, p.123).

The government responses to the impact of the financial crisis were also crucial. Their strategies can be divided in three categories: specific employment policies; macro-social policies; and macro-economic policies. All the countries adopted similar policies regarding employment services, job creation, and training and retraining strategies. All countries strengthened their employment services to provide thorough and up-to-date job information to the unemployed. Singapore have initiated training and retraining programmes for the unemployed, to equip them with more updated and relevant skills. In other words, the countries have adopted a liberal market approach to support employment.

Poverty relief measures included regulating the price of essential items and financial assistance. For example, Indonesia implemented the food subsidies and regulation food costs when the crisis was at its worst. Another policy, adopted in Thailand and Indonesia, provided extended assistance to the poor to cover their health and education expenses. Thailand attempted to expand its social security programme to include the unemployed, but failed due to lack of financial resources. In Singapore, the public assistance programme and various aid programmes operated by voluntary welfare organisations helped families in need (although there was not a sharp increase in the number of applicants during the crisis).

Macro-economic policies included supporting the economy by using public funding, supporting business by fostering a positive environment, restructuring the economy to meet the challenge, and revising taxation and wage policy. Almost all governments deployed large amounts of public funding to restore the economy. To encourage the revival of the business sector, the governments of Singapore and Malaysia also tried to suppress wage increases and to manage wage decreases to protect employment (Chan and Li, 2000, pp.11-16).

These responses illustrate the typical welfare arrangements and strategies adopted in Southeast Asian countries. When individuals face economic problems, such as unemployment, their first response is to try to find another job, sometimes with government support. At the same time, the household strategies may be adopted to relieve the pain. When individuals are unable to buy necessary items, they may turn to the state for assistance. This put pressure on the state. Community mobilisation occurred in some countries, as a result of the community's own initiative or with the aid of government or overseas organisations. However, the government must continue to mobilise resources to cope with the increasing demands to improve employment and to relieve hardship. Singapore and Malaysia can mobilise public resources to meet the increasing demands. The governments of Indonesia and Thailand, however, were required to adopt more stringent measures to contain their expenditure and, with the support of international organisations, to mobilise resources to strengthen their safety nets. Generally speaking, a neo-liberal approach was used to cope with the crisis, with an emphasis on familialism and communitarianism. The governments believe that the restoration of economic growth and, promoting traditional values of self-reliance and mutual support, are the best strategy to tackle the social crisis.

The financial crisis and its social impacts have led to important realisations. The crisis revealed the degree to which most governments and their welfare systems were unprepared for such a challenge. The past decades of economic achievement and development have, to certain extent, conditioned both the governing and the governed to believe that economic development could be taken for granted and that the current welfare system could effectively meet most, if not all, social demands and, at the same time, contribute to economic development. As a result of the crisis, they realised that growth cannot be taken for granted, and, for some, public resources are inadequate to deal with the sudden increase of social demands. In a time of hardship, it was found that the social safety nets in some of the countries were insufficient, and that households and communities cannot be relied upon to offer support to a large number of people in need (Atinc, 2000; Chan, 2001; Ramesh, 2000).

Changing Social Trends and their Impact on the Asian Welfare Systems

Not only were the government and the state welfare system unprepared to cope with a crisis on such a scale but the core of the Asian welfare system, the household and the community, were also facing difficulties. Social trends in Southeast Asia have had, and will continue to have, a negative impact on the ability of households and communities to provide welfare and support to their members. Unlike the more developed East Asian countries, Southeast Asia countries are not facing the problems of an aging society. They are not facing a pressing demand for care of the elderly. The major concerns in Southeast Asia are the common trends of an increasing divorce rate, declining fertility rate, and an increasing female participation in the labour force, which are weakening the stability and integrity of the family as a cohesive and strong unit, capable of supporting its members (Table 7.10).

Table 7.10 Social trends (%)

	Indonesia	Malaysia	Philippines	Singapore	Thailand
Crude divorce rate[a]	0.8 (1986)	--	--	1.3 (1990) 2.4 (2000)	2.1 (1990) 1.9 (2000)
65 & above as % of total population	3.3 (1980) 4.5 (1999)	3.7 (1980) 4.0 (1999)	2.8 (1980) 3.7 (1999)	4.5 (1980) 5.5 (1999)	3.5 (1980) 5.5 (1999)
Total fertility rate	4.3 (1980) 2.4 (2000)	4.2 (1980) 3.0 (1999)	4.8 (1980) 3.3 (2000)	1.7 (1980) 1.5 (2000)	3.5 (1980) 1.9 (1999)
% of female to total labour force	35 (1980) 41 (1999)	34 (1980) 38 (1999)	35 (1980) 38 (1999)	35 (1980) 39 (1999)	47 (1980) 46 (1999)
Female economic activity index[c]	115 (1999)	111 (1999)	107 (1999)	105 (1999)	97 (1999)

Note:
a. Per 1,000 population
b. Thailand's figures refer to the percentage of divorced and separated population
c. 1985 = 100

Sources: Demographic Yearbook; Human Development Report; World Development Report

In Thailand, the mean number of children born to ever married women aged 15 to 49 decreased from 2.4 in 1990 to 1.7 in 2000.[6] In the Philippines, the country with the highest total fertility rate, the National Demographic and Health Survey in 1998 found that 51.4 percent of married women interviewed preferred to have no more children, 10.4 percent had already been sterilised, and 18.7 percent wished to have another child later. It was found that vast majority of the married women wanted either to wait before their next child or to cease childbearing.[7]

In Singapore, the divorce rate, measured by the number of divorced people per thousand married residents, has been higher than 6 percent since 1995 and is steadily increasing (for males, the rate increased from 5.0 percent in 1989 to 6.9 percent in 1999; for female, it was 4.5 percent in 1989 and 7.1 percent in 1999). The average number of children per each ever-married female also dropped from 2.8 in 1990 to 2.5 in 2000 (Department of Statistics, 2001b). These changing demographic trends will have far-reaching impacts on society (Cheung, 1999). In the

Philippines, the number of divorced people increased from 280,136 in 1990 to 332,729 in 1995.[8] Another worrying trend is the impact of migration, especially female migration which is more popular in the Philippines and Thailand, both internal and external, on the integrity of families and their ability to take care of each other. The gradual increase of female participation in the workforce, except Thailand, is also likely to lead to the decline of the fertility rate and a weakening of family responsibilities in caring for the members in need.

Currently, there is no sign that family members have abandoned their responsibility to take care of their elders, although the percentage of co-residence is declining. As Mason observes, 'inter-generational co-residence and support of the elderly by their children also appear to be less common in the more "modernized" sectors of the population, for example, among those with advanced education, modern-sector occupations and high levels of income' (1992, p.26). A World Bank study found that more than two-thirds of those aged 60 and above still reside with an adult child in Malaysia, the Philippines, and Thailand (2000a, p.131). Chan (1997) observes that, in Singapore, the majority of those over 60 still receive support, both financial and house keeping, from their children. In a survey conducted in Thailand in 1986, more than 50 percent of the elderly still received regular support, food, clothing, and money (Knobel et al., 1992). On the basis of the Philippines survey on the near elderly and elderly in 1996, Natividad and Cruz, note that more than 80 percent of the elderly receive money and non-monetary support from their children, although only 21 percent have received a significant amount of money (1997).

It would be an exaggeration, then, to maintain that family system in Southeast Asia is collapsing; however, the ability of the family to offer protection to its members may be diminishing due to the weakening of the family system. In fact, statistics show that, even before the financial crisis, some families were unable to provide adequate support to their members in need. In countries, such as the Philippines, Indonesia, and Malaysia, transfers within families only accounted for 9 to 20 percent of household income (Gough, 2000c). Hirtz's analysis of the situation in the Philippines shows that support for poorer members of a family is often very limited since their kin system is also poor (1992). Recognising the possibility that the younger generation may abandon their filial responsibilities, Singapore enacted the Parents Maintenance Act in 1996.

It is also doubtful that the 'community' has the capacity to fulfill its expected role in the welfare system. The informal community may often lacks the resources to provide large-scale and continuous assistance to those in need, though it may be able to help on an ad hoc basis. Statistics showing the extent of volunteer participation are not available, but a survey in Singapore found that only 6 percent of the residents participate in volunteer work (Ramesh, 2000, p.195). This suggests that the percentage of the population engaged in volunteer work in Southeast Asian societies can be lower than it is in North America (55.5 percent in USA and 31.4 percent in Canada).[9]

As van Rooy notes, the concept and structure of civil society are historical products. Asia lacks the necessary historical foundation. There is neither a strong civil society nor a sense of collectivity, and most charity activities are outgrowths of family care (1998, p.21). NGOs have limited power and are non widely presented in some countries; they are financially weak (Gough, 2001b) and rely heavily on external funding sources to maintain their operation (Gough, 2000a, p.25). Hewison studied the popular localism that emerged in Thailand after the financial crisis, which emphasised self-reliance, self-sufficiency, culture, community, and resistance to globalisation. However, Hewison notes that such localism is often a romantic construct, which cannot resist the global impact on national economy (2000).

The above discussion paints a bleak picture of the ability of households and communities to provide adequate and stable care and support to their members. Of course, this is not to say that households and communities have become, or will become, redundant in the Asian welfare systems. This cursory review, however, reminds us that we should not assume that these systems can be relied on now and in the future. The capacity for self-reliance and family care may be further threatened by the rather pessimistic medium-term forecast of economic growth in this region, as economic growth provides the impetus for the creation of jobs, which in turn constitute major portion of individual income. In Indonesia, the Philippines, Malaysia, and Thailand, the Asian Development Bank predicts that the average growth rate will decline from an estimated 7.1 percent in 2000 to 4 percent in 2001 (ADB, 2001). The World Bank also predicts that the economic prospects of the Asia-Pacific region in the period from 2000 to 2010 are bleaker than those of the previous decade, and that in Indonesia, the Philippines, Malaysia, and Thailand, the average growth rate for the first decade of the 21st century will lower than that of 1999 and 2000 (World Bank, 2000c). The slowdown in the global economy may also aggravate Southeast Asia's debt problem of these countries (except Singapore) in which the debt stock to GDP ratio ranges from 25 percent in Thailand to 91 percent in Indonesia. Debt repayment in Indonesia accounted for 36 percent of government tax revenue in 1999. This will certainly constrain the state's capacity to fund social programmes (UNESCAP, 2001, p.100). We also must take into account the effects of ongoing mass layoffs due to corporate restructuring and the need to maintain competitiveness. The result will probably be an increasing number of permanent or long-term unemployed.

The Sustainability of the Asian Welfare System in Southeast Asia

The welfare systems in Southeast Asian countries share certain characteristics: limited but strategic state intervention in services; strong emphasis on individual self-reliance through work; mutual care in families and communities. This is not a very residual system as the state has assumed more and more responsibility in taking care of its citizen. The system is a work- and family-based system, situated in a capitalist economy, but vested with traditional norms and beliefs. These characteristics are similar to the general principles of the systems in other developed East Asian countries. Of course, the details of the system and extent of provision are different, and the problems that arise are also different.

Chan (2001), based on Gough's analysis (2000a, Figure 1), describes the structure of, and demands on, the Asian welfare model. In the aftermath of the financial crisis, and the current, and possible future economic and social trends, the effectiveness and sustainability of the system is in doubt. The efficacy of the system during the period of economic growth was due to high employment and a rapid accumulation of wealth. These factors made consumption of private market services feasible and significant amount of intra-household transfer possible (Table 7.11). In times of prosperity, the state can maintain a relatively minimal role (though it has, on occasion, intervened extensively in selected services for maintaining economic growth) and a limited budget. When the government cannot cope with demands, due to lack of resources or loopholes in the welfare system, there will be widespread social problems, discontent, and instability.

The impacts of these threats vary from country to country. For example, in countries where the majority of people are still engaged in agriculture, such as Indonesia, Thailand, and the Philippines, less people will be vulnerable to formal unemployment. Those affected may retreat to agricultural or informal economy to gain income for their own survival. Southeast Asian countries face less pressure from aging society and less family disintegration than their East Asian counterparts (Chan, 2001). The caring capacity of families has been weakened, but the caring burden has not been greatly increased. Comparatively speaking, Southeast Asian countries, with the exception of Singapore, are less gloablised, in terms of trade and foreign direct investment, and, theoretically, less vulnerable to global influence. However, the fact that their economies still rely heavily on export to countries apart from the ASEAN community means that they are affected by global trends. The labour force is the most vulnerable, and Southeast Asian countries are inclined to reduce labour costs (wage and protection) to attract foreign investment.

In places such as Singapore, where there has been a high economic growth rate, which has led to sound public finances, resources are still available. In country that have established relatively strong social safety net and social security system, the short-term impacts will be less severe. However, the financial crisis revealed that most governments have very limited budgets, which are unable to meet demands of a dire situation, not the mention the existing demands of poverty, health problems, increasing investment in education; slums, and housing shortages. The strategies adopted to tackle the financial crisis reveal that the governments took a conventional liberal capitalist attitude and relied on traditional values of individual, family and community, when faced with greater demands. However, this attitude requires a more careful examination; it may no longer be practicable.

Table 7.11 The Asian welfare system and its current threats

Systems	Characteristics in Southeast Asia	Current Threats
State	Limited social entitlement Low public spending and low tax	Globalised competition Lower tax Limited public finance
Market	Improved workfare, income, and labour standard Employment protection Private consumption in private market (e.g., education and health)	Lower-income growth rate Higher unemployment rate and risk Loosening of standards and weakened labour movement for labour protection Lower consumption of private market services
Community	Private charity donation Volunteer organisations Localised community Self-help organisations	Weakened community bonding and weak civil society Financial limitations of NGOs
Household	'Private' mutual care High saving rate and intra-household income transfer Modified stem family Remittances	Family 'disintegration' Weakening of caring capacity (decreasing fertility rate, increasing migration and women's participation in the workforce)

The author is grateful for comments by Kevin Hewison on the draft of this chapter.

Notes

1. Information retrieved July 26, 2001 from World Wide Web: http://www.hsd.ait.ac.th/ihsa/si/a13lc/jakarta/hou/phph.html and http://www.hsd.ait.ac.th/ihsa/si/a13lc/jakarta/hou/kam.html
2. Information retrieved July 26, 2001 from World Wide Web: http://www.hsd.ait.ac.th/ihsa/si/a13lc/manila/hou.html
3. Information retrieved July 22, 2001 from World Wide Web: http://www.worldbank.org/eapsocial/
4. Indonesia had an improved Gini coefficient, from 0.36 to 0.32, during the period of 1996 to 1999. The income share of the top 20 percent of households actually dropped, while the other 80 percent recorded a slight increase. Retrieved April 22, 2001 from World Wide Web: http://www.worldbank.org/research/povmonitor/countrydetails/indonesia.htm
5. The savings rate in Asian countries is relatively high by international standards. For example, in 1997, savings as a percentage of GDP were 51.3 percent in Singapore, 35.2 percent in Indonesia, 35.6 percent in the Philippines, and 12.1 percent in Malaysia (1995). See Flynn, 1999, Table 6.2. The saving pattern did not change after the crisis; in fact, the amount of saving actually increased.
6. These figures are from a survey conducted by National Statistical Office in Thailand in 2000. See website: http://www.nso.go.th
7. See National Statistics Office, Philippines. See: http://www.nso.gov.ph
8. *ibid*
9. Figures quoted from a survey of social development trends in Taiwan, and retrieved April 15, 2001 from World Wide Web: http://www.dgbas.gov.tw/census~n/three/social88.htm

References

Agus, M.R. (2000), 'Public Housing Policy in Malaysia', in J. Doling and R. Omar (eds), *Social Welfare East and West: Britain and Malaysia*, Ashgate, Aldershot, pp. 157-72.

Asian Development Bank (1999), *Asian Development Outlook 1999*, Asian Development Bank, Manila.

Asian Development Bank (2001), *Asia Recovery Report, 2001 March Issue*, Asian Development Bank, Manila.

Atinc, T.M. (2000), *Coping with Crises: Social Policy and the Poor*, Paper presented in the Parallel Session to the Annual World Bank Conference on Development Economics, June 27, 2000, Paris.

Bakar, S.H.A. and Yunus, F. (2000), 'Social Security Policies in Malaysia', in J. Doling and R. Omar (eds), *Social Welfare East and West: Britain and Malaysia*, Ashgate, Aldershot, pp. 39-51.

Bidani, B., Ferreira, F., Walton, M. and Ahuja, V. (1997), *Everyone's Miracle?: Revisiting Poverty and Inequality in East Asia*, World Bank, Washington D.C.

Booth, A. (1997), 'Poverty in South East Asia: some comparative estimates', in J. Dixon and D. Drakakis-Smith (eds), *Uneven Development in South East Asia*, Ashgate, Aldershot, pp. 45-74.

Booth, A. (2000), 'The Impacts of the Indonesian Crisis on Welfare: what do we know two years on?' in C. Manning and P. van Diermen (eds), *Indonesia in Transition: social aspects of reformasi and crisis*, ISEAS, Singapore, pp. 145-62.

Buracom, P. (1987), *Limits of State Intervention: the political economy of housing policies in Thailand*, PhD thesis, Northwestern University.

Chan, A. (1997), 'An Overview of the Living Arrangements and Social Support Exchanges of Older Singaporeans', *Asia-Pacific Population Journal*, vol.12 no.4, pp. 35-50.

Chan, R.K.H. (1996), *Welfare in Newly-industrialising Society – the construction of welfare state in Hong Kong*, Avebury, Aldershot.

Chan, R.K.H. (2001), *The Sustainability of the Asian Welfare System after the Financial Crisis: Reflections on the Case of Hong Kong*, Southeast Asia Research Centre, City University of Hong Kong, Hong Kong.

Chan, R.K.H. and Li, C.F. (2000), *Unemployment in Asia: Challenges and Responses*, Research Centre on Comparative Public Management and Social Policy, City University of Hong Kong, Hong Kong.

Chan, R.K.H. and Moha Asri, A. (1999), *Foreign Labour in Asia: Issues and Challenges*, Nova Science, Commack, NY.

Cheung, P. (1999), 'Needs and Challenges of New Demography', in L. Low (ed), *Singapore: Towards a Developed Status*, Centre for Advanced Studies, National University of Singapore, Singapore, pp. 194-209.

Department of Statistics, Singapore (2000), *Is Income Disparity Increasing in Singapore?* Department of Statistics, Singapore.

Department of Statistics, Singapore (2001a), *Singapore Census of Population, 2000 Advance Data Release No.7 – Household Income Growth and Distribution*, Department of Statistics, Singapore.

Department of Statistics, Singapore (2001b), *Singapore Census of Population, 2000 Advance Data Release No.8 – Marriage and Fertility*, Department of Statistics, Singapore.

Department of Statistics, Singapore (2001c), *Singapore Census of Population, 2000 – Quick Count*, Department of Statistics, Singapore.

Doling, J. and Omar, R. (eds) (2000), *Social Welfare East and West: Britain and Malaysia*, Ashgate, Aldershot.

Esping-Andersen, G. (1990), *The Three Worlds of Welfare Capitalism*, Polity, Cambridge.

Flynn, N. (1999), *Miracle to Meltdown in Asia – Business, Government and Society*, Oxford University Press, Hong Kong.

Goh, C.T. (1997), *A Study of the Home Ownership Polices of Public Housing in Singapore and its Transferability to Thailand*, School of Building and Real Estate, National University of Singapore, Singapore, retrieved in June 24, 2001 from World Wide Web: http://members.tripodasia.com.sg/re4group4/nem3.html

Gough, I. (2000a), *Welfare Regime in East Asia and Europe*, paper presented in the Annual World Bank Conference on Development Economics, June 27, 2000, Paris.

Gough, I. (2000b), *Globalisation and Regional Welfare Regimes: The East Asian Case*, paper presented in Conference on Social Protection in the New Era, August 2000, Tilburg University.

Hewison, K. (2000), 'Resisting Globalisation: a study of localism in Thailand', *The Pacific Review*, vol.13 no.2, pp. 279-96.

Hirtz, F. (1992), 'The State, Family, and the Social Welfare: Notes on the Philippines Experience', *Social Development Issues*, vol.14 no.1, pp. 71-82.

Holliday, I. (2000), 'Productivist Welfare Capitalism: Social Policy in East Asia', *Political Studies*, vol.48, pp. 706-23.

Jones, C. (1990), 'Hong Kong, Singapore, South Korea and Taiwan: Oikonomic Welfare State', *Government & Opposition*, vol.25, pp. 446-62.

Jones, C. (1993), 'Pacific Challenges: Confucian Welfare State', in C. Jones (ed.), *New Perspectives on the Welfare State in Europe*, Routledge, London, pp. 198-217.
Knodel, J., Chayovan, N. and Siriboon, S. (1992), 'The Familial Support System of Thai Elderly: An Overview', *Asia-Pacific Population Journal*, vol.7 no.3, pp. 105-26.
Knowles, J.C., Pernia, E.M., and Racelis, M. (1999), *Social Consequences of the Financial Crisis in Asia – The Deeper Crisis*, paper presented in Manila Social Forum: The New Social Agenda for East and Southeast Asia, November 8-12, 1999, Manila.
Koswara, M. (1997), 'Urban Housing and Infrastructure Provision and Financing in Indonesia', in G.W. Jones and P. Visaria (eds), *Urbanization in Large Developing Countries: China, Indonesia, Brazil, and India*, Clarendon Press, Oxford, pp. 180-97.
Kwok, J.K.F, Chan, R.K.H. and Chan, W.T. (2002), *Self-Help Organizations of People with Disabilities in Asia*, Auburn House, Westport CT.
Kwon, H.J. (1997), 'Beyond European welfare regimes: comparative perspectives on East Asian welfare systems', *Journal of Social Policy*, vol.26, pp. 467-84.
Lim, B.H. (1994), *Family Values – speech at the opening of the NTUC Seminar on Family Values*, retrieved in July 11, 2001 from World Wide Web: http://www.gov.sg/mita/speech/speeches/v18n6011.htm
Lim, C.Y. (2001), *Southeast Asia – The Long Road Ahead*, World Scientific Publishing Company, Singapore.
Mason, K.O. (1992), 'Family Change and Support of the Elderly in Asia: what do we know?' *Asia-Pacific Population Journal*, vol.7 no.3, pp. 13-32.
McLaughlin, E. (1993), 'Hong Kong: a residual welfare regime', in A. Cochrane and J. Clarke (eds), *Comparing Welfare States*, Sage, London, pp. 105-40.
Ministry of Education, Singapore (2000), *Report of the Committee on Compulsory Education in Singapore*, Ministry of Education, Singapore.
Na Ranong, A. (2001), *Vulnerability and Poverty*, paper presented in The Third Asia Development Forum, June 11-14, 2001, Bangkok.
National Economic and Social Development Board (NESDB), Thailand, (1996), *Eighth National Economic and Social Development (1997-2001)*, National Economic and Social Development Board, Bangkok, retrieved in June 18, 2001 from World Wide Web: http://www.nesdb.go.th/New_menu/plan8e/plan8c3.html
Natividad, J.N. and Cruz, G.T. (1997), 'Patterns in Living Arrangements and Familial Support for the Elderly in the Philippines', *Asia-Pacific Population Journal*, vol.12 no.4, pp. 17-34.
Pongprayoon, C. (1997), 'Urbanization and the housing situation in Phuket, Thailand', in H. Schneider and K. Vorlaufer (eds), *Employment and Housing: central aspects of urbanization in secondary cities in cross-cultural perspective*, Avebury, Aldershot, pp. 79-95.
Porananond, U. (1997), 'Housing for the poor in Chiang Mai, Thailand', in H. Schneider and K. Vorlaufer (eds), *Employment and Housing: central aspects of urbanization in secondary cities in cross-cultural perspective*, Avebury, Aldershot, pp. 67-78.
Ramesh, M. (1995), 'Social security in South Korea and Singapore: explaining the differences', *Social Policy and Administration*, vol.29, pp. 228-40.
Ramesh, M. (with Asher, M.G.) (2000), *Welfare Capitalism in Southeast Asia: Social Security, Health and Education Policies*, Macmillan, London.
Schmidt, J.D. (1997), 'The challenge from South East Asia: social forces', in J. Dixon and D. Drakakis-Smith (eds), *Uneven Development in South East Asia*, Ashgate, Aldershot, pp. 21-44.
Tarmidi, L.T. (2001), *Poverty and Inequality in Indonesia: Before and After the Crisis*, paper presented at the 5th ASEAN Inter-University Seminar on Social Development, May 23-25, 2001, National University of Singapore, Singapore.
United Nations, *Demographic Yearbook*, various years, United Nations, New York.

UNDP (2001), *Human Development Report 2001*, UNDP, New York.
UNESCAP (2001), *Economic and Social Survey of Asia and the Pacific, 2001*, UNESCAP, Bangkok.
UNESCO (1993), *World Education Indicators*, UNESCO, Montreal.
UNESCO (2000), *World Education Indicators*, UNESCO, Montreal.
van Rooy, A. (ed) (1998), *Civil Society and the Aid Industry: the politics and promise*, Earthscan, London.
White, G. and Goodman, R. (1998), 'Welfare Orientalism and the search for an East Asian Welfare Model', in R. Goodman, G. White and H.J. Kwon (eds), *The East Asian Welfare Model: Welfare Orientalism and the State*, Routledge, London, pp. 3-24.
Wilding, P. (1997), 'Social policy and social development in Hong Kong', *Asian Journal of Public Administration*, vol.19, pp. 244-75.
World Bank (1994), *Averting the Old Age Crisis*, Oxford University Press, Oxford.
World Bank (2000a), *East Asia: Recovery and Beyond*, World Bank, Washington D.C.
World Bank (2000b), *Poverty Trends and Voices of the Poor*, World Bank, Washington D.C.
World Bank (2000c), *Global Economic Prospects and the Developing Countries 2001*, World Bank, Washington D.C.
WHO (1999), *World Health Report 1999*, WHO, Geneva.
WHO (2000), *World Health Report 2000*, WHO, Geneva.
Yunus, F. and Bakar, S.H.A. (2000), 'Community care in Malaysia', in J. Doling and R. Omar (eds), *Social Welfare East & West: Britain and Malaysia*, Ashgate, Aldershot, pp. 101-14.

8 Social Security and Safety Net Development in Southeast Asia Amongst the Asian Financial Crisis

RAYMOND M H NGAN

Social Security and Economic Insecurity

The currency crisis which began in Thailand in mid-1997 had spread quickly to affect other countries in Southeast Asia, notably Malaysia, Indonesia, the Philippines and Singapore. Up to now, although some of the crisis-hit economies have shown signs of economic recovery, adverse effects are still being widely felt throughout these countries. The UNESCAP (2001) observed that there is increasing recognition that the damage extends beyond purely economic or financial realms. The economic crisis has developed into a crisis of poverty, hunger, malnutrition, inequality and social conflict which requires much attention and solutions. At the 1998 meeting in Kuala Lumpur, APEC economic leaders noted that intensified efforts to address social impacts of the Asian financial crisis should be a matter of high priority. Concrete actions aimed at strengthening social safety nets should be formulated to alleviate household insecurity and financial hardship (World Bank, 2000).

The 1997 Asian financial crisis appears as a sourly re-awakening of the rightfulness of the development strategies by Southeast Asian ruling regimes on their hitherto emphasis of lopsided economic growth. Instead of heralding the success of the East Asian Miracle on economic growth and public policy (World Bank, 1993), the recent financial crisis has brought about intensified problems of currency devaluation, soaring inflation, rising unemployment and underemployment rates, increasing income inequality and persistent pockets of poverty (Jomo, 1998; Thailand Development Research Institute, 2000; UNESCAP, 2001). With insufficiently constructed social safety nets, notably the widespread absence of unemployment insurance in Thailand, Malaysia, Indonesia, The Philippines and Singapore, societies in the Southeast Asia region have suffered a disastrous fall-out from the crisis, although Singapore fared slightly less seriously than the other aforesaid countries.

This chapter will discuss firstly, the safely net functions of social security in the context of lopsided economic growth for past decades in Southeast Asia. Secondly, it will examine whether or not the safety net functions have been gone amongst the recent Asian financial crisis. Thirdly, what are the social security measures adopted by ruling regimes in the Region to cope with such crisis and lastly, a critique of social security development in Southeast Asia in the context of increasing inequality and inequity. Policy implications and recommendations will also be identified. Social Security and Safety Net Functions: Development and Underdevelopment in Southeast Asia

The International Labor Organization (ILO) formulated a set of Minimum Standards on Social Security in 1952 (ILO, 1958). It also acknowledged that social security and safety net programmes are crucial to ensure that various segments of the population have reasonable access to minimal income and basic social services in the event of diverse contingencies such as involuntary unemployment, old age or sudden economic crisis. The ILO identified that only those schemes which provide the citizen with benefits designed to prevent or cure disease, to support him when he is unable to earn and to restore him to gainful activity as social security (ILO, 1942, p.80). As a supernational agency on labour welfare and rights, the ILO called forth that policy regimes should always consider it important that social security programmes should be widely developed in the following social safety net protection domains: unemployment, poverty alleviation, emergency relief, old age and medical care (ILO, 1947). Social safety nets serve primarily two important functions: first is the risk-reduction function which is to protect individuals, households and communities against uninsured income and consumption risks. The second is the redistributive function which is to reduce the impact of poverty on the poor and disadvantaged social groups who are often found to be incapable of pursuing gainful employment owing to lack of education, training and financial resources (World Bank, 1999).

However, the UNESCAP (2001) observed that the coverage of these safety net social security programmes in Southeast Asian countries has not been comprehensive and is largely confined to the urban population and civil servants (Ramesh, 2000a). Unemployment insurance has not been enacted in Thailand, Malaysia, Singapore, Indonesia and the Philippines (Tang, 2000). However, the recent Asian financial crisis has caught many Southeast Asian countries unprepared to deal with the scale and the intensity of social deprivation resulting from increased unemployment and aggravated poverty. To a considerable extent this was because of inadequate attention to social aspects of development in the past (Ramesh, 2000b). In several countries hit by the crisis, the growth of public expenditure on social sectors over the decade ending in 1997 barely kept pace with or indeed fell considerably short of growth in GDP during the same period (UNESCAP, 2001). The UNESCAP commented that decades of lopsided growth have masked rising income inequality, outmoded labour-market policies, strained industrial relations, persistent pockets of poverty, and rising need for formal mechanisms to support household security. The financial crisis has brought to light underlying social vulnerabilities. With insufficiently constructed social safety nets and inadequate social security coverage, most Southeast Asian countries have suffered from major currency devaluation, soaring inflation, slumping markets and a fundamental disastrous fall-out from the financial crisis.

In general, Thailand, Malaysia, Indonesia, Singapore and the Philippines have not adequately developed formal 'western-style' social security social safety nets (Reddy, 1998). Mostly, there is a limited mandatory compensation in the form of severance pay or other benefits for those who are laid off; there is no unemployment insurance, and other social security benefits for the unemployed are also very limited (Thailand Development Research Institute, 2000). Furthermore, most of the social security benefits are not available to the self-employed or workers in the informal sector who comprise the majority of the workforce in these countries (except Singapore which is largely an urban industrialised state) (Ramesh, 2000a; Tang, 2000). Table 8.1 shows the types of social security programmes provided by the captioned five countries. Although all countries have developed social security programmes to cover the risks of old age, disability, death and work injury, unemployment insurance and family allowance are not being covered as a social safety net.

It is commonly believed that the ever-growing economy of Southeast Asia grew as fast as they did in the 1980s and 1990s because they concentrated on economic development and avoided western welfare state social welfare programmes (Tang, 2000). Ramesh (2000b) pointed out that, contrary to popular perceptions, most countries in Southeast Asia have a range of social security programmes, notably retirement and health care. He argued that it is not the absence of such safety net programmes but rather their bias towards state employees, and the well-off generally, with inadequate protection for those most in need of state protection. Fundamental to this gap in social protection, social security programmes in these countries suffer from a problem of inequality in coverage to most people in need, and a lack of provision to cover the risks of massive unemployment and problems of a large family (as in the case of absence of family allowances) (Midgley, 1984). Thus when the financial crisis came in 1997, it spread quickly among the Asian Tigers' economies which plunged steeply. Indonesia, hit early in the crisis, was among the worst off, with 30 million more people earning less than US$1 a day than it had before the financial collapse (Tang, 2000; World Bank, 1998a). Not only are the poor being the ones hardest hit by the financial crisis as demand for their labour falls, prices for essential commodities rise, social services are cut, and crop failures occur in drought-stricken economy, other social groups fare poorly as well. In a crunch, female employees are often the first target for lay-offs, and many families in oriental cultures tend to pull girls out of school to stay at home to care for younger siblings (Thailand Development Research Institute, 2000). One begins to ask as if the risk-reduction function and redistributive function of social safety nets have been withered away by the crisis.

Table 8.1 Types of social security programmes, 1999

Countries	Old age, disability, death	Sickness, maternity and medical care	Work injury	Unemployment	Family allowance
Indonesia	✓	--	✓	--	--
Malaysia	✓	--	✓	--	--
Philippines	✓	✓	✓	--	--
Singapore	✓	✓	✓	--	--
Thailand	✓	✓	✓	--	--

Source: Social Security Administration, 1999

Under-development of Safety Net Programmes in Southeast Asia

To recapitulate, it is not the absence of social security programmes but rather inequality in their coverage and their limited provisions which leave most people uncovered to cope with the financial crisis. Somehow this has its cause in the mindset of ruling regimes who have been aversive to western-style welfare state universal and non-means tested social security programmes. Singapore, in particular, is a prominent example. As a ruling party, the People's Action Party (PAP) in its 1998 budget reasserted its anti-welfare ideology: 'We believe that extensive welfare programmes damage the fabric of our society as they discourage individual responsibility, self-reliance, community support and the work ethic' (Lee, 2001). Instead, co-funding, provident fund approaches and voluntarism have been upheld. 'Our approach is one of many helping hands, with co-funding from government and public donations and services rendered by volunteers and members of the community (Lee, 2001; Tang, 2000).'

Table 8.2 shows the main types of social security schemes in Indonesia, Malaysia, Philippines, Singapore and Thailand. The following characteristics are identified:

1. As a whole, western-style social insurance is sparingly used in Southeast Asia with the exception of the Philippines and since 1999, Thailand. However, the GSIS programmes in the Philippines are for civil servants and the military. It is only the SSA in Thailand which is for private sector employees, but they are confined to those who are working members of the labour force rather than to the whole population.
2. All the aforesaid five countries in Southeast Asia, and except the Philippines, have relied mostly on the Provident Fund approach to provide contributory retirement protection from both employers and employees. Malaysia and Singapore have relied on this mechanism for protecting private sector workers since the 1950s, with Indonesia and Thailand since more recently. Thailand, which had no experience with a provident fund, now has a compulsory savings scheme for state employees and a voluntary scheme for private sector employees (Ramesh, 2000a).
3. Voluntary occupational and optional personal pension plans are also evident in the five countries (see Table 8.2), and notably in Indonesia which accounts for a significant portion of retirement saving assets. However, these schemes are largely confined to employees of large private and state enterprises to the exclusion of the ordinary workers in small working units and informal sectors.

Table 8.2 Main types of social security programmes in Southeast Asia

	Government-financed	Provident Fund	Social insurance	Voluntary, tax-assisted
Indonesia	TASPEN for civil servants; ASABRI for military personnel.	JAMSOSTEK for private sector employees		Optional provident fund for workers in private and state-owned firms
Malaysia	Pension schemes for civil servants and military	EPF mainly for private sector employees	SOCSO	Optional occupational pension
Philippines			GSIS for civil servants and military; SSS for private sector employees	Optional occupational pension
Singapore	Pension schemes for civil servants and military	CPF mainly for private sector employees		Optional occupational pension
Thailand	Pension schemes for civil servants and military	Provident fund for state employees	SSA for private sector employees	Partially voluntary provident fund for private sector workers

Source: *Ramesh, 2000a*

4. Inequality in coverage among government financed retirement schemes is evident in Southeast Asia as nearly all ruling regimes except the Philippines rely on their general revenues for funding these programmes for their civilian and military employees whereas workers in private enterprises have to contribute their wages for their own provident fund schemes.
5. Table 8.3 shows that although most states have their social security expenditure on the increase, such expenditures when expressed as a percentage of GDP, still remain at very low levels, around 0.55 to 1.47 percent in 1990-1995.

Table 8.3 Share of government expenditure on social security, annual average (%)

	Total government expenditure			GDP		
	1972-79	1980-89	1990-95	1972-79	1980-89	1990-95
Indonesia	n.a.	n.a.	5.75*	n.a.	n.a.	0.88*
Malaysia	3.11	3.99	5.51	0.77	1.25	1.47
Philippines	2.60	1.61	2.25	0.34	0.21	0.43
Singapore	1.56	1.47	3.04	0.28	0.37	0.53
Thailand	3.68	3.13	3.61	0.61	0.57	0.55

*1994 and 1995 only

Sources: Ramesh, 2000a; World Development Indicators, 1998b.

6. Table 8.4 shows that social security programmes in the Region tend to have a low coverage of the total population. Ramesh (2000a) pointed out that more than half of the workforce in Indonesia, the Philippines and Thailand, and in excess of one-third in Malaysia, are in non-wage employment and are thus being excluded from regular wage-employment based type of Provident Fund contribution schemes. Singapore, being an urban industrialised state, appears slightly better in terms of the coverage for its Central Provident Fund for the entire labour force.

Table 8.4 Coverage of all social security programmes (%), 1992-1995

	Population	Labour force
Indonesia	9	20
Malaysia	20[a]	50[a]
Philippines	29	73
Singapore	39[b]	81[b]
Thailand	18[c]	32[c]

Notes:
a. Includes only active contributors to provident fund schemes
b. Includes only active contributors to provident fund schemes. CPF contributors as a percentage of labour force is only 65.3 if the Government of Singapore data is used
c. Excludes civil servants

Source: Ramesh, 2000a

Summing up, social security schemes in the Southeast Asia region are mostly applicable to employees of the non-agricultural, urban sectors, but non-agricultural workers constitute only a small part of the total workforce (UNESCAP, 2001). The agricultural sector still employs a large number of persons who are mostly self-employed and therefore remain outside many formal provident fund and unemployment insurance schemes. Thus, before the recent financial crisis, there already existed a considerable segment of residual workers and the self-employed who are not covered by any form of social protection during periods of unemployment. Midgley (1984) commented that the regressive consequences of present-day social security policies in the Third World must be modified; these schemes must help to reduce and not maintain inequalities, and by extending protection to the neediest sections of the population.

The Asian Financial Crisis: Withering up of the Safety Net Functions of Social Security Programmes in Southeast Asia?

Although countries in the Southeast Asia region have some form of social security programmes as the safety nets for its citizens, these programmes are not exhaustive nor being extensive in its coverage, their benefit levels are rather limited, and are largely unprepared to cope with the adverse social impacts posed by the Asian financial crisis in 1997, especially in regard to problems of unemployment, underemployment and poverty. The following are the social impacts posed by the crisis in Thailand, Indonesia, Malaysia, the Philippines and Singapore.

Social Impacts of the Crisis in Thailand

In 1988, Thailand recorded a record-high growth in its GDP which reached 13.3 percent. However, ten years later, the same rate was recorded at minus 8 percent in 1998 which is the lowest in recorded history. Table 8.5 shows the incidence of poverty in Thailand during the years 1988 to 1998. It is noted that there was a noticeable drop in the percentage of the poor from 32.6 percent in 1988 to 11.4 percent in 1996, but then it rose to 12.9 percent in 1998 mainly as a result of the financial crisis. Kakwani attributed that the impact of the crisis had caused the incidence of poverty to increase by about 19.7 percent (Kakwani, 1999).

Table 8.5 Incidence of poverty, Thailand, 1998-1999

Period	Percentage of the poor	Poverty gap ratio	Severity of poverty index	Number of poor in million
Percentage				
1988	32.6	10.4	4.6	17.9
1990	27.2	8.0	3.3	15.3
1992	23.2	6.8	2.8	13.5
1994	16.3	4.3	1.7	9.7
1996	11.4	2.8	1.1	6.8
1998	12.9	3.2	1.2	7.9
Percentage change				
1988-1990	-16.6	-23.1	-28.3	-14.5
1990-1992	-14.7	-15.0	-15.2	-11.8
1992-1994	-29.6	-37.0	-39.9	-28.5
1994-1996	-30.2	-34.7	-34.6	-29.6
1996-1998	12.9	14.1	7.9	15.8
Crisis index	19.7	22.5	16.5	22.3
Expected value	10.8	2.6	1.0	6.4

Source: National Economic and Social Development Board, 1999

In terms of the number of poor during the crisis, the last column in Table 8.5 shows that, without the crisis, the expected number of poor would be 6.4 million. The fact that the actual number is 7.9 million means that there was a 22.3 percent increase in the number of the poor between 1996 to 1998 (National Commission on Social Welfare, 1999; World Bank, 1999).

A second major social impact of the crisis was a marked fall in employment opportunities. A study by Thailand's National Economic and Social Development Board (1998) shows that although the total workforce increased from 32.7 million in 1995 to 33.1 in 1998 (see Table 8.6), the labour force participation rate declined from 76.2 percent to 73.6 percent during that period. This decline was more evident for women than for men.

Table 8.6 Employment situation in Thailand, 1995 and 1998

	1995			1998		
	Total	Male	Female	Total	Male	Female
Total labour force ('000)	32,670	17,586	14,884	33,141	18,211	14,930
Labour force participation rate	76.2	83.5	68.9	73.6	81.5	65.8
Unemployment rate	1.1	0.9	1.3	3.4	3.4	3.4
Average hours worked per week	52.3	53.3	51.2	51.1	52.0	50.0
Percentage of employed persons available for additional work	6.1	6.2	6.0	9.5	9.9	9.0

Source: Ministry of Labour and Social Welfare, 1998

For those who were employed, their average working hours per week declined from 52.3 hours in 1995 to 51.1 hours in 1998. The percentage of persons who would like additional work increased from 6.1 percent to 9.5 percent. Thus the impact of the crisis resulted in higher open unemployment, higher under-employment and a lower rate of increase in the nominal wage rate (Thailand Development Research Institute, 2000).

Another major concern of the social impact posed by the crisis is the increase in long-term unemployment. During the crisis period, the 1998 labour force survey showed a high share of long-term unemployed among the labour force in Bangkok, the high-educated (ranging from 6 percent to 7 percent during the period 1998-1999) and the relatively young labour force (12 to 14 percent in the dry seasons of 1998 and 1999 and 7.5 percent in the wet seasons of 1998) (Thailand Development Research Institute, 2000, p.61).

Government Responses Thailand's National Commission on Social Welfare (1999) commented that when the crisis hit, both the government and the people were at a loss of what to do. There were no government policies or mechanisms that could be diverted to help the poor in cases of emergency and financial hardship. Despite the high economic growth rates of the past decade, there had been no active nor effective social policies to deal with the problems of the poor, especially the urban unemployed and the rural poor. Many public resources did not reach those who needed them most: the ultra-poor in rural areas and the newly-poor due to rising urban unemployment resulting from the financial crisis.

What have happened to the safety nets programmes? Have they been able to offer effective help to aid people in need escape from the crisis? To start with, current safety net programmes are few and restricted in their coverage. The first safety net is provided by the severance payments but they are only available for those who are in regular employment in the formal sector. At first they were paid up to six months for those who had worked for at least three years. Due to the onset of the financial crisis and the massive laid-off, the severance payments were raised to ten months' maximum claim since August 1998. Despite the government's good intention to offer better benefits for laid-off workers, it had been observed that employers tended to continue to reduce their labour costs in a shrinking economy by keeping workers highly underemployed rather than immediately lay them off (Thailand Development Research Institute, 2000, p.39). The result is a subsequent marked increase of under-employment rates moving from about 5.7 percent in mid-1997 to 10 percent in mid-1998 (Ministry of Labour and Social Welfare, 1999). Furthermore, more employers tended to dismiss redundant workers before the increase in severance payments going to be implemented, thus contributing to a sharp drop in private employees in August 1998. Besides, as the bulk of Thailand's population are largely rural and agricultural workers, many people are non-regular wage-workers who work mostly in high seasons in primary industries, a large portion of workers could not be able to become eligible for the severance payment safety net which requires a continuous three-year working record.

The second line of safety net protection in the social security system is the Social Security Act (SSA) which requires a contribution of 1.5 percent of the wages each from employer, employee and the government so that a gross total of 4.5 percent of workers' monthly wages would be accumulated as retirement pension for most workers working in private enterprises. However, retirement pension under the SSA is only available to those workers who have contributed for at least fifteen years and who are at least 55 years old. But the SSA was not implemented until 1991. Thus benefits will not be available until the year 2014. To most workers the SSA appears rather remote to provide the needed assistance in financial crisis. In 1997, in order to cope with the crisis, the Government had temporarily reduced the SSA contribution rate from 1.5 percent to 1 percent each for employers, employees and the government for three years. Somehow the ruling regime hoped that this benevolent measure would help to reduce the financial plight of workers and employers at times of economic crisis. Yet most workers found the SSA ineffective to help them when they were unemployed during the crisis. By nature, the SSA is not an unemployment insurance. Initially it provided only sickness, maternity, invalidity and death benefits. It was not till December 31, 1998 that the Old Age Pension and Child Allowance programmes came into effect. The SSA appears too remote as an effective safety net to help unemployed workers.

It appeared that people working in public sector survived relatively better than private enterprise workers. Civil servants, police cadets, army officers and military personnel, and workers in public enterprises are all covered by the Government Officials Pension Act (GOPA) as early as 1951. It is a non-contributory pension scheme funded entirely by the government. Despite the financial crisis, public sector employees were seldom sacked, though they had their salary being cut by about 5 percent in 1998. But private sector employees even had a higher drop in their salaries - a drop of 10 percent in 1998 (Ministry of Labour and Social Welfare, 1999). Workers in private enterprises were badly hit than their counterparts in the public sector who already possess a superior and non-contributory pension (i.e. GOPA).

As of September 1999, the beneficiaries of the SSA and the GOPA in Thailand were 5.53 million workers. But it covers only 15 percent of the total workforce in 96,643 business establishments, of which 39 percent were based in Bangkok (Statistical and Planning Office, 2000). With massive lay-off and rising unemployment during the crisis years, a rising number of the unemployed were seriously affected due to the lack of comprehensive social insurance which normally covers unemployment. To lessen the plight of laid-off workers, the government introduced a voluntary insurance whereby laid-off workers could apply within six months to get a social security benefit from six to 12 months and to have their SSA monthly contribution reduced by one-third.

The Thailand Development Research Institute (2000) found that the majority of the vulnerable who lost employment were unlikely to receive any compensation because about 75 percent of those who lost jobs in 1998 did not receive any social security benefit nor severance payments, while only 12 to 15 percent received one to three months' salary as compensation. It seems that the relief measures came too late and were not effective in reaching-out to the ultra-poor in urban and rural areas who have been largely working as irregular workers in informal sectors or who are mostly self-employed people working in the farm. It is evident that other social safety nets in addition to current social security benefits are needed badly.

A new social safety net was created through the World Bank loans of US$300 million, disbursed through the Social Investment Programme (SIP), aimed for promoting job-creating programmes in communities and local governments in urban and rural areas. As of February 2000, there were 1,722 supported projects, using a total budget of 1,915 million baht and benefiting about 2.7 million people. Most of these SIF projects are concentrated mostly in the Upper North and Lower Northeast regions, with the aim to increase social capital, creating jobs and environment preservation. However, the ILO estimated that only 7 percent of the unemployed would be re-employed under these SIP programmes (Lee, 1998, p.55). The International Monetary Fund (IMF) (1998) also admitted that none of the studies on social impacts provide a clear answer to the question of how much impact unemployment has had on the reduction in household income. The ILO concluded that whether these employment creation programmes will become proper 'safety nets' remains a question, since they provide only a fraction of relief to those who need it (Lee, 1998).

To revitalise the Thai economy, the Unemployment Mitigation Plan was introduced in 1999 with the aim to generate 1.48 million jobs through a budget of 61.4 billion bath (National Commission on Social Welfare, 2000). It has the following measures:

1. Thai help Thai through social assistance;
2. Job creation in rural areas;
3. Repatriation of illegal workers;
4. Promotion of new agricultural method;
5. Employment promotion in industry;
6. Career and occupational guidance;
7. Job creation in community; and
8. Temporary employment of the graduates.

It is hoped that the above measures would be able to reduce financial hardship of the unemployed by providing essential goods at subsidised prices, while others provide small loans for those who want to start their own businesses. As they are just being implemented, the effectiveness of the Unemployment Mitigation Plan remains to be seen.

The government also introduced the Miyazawa Plan in 2000 with the goal to stimulate consumption and the economy. It aims to create 486,000 jobs with a budget of 13 billion baht, out of the main budget of 53 billion baht (Vasuprasat, 1999). Despite its ambitious objective, a preliminary evaluation found that the lack of coordination among various local and provincial committees which plan and implement the job-creation programmes plus the lack of up-to-date and reliable data are creating barriers which tend to reduce programme effectiveness.

In retrospect, social security responses during the crisis are unlikely to address the core issues of lopsided development effectively. Current social security schemes cover only a minority in the labour force (about 15 percent of the total workforce). The increase in severance payments from six to ten months also tends to benefit those in the formal sector and large-size establishments as the majority of workers are not eligible for severance pay. Disadvantaged groups notably children and women, the elderly living under poverty conditions, the urban and rural poor, and minority Thais and indigenous peoples are still left without an effective safety net. It is not a matter of the withering away of social protection function of current social security schemes. Rather, the core problem is due more to the inequality in coverage to public sector employees and private enterprise workers with a steady job in the formal sector. The self-employed, the unemployed, and those people working in the informal sector are still largely left excluded in the social security safety net in Thailand.

Social Impacts of the Crisis in Indonesia

Economic impacts of the financial crisis which broke out in 1997 were most severe in Indonesia than other Southeast Asian countries. Radelet and Woo (2000, p.165) remarked that 'it is hard to have a more obvious indicator of extreme economic distress than a 36 percent collapse in real fixed investment in one year and a further 21 percent drop in the following year. Such was the dismal economic picture in Indonesia in 1998 and 1999.' They further observed that after economic growth which had averaged 7.7 percent per year during the early 1990s and declined to 4.7 percent in 1997, the economy contracted by 13.2 percent in 1998. It was observed that the Rupiah, which depreciated to over Rp/$16,000 in the aftermath of the May 1998 riots, appreciated to Rp/$8,025 at the end of 1998 and then to Rp/$7,085 by the end of 1999. High inflation led to more than 30 percent decline in real income and a marked increase in underemployment from 35 percent in 1997 to 39 percent in 1998. Unemployment also increased from 4.8 percent in 1997 to 5.4 percent in 1998 and 6.4 percent in 1999 (Thailand Development Research Institute, 2000).

The crisis aggravated the extent of poverty in Indonesia. Before the crisis, poverty declined from about 11 percent in 1996 to about 7 percent to 8 percent in mid-1997. During the crisis, poverty increased to about 17 percent to 18 percent at the peak in August 1998, and then declined back to about 11 percent in August 1999 when political order was eventually restored in Indonesia. With wide fluctuations in the Rupiah exchange rate, it was observed that food prices had increased by about 118 percent in 1998, compared with the 78 percent increase in general inflation, and 17 percent increase in nominal wages on average (Thailand Development Research Institute, 2000). Data on rice prices was even more shocking. The average price of rice increased from around Rp.1,000/kg just before the crisis in 1997 to around Rp.2,750 (275% increase) in early 1999 (BULOG, National Logistic Agency, 2000).

Table 8.7 Per-capita GDP during the crisis, Indonesia, 1997-1999

	1997	1998	1999
In Rupiah at current price	Rp.3,100,707	Rp.4,647,500	Rp.5,421,600
Growth of nominal GDP per capita	15.5%	50%	17.1%
Growth of real GDP per capita	3.0%	-14.3%	-5.5%
In US$ at current price	US$1,082.9	US$465.0	US$691.5
Growth of GDP in US$	-6.0	-57%	-48.7%

Sources: Central Bureau of Statistics, Indonesia, various years; Thailand Development Research Institute, 2000

The government's social safety nets programmes Despite the severity of the problem in living, while the need for social safety nets programmes was widely acknowledged in the fall of 1997, it was only in June 1998 when such programmes were spelled explicitly in the International Monetary Fund (IMF) reform package, almost one-year late since the onset of the crisis. Table 8.8 shows the social safety nets programmes (SSN) in the revised government budget drafted in June 1998 (World Bank, 1998c; UNSFIR, 1999). It can be seen that around 7.4 percent of GDP or Rp.70.46 trillion were allocated for the SSN programme. Among this huge sum, around 83.5 percent or Rp.58.8 trillion was allocated for various subsidies. The remainder or 16.5 percent or Rp.11.7 trillion was planned for employment generation programmes, support for education in the form of block grants, and other expenditure for health related services. However, within the total expenditure for subsidies, 51.06 percent was allocated for fuel and electricity subsidies, while food subsidy was allocated at only 19.63 percent of total subsidy. The subsidy for medicine was much more meagre at 1.25 percent of total allocated subsidy. The fact that the majority of the budget was allocated for fuel and electricity subsidy suggested that the SSN programmes were not reaching the poorest people in society especially in rural areas (Thailand Development Research Institute, 2000). It was reported by the UNSFIR (1999) that only about 30 percent to 40 percent of the SSN fund was actually used because the SSN programmes did not reach the poor effectively and even the money was corrupted. As a result, the World Bank had to delay the disbursement of the loan to Indonesia.

Table 8.8 Allocated government expenditure for the social safety net programmes, Indonesia, 1998

	In trillion rupiah	%
Based on government drafted budget June 1998		
All programmes	70.46	100.00
Subsidies	58.81	83.42
Food	13.84	19.63
Based on government drafted budget June 1998		
Fuel	27.53	39.05
Electricity	8.47	12.01
Medicine subsidies	0.88	1.25
Other subsidies	8.08	11.46
Employment generation	9.68	13.73
Support for education	0.70	0.99
Support for health services	1.00	1.42
Other programmes	0.27	0.39
Based on UNSFIR (1999)		
Total	17.94	100.00
Core SSN programmes	9.34	52.07
Food security	0.63	3.53
Social protection (health and education)	4.96	27.64
Employment creation	3.75	20.90
Non-core SSN (such as fuel and electricity)	8.6	47.94

Sources: UNSFIR, 1999; World Bank, 1998

The IMF relief packages call forth the need for a comprehensive SSN Programme. This was announced by the Indonesian government in July 1998. It was consisted of four subsidy programmes. The first was a food security programme to guarantee the availability and affordability of food throughout the country, which included the promotion of local production of food, as well as the development of a reliable distribution system. The second is a public works programme, especially in labour-intensive industries, to promote employment. The third is a social protection programme to protect the health and education facilities, and the fourth is the promotion of small and medium enterprises. It was reported by the local media (Kompas, September 20, 1998) that the total subsidy was boiled down to around Rp.17 trillion (6.5% of government budget) rather than the budgeted sum of 25.5 trillion in the government budget draft in June 1998 as the government was under budgetary constraint (UNSFIR, 1999).

As the average cost of food had increased by about 40 percent in 1998, it was reported that whilst some people would go back to work in farmlands and in informal sectors, unemployed married workers had become dependent upon local credit from food shops from between one to three months, while the less fortunate borrowed from money lenders who gouge the interest rates (Thailand Development Research Institute, 2000). It is evident that Indonesia needs to develop some forms of effective safety nets especially for the poorest vulnerable groups notably the unemployed, poor children in large-sized families, the elderly and women.

Where have social security programmes been gone as social safety nets during the crisis? By and large they failed to reach the poorest and the hardest hit people by the crisis. Formal social security programmes cover civil servants and people working in private-sector with firms having at least ten employees. The latter tends to exclude a vast majority of Indonesians who work mostly in the informal sector, in farms and as self-employed workers having irregular employment patterns (high and low seasons). Thus, when the crisis came in mid-1997, civil servants were already being protected by the TASPEN (the Government Civilian Employees' Saving and Insurance Scheme) and pension. It was set up in 1963 as an endowment insurance scheme but was expanded in 1981 to provide life insurance to civil servants, their spouses and children (Ramesh, 2000b). Members contribute 3.25 percent of their monthly salary to TASPEN for their retirement pension. Private sector workers were covered by ASTEK between 1977 to 1992, when it was replaced by JAMSOSTEK to include provident fund, health care, employment accident insurance and death insurance. The rate of contribution to the provident fund component is 5.7 percent of monthly salary, with employer paying 3.7 percent and employee 2 percent (Ramesh, 2000b). However, the contribution was too small to be adequate as a retirement pension especially in times of high inflation. Besides, the JAMSOSTEK does not cover the risk of unemployment and covers only 9 percent of the population in Indonesia (see Table 8.4). The low coverage is largely a result of exclusion of the unemployed or those employed in informal sectors or in small firms

(Ramesh, 2000b, p.539). Apart from these drawbacks, the JAMSOSTEK suffers from a low replacement ratio of only 10 percent, because of the following reasons: low contribution rates by employers and employees, high inflation, high administrative costs and poor returns on investment. There is no unemployment insurance to protect lay-off workers during the crisis. There is a fundamental need for an effective social security safety net to cover most people in Indonesia, especially those working in the informal sector, the unemployed and the poorest.

Social Impacts of the Crisis in Malaysia

The currency and financial crises, triggered by the collapse of the Thai bath in July 1997, led Malaysia to economic recession. However, it has to be noted that the financial crisis was not as severe in Malaysia (Jomo, 2000). The Malaysian economy and population were not as adversely affected as its counterparts in Thailand and Indonesia. The 1997 to 1998 crisis only reversed the preceding decade-long boom, taking the economy into its most severe recession of the post-war era (Jomo and Lee, 2000). The real GDP went down to –7.5 percent in 1998 but was able to rise back to 5.4 percent in 1999 (see Table 8.9). The Malaysia Ringgit depreciated from around RM2.50 per US dollar in July 1997 to about RM4.80 per US dollar at its worst point in January 1998. Although it recovered somewhat after that, it was hovering around the RM4.00 mark when its value was pegged at RM3.80 per US dollar on September 2, 1998 when capital and exchange controls were imposed. This represented a 38 percent depreciation (Pillay, 2000). In 1999, the economy recovered from a smaller contraction of 1.3 percent in the first quarter to an expansion of 4.1 percent in the second quarter and 8.1 percent in the third quarter of 1999 (Jomo and Lee, 2000).

Despite the crisis and the depreciation of the Ringgit, official estimates of unemployment rates in Malaysia were low - 3.2 percent for 1998. This rise in unemployment was surprisingly small. Jomo and Lee (2000) pointed out that the official definition of employment in Malaysia, i.e. working at least one hour per week, tended to understate the extent of under-employment. It also excluded the bulk of unskilled casual workers in the construction industries who were mostly foreign immigrants (Wong, 1998). Jomo and Lee (2000) observed that women comprised 42.3 percent of retrenched workers in 1998, with 64.5 percent of retrenched women from the manufacturing sector, where weaker unionisation among women made them more vulnerable to coercion and exploitation. Inflation rose markedly from 2.7 percent in 1997 to 5.3 percent in 1998. The price of food increased from 4.1 percent in 1997 to 8.9 percent in 1998 but lowered to 4.6 percent in 1999 (Bank Negara

Malaysia, 1999). The crisis had caused more households to slip into poverty. Poverty rate increased from 6.7 percent in 1997 to 8.05 percent in 1998, reversing the long-standing trend of declining poverty from 8.9 percent in 1995. The incidence of hardcore poverty, defined as households receiving less than half the poverty line income, rose from 1.4 percent to 1.7 percent (Thailand Development Research Institute, 2000, p.217).

Table 8.9 Selected macroeconomic indicators, Malaysia, 1991-1999

Year	Real GDP (%)	Inflation (%)	Unemployment (%)	Fiscal balance (% of GDP)	Current account (% of GDP)
1991	8.7	4.4	4.0	-2.0	-9.2
1992	7.8	4.7	3.7	-0.8	-3.8
1993	8.3	3.6	3.0	0.2	-4.8
1994	9.2	3.7	2.9	2.3	-6.3
1995	9.5	3.4	2.8	0.9	-8.5
1996	8.6	3.5	2.6	0.7	-4.9
1997	7.7	2.7	2.6	2.4	-5.1
1998	-7.5	5.3	3.2	-1.3	12.9
1999	5.4	2.8	3.0	0.2	14.0

Sources: Bank Negara Malaysia Annual Report, 1996, 1998 and 1999; Jomo and Lee, 2000, p.173

Government responses and social safety nets measures The government's Social Safety Nets (SSN) measures were primarily credit schemes in the form of loan and subsidies for poverty development programmes as follows:

1. The Fund for Food programme, with an initial start-up allocation of RM300 million, was established to increase food production through provision of low-interest loans to small farmers and Farmers' Associations;
2. An additional allocation of RM100 million for the Hardcore Poverty Development Programme was designed to provide loans to the hardcore poor for income-earning activities through Amanah Ikhtiar Malaysia (AIM);
3. The Small-Scale Entrepreneur Fund (RM100 million) and Economic Business Group Fund (RM150 million) were set up to provide

assistance to pety traders, hawkers and small entrepreneurs, including women entrepreneurs, in urban areas;
4. The Small and Medium-Scale Industry Fund, with start-up financing of RM750 million, was mandated to aid small and medium scale businesses to expand production. Loans were mainly channeled for the purchase of equipment and machinery;
5. The National Higher Education Fund, with an initial RM320 million allocation, is meant to provide financial assistance to students in local universities and colleges (Jomo and Lee, 2000).

It seems that the Malaysian government's active responses in social safety net measures tended to reflect her strong commitment for a marked social and economic recovery to the crisis. Whilst the real impacts of the above-mentioned SSN measures remain to be seen, the ruling regime's special efforts to help small and medium-sized enterprises have been able to reach a broader and wider sectors of the population in need of aid and economic recovery (Haggard, 1999). Jomo and Lee (2000) remarked that their financing has been far more modest and successful than the funding for bailing-out the banking system which is now in excess of RM645 billion.

Formal social security schemes protect those workers in regular wage employment in private sector and civil servants. Those who are engaged in the informal sector, being mostly farmers, casual labourers, seasonal workers, domestic servants and the self-employed are mostly excluded from the Employee Provident Fund (EPF) which was set up since 1951 mainly acts as a compulsory saving pension for retirement. The rate of contribution has been increased from the original 5 percent each from employer and employee to 11 percent for employees and 12 percent for employers since 1995. However, Ramesh (2000a) commented that the EPF still barely covers half of the labour force. A survey commissioned by the EPF found that 65.8 percent of the retirees had income of less than M$500 per month. Of these, more than two-thirds (68.6 percent) said their EPF savings were inadequate to sustain their living after retirement (Mokhtar, 1995). This somehow has a close relationship to the low contribution rates and low salary levels for most workers during the early years of the EPF. Public sector employees are covered by the Public Service Pension Scheme since 1951. It is a non-contributory pension with the government contributing 17.5 percent of the employee's monthly salary which turns out to be a highly generous scheme compared to the EPF to workers in the private sector.

However, the EPF does not cover workers who are retrenched. This gap seems to be covered by the Employment Act, 1955 which stipulates that employers are obliged to compensate employees at between 1.25 to 1.75 of the last drawn monthly pay for each year of service to give retrenched workers some respite while searching for a new job. Jomo and Lee (2000) noted that compliance with these regulations has not been commendable. In October, 1998, it was found that RM56.7 million due as compensation to 43,889 workers retrenched during the first seven months of 1998 had not been paid by their 2,094 employers. That is to say, about 23 percent of the legally prescribed compensation was still due and unpaid to retrenched workers (Ishak, 1999). It seems that tougher law enforcement measures are needed to ensure strong compliance plus the need to re-design effective social safety nets for the unemployed and the poorest people in the country.

Social Impacts of the Crisis in the Philippines

While the 1980s saw the ASEAN countries grew by leaps and bounds, for the Philippines, it was a lost decade. GDP during the period grew by a meager average of 1.8 percent amidst double-digit inflation and high external debt. The economy grew faster in the early 1990s, with GDP grew in an annual average of 2.8 percent. However, the crisis in 1997 induced the following negative impacts: the rise in the number of lay-off workers due to closures and retrenchments, mostly in the manufacturing, wholesale and retail trade and finance, insurance and real estate. Moreover, most of the affected firms were located in Metro Manila. Job contraction was most pronounced among the lower job scale in production, clerical and agricultural workers (Pasadilla, 2000). The Peso depreciated from the pre-crisis level of P26.3 average peso to US dollar value in mid-1997 to between P39.95 to a dollar by the end of 1997, with a 65.8 percent depreciation. Nevertheless, subsequent improvements throughout East Asia further stabilised the peso in 1998 and recouped some of the value it had lost a year ago to about P33 to P35 per US dollar. The real GDP fell by a slight of –0.5 percent in 1998 and was able to recover to a rise of 3.23 percent in 1999 (Thailand Development Research Institute, 2000).

The unemployment rate, however, stood at the highest level since 1990. It rose to 10.1 percent in 1998 (Ministry of Human Resources, 1999). In absolute number, unemployment levels increased by 504,000 persons on the average, bringing the total unemployed persons to 3.1 million in 1998 (Thailand Development Research Institute, 2000, p.255). It was found that the younger 15 to 24 age bracket school leavers were mostly hit as most of the retrenched jobs were in short-tenure and temporary jobs rather than full-time and long-tenure ones. Inflation rates increased to 10 percent in 1998. It was found that much of the increase was in the price of food which comprised more than 55 percent of the consumption basket. It grew by 8.8 percent in 1998. However, real minimum wages decreased by 2.51 percent in 1998 (National Statistical Office, 1999). A survey by the National Statistical Office shows that 97 percent of families surveyed were affected most by the increased prices of commodities while only about 25 percent suffered from job losses or retrenchment of migrant workers (National Statistical Coordination Board, 1999).

Government responses and social safety nets programmes In regard to formal social security social safety nets, there are two main schemes: the Social Security system (SSS) for the private sector and the Government Service Insurance System (GSIS) for the public sector. However, their coverage is limited in form and in the number of people they are able to reach. They were only able to cover 29 percent of the total population in 1995 (Ramesh, 2000a).

How successful are these two social security schemes as social safety nets during the crisis? It was noted that the SSS granted a total of P25.2 billion in short and long-term benefits while GSIS granted P7.7 billion in social security benefits, including retirement, employees' compensation and survivorship. But only a very small fraction of this would directly benefit people affected by the crisis as coverage for most people is limited to claims for retirement pension. It was observed that left with little options during the crisis, many people resorted to early retirement (Pasadilla, 2000). Benefits such as sickness, disability and hospitalisation would not apply to the direct unemployment consequences of the crisis. Instead, the SSS are more readily available to provide help as loans for displaced workers. It was noted that in 1998, the Employees Compensation Commission under the SSS offered about P135 million as loans in the form of Emergency Loan Programme to improve the living of 16,000 retrenched workers (The President's Socioeconomic Report, 1998). This loan lends a maximum of P12,500 to retrenched members of SSS at an annual interest of 6 percent. Besides, the SSS was asked to work with the Guarantee Fund for Small and Medium Enterprises in providing funds for the newly created Enterprise Stabilization Guarantee Fund (ESGF). This programme is supposed to guarantee up to 50 percent of the principal loan balance. Its finance requirement is P1 billion (Haflah, 1999). ESGF is supposed to help small and medium enterprises experiencing liquidity problems. Pasadilla (2000) remarked that this poses a problem for the SSS. Its funds are not even sufficient to cover unemployment or other benefits for displaced workers or even provide more comprehensive health coverage for its members. This is because the total contribution rate for the retirement component of the SSS is only 8.4 percent of the salary, with the monthly salary ceiling of P12,000 (Ramesh, 2000a). Compared with the 23 percent contribution rate for the EPF in Malaysia, the SSS suffers from low contribution rates but being tapped for quite a large variety of crisis-loan back-up for retrenched industries and displaced workers.

The World Bank (1994) noted that the GSIS will become negative in its financial viability sometime between the years 2007 and 2018 and the pension funds will be depleted between 2014 to 2019. It is observed that expenditures have been increasing faster than receipt from contributions. Between 1998 and 1993, member contributions increased by 22.3 percent per annum, whereas benefit payments increased by 25.8 percent (Ramesh, 2000a). The World Bank (1994) alerted that in future, GSIS is expected to face even greater problems than SSS because its members are likely to age faster, its investment returns have been lower and its operating expenses higher. Besides, the GSIS also suffers from a rather generous benefit payment. Most members who complete 35 years of service will receive a pension of 100 percent of their final salary.

The Asian crisis alerts the need for structural reforms not only in the financial sectors of the erstwhile tiger economies but also in re-designing suitable and effective social safety nets programmes on a long-term basis to help the urban poor, the unemployed and displaced people in rural areas. Formal social security schemes have to be reformed with a comprehensive coverage not only to the general population but also to include unemployment as a major contingency.

Social Impacts of the Crisis in Singapore

Singapore, one of the five Asian tigers, was least affected by the financial crisis and is likely to recover first (Huong, 2000). Singapore achieved a marked GDP growth rate of 7.8 percent in 1997 and 5.6 percent in first quarter 1998, but down to 0.5 percent to and − 1.5 percent in the first and second quarters 1998 and 0.4 for the 1998 year as the deteriorating financial and economic conditions in the Southeast Asian Region took their toll (Arndt and Hill, 1999). In 1998, retrenchments had been on the rise with 23,500 workers lost their jobs. Recent data showed the number of unemployed workers was down by 2,800 in the first quarter of 1999, which represented a drop from the 8,000 retrenchments in the last quarter of 1998 (Tang, 2000). Although the crisis has impaired Singapore's economic growth performance, it has not led to a collapse of the Singapore dollar nor jeopardised the health of the financial sector. In 1999 the economy showed signs of recovery with a growth rate of 1.2 percent in the first quarter, though still with a bleak outlook in rising unemployment rates to 3.5 percent (Asian Development Bank, 2000).

Government responses to the financial crisis There is a marked absence of western welfare state social safety nets in Singapore as the country is opposed to provide 'free meals'. The ruling regime, the People's Action Party (PAP), has a strong anti-welfare stance. Despite the financial crisis, Singapore still turns a deaf ear to the call for the need for an unemployment insurance and to improve the meager benefit levels of the Public Assistance Scheme for displaced workers. Instead, the government resorted to on active self-reliance measure and active labour retraining schemes. It adopted measure as in the second half of 1998 to reduce labour costs and stimulate domestic demand. It bolstered the fiscal stimulus by providing rebates on Property tax, and expanding credit loans for small business (Tang, 2000). Active measures to reduce labour costs include:

1. a reduction in employers' contribution to the Central Provident Fund by 10 percent since 1998 so that employers now only need to contribute 10 percent of workers' monthly salary, instead of the former high level of 20 percent to 25 percent to the CPF;
2. senior civil servants had their salaries decreased by 5 percent, ministers by 10 percent and overall labour costs to be reduced by a further 5 percent;
3. a 10 percent rebate on corporate taxes for 1998;
4. a 55 percent property tax rebate;
5. reduction in customs duty, excise duty on gasoline, airport landing fees, port rents and dues;
6. no mid-year National Wages Council wage adjustment in 1999;
7. invest in education, notably IT and active labour retraining courses and to attract foreign talent.

It is claimed that the above measures could be able to reduce the labour costs by at least 15 percent. This, together with employers' 10 percent reduced CPF contributions, could be able to make Singapore much competitive to attract foreign investment during the crisis (*Straits Times*, June 22, 1999). Nevertheless, the government has also raised the income eligibility and financial assistance extended to low income families staying in Housing Development Board (HDB) rental flats who need temporary assistance to pay for rent, utilities and conservancy charges (Ministry of Community Development and Sports, October 18, 2001). This policy is going to be implemented from November 1, 2001 in view of the current economic recession being prolonged. Under this scheme, these poor families will be given monthly vouchers for their rent, utilities, and conservancy payments for a period of six months.

For the able-bodied Singaporeans, the CPF is their mainstay social safety net in old age, sickness, education and housing. It was set up in 1955 with the initial contribution rates at 5 percent of the wages each by employer and employee in the 1950s and 1960s, then increased to 25 percent each in the early 1980s, and 20 percent each in the mid-1990s. Since January 1999, the rate has been reduced to 10 percent of the wages for employers and 20 percent for employees. A major change took place in 1968 when people were allowed to borrow their CPF funds to purchase HDB flats to promote home-ownership, so that high home-ownership existed before the crisis took its spell among retrenched workers in 1998.

However, since the onset of the financial crisis and the depreciation of the Singapore dollar, CPF savings face some risks. As the savings are not indexed against inflation and wage-cuts, the real rate of return will suffer and the accumulated savings would be affected. A prolonged recession will worsen the situation causing further depletion of savings that would infringe upon other withdrawals such as housing and medical schemes (Lee, 2001).

Conclusion: Effective Social Safety Nets as the Important Social Care Agendum

With the outbreak of the Asian financial crisis in mid-1997, the success story of East Asian Miracle on maintaining economic growth and full employment without spending much public pulse on welfare now becomes a classic in history rather than a noble nor pride path in development. The current economic crisis in the Southeast Asia Region has done much to further highlight the need for statutory social security and hasten efforts to expand it (Ramesh, 2000b). The Indonesian government budget for 1999 already allocated larger spending for social security. The Thai government established three major formal social security schemes in 1998: Children's allowance, pension schemes for the aged and unemployment insurance law. The Philippines government also encouraged increased spending as credit loans to help small and medium sized enterprises. Malaysia had much more public funds designated as subsidies for food, utilities, and education. Singapore also adopted active measures to reduce labour costs and to spend public funds to further the education and retraining needs of its displaced workers.

The recent financial crisis also calls forth the attention of ruling regimes in Southeast Asia to effectively re-design their formal social security programmes so that they can be able to reach the hardest hit population by the crisis in both urban and rural areas. The need to include unemployment insurance in formal social security programmes is imminent as a preventive measure to hedge against future massive lay-off in financial crisis. With the absence of such protection, unemployed workers in Southeast Asia will find their states rather uncaring, should their economies worsen in future (Tang, 2000).

A new social care agendum emerges for most Southeast Asian states. The UNESCAP (2001) calls for the need for a comprehensive and effective Social Safety Nets Programme to cover the following essential areas:

1. Employment security: enabling full employment with decent wage levels and helping the unemployed back to work is the best way to provide household security. An active employment security strategy should aim to promote adequate job opportunities. Macroeconomic policies such as stimulating domestic demand, implementing public infrastructure projects, loosening monetary policy, loaning start-up capital to enterprises, and cutting taxes, have been implemented with some success in most APEC economies. Training programmes for job transition and technology upgrading are active human resource training measures for displaced workers.
2. Social Risk Pooling approaches, based on the principles of social adequacy and individual equity, across individuals and their life cycles, have been a well-developed policy to minimise the shocks caused by unemployment, sickness, disability and old age. The coverage, benefit levels, administration and financing of social insurance schemes are pivotal in determining the sufficiency and effectiveness of the social safety nets support and protection provided.
3. Social assistance system should be developed as effective relief measures for vulnerable social groups at times of high unemployment not only for the unemployed but also for their young family dependents. Schemes of income support, price controls for basic necessities, food subsidies for growing children should be devised to help the weak and displaced workers.
4. Promoting economic development through active social policies by encouraging much interface between welfare relief payments and active labour retraining job referrals, offering credit loans to small and medium sized enterprises, creating job opportunities by increasing public spending on environmental improvement schemes and public works programmes in both rural and urban areas, and giving small loans to encourage self-employment.
5. Expansion of existing social protection programmes: those people who are not covered in social safety nets require the most attention by ruling

regimes. Interim measures should be created and existing SSN programmes should be expanded to their largest caring capacities. Those programmes offering basic protection such as food security, subsidised health care for the poor, keeping children in school, should be specially emphasised. Consideration should be given to extending coverage to home workers and the informal sectors, where social protection is traditionally lacking.

The above recommendations by UNESCAP are to call for the need to have comprehensive and formal social security safety nets programmes to cover most people in society, with an emphasis on the social dimensions of development (Hardiman and Midgley, 1989). It is increasingly clear that both the western welfare states model of development and the East Asian Miracle on lopsided economic growth are not suitable for Southeast Asian countries. The need to have their own unique models of social and economic development is an important research agendum for scholars of the East Asian welfare models (Kwon, 1997; Ku, 1997; Lee, 1999; Lee, 2000; Midgley, 1992, 1996, 1997, 1999; Park, 1990; Tang, 2000, Tang and Ngan, 2001; White and Goodman, 1998).

References

Arndt, H.W. and Hill, H. (eds) (1999), *Southeast Asia's Economic Crisis*, Institute of Southeast Asian Studies, Singapore.
Asian Development Bank. (2000), *Asian Development Outlook 2000*, Oxford University Press, New York.
Bank Negara Malaysia (BNM), *Monthly Statistical Bulletin*, various issues, BNM, Kuala Lumpur.
BULOG (2000), *Movement of Food Prices*, National Logistic Agency, Jakarta.
Haflah, P. (1999), *The Social Impact of the Asian Crisis: Malaysian Country Paper*, Malaysian Institute of Economic Research For Asian Development Bank, Manila.
Haggard, S. (1999), *The Social Fallout: Safety Nets and Redrafting the Social Contract*, Thailand Development Research Institute, Bangkok.
Hardiman, M. and Midgley, J. (1989), *The Social Dimension of Development*, Wiley, London.
Huong, H. (2000), 'ASEAN's Position in the New Asian Order after the Economic Crisis: Management Strategies of Singapore: Present Pain for Future Gain', in Richter, F.J. (ed.), *The East Asian Development Model: Economic Growth, Institutional Failure and the Aftermath of the Crisis*, St. Martin's Press, New York, pp. 239-50.
ILO (1942), *Approaches to Social Security*, ILO, Montreal.
ILO (1947), *Problems of Social Security*, ILO, New Delhi.
ILO (1958), *The Cost of Social Security*, ILO, Geneva.
IMF (1998), *World Economic Outlook*, IMF, Washington D.C.
Ishak, S. (1999), *Social Impact of Financial Crisis: Malaysia*, Report submitted to the United Nations Development Programme, Kuala Lumpur.

Jomo, K.S. (ed.) (1998), *Tigers in Trouble: Financial Governance, Liberalisation and Crises in East Asia*, Hong Kong University Press, Hong Kong.
Jomo, K.S. (ed.) *Malaysian Eclipse*, Zed Books, London.
Jomo., K.S. and Lee, H.A. (2000), 'Some Social consequences of the 1997-8 Economic Crisis in Malaysia', in Thailand Development Research Institute (ed.), *Social Impacts of the Asian Economic Crisis*, Thailand Development Research Institute, Bangkok.
Kakwani, N. (1998), *Impact of Economic Crisis on Employment, Underemployment and Real Income*, Thailand Development Research Institute, Bangkok.
Ku, Y.W. (1997), *Welfare Capitalism in Taiwan: State, Economy and Social Policy*, Macmillian, Basingstoke.
Kwon, H.J. (1997), 'Beyond European Welfare Regimes: Comparative Perspectives on the East Asian Welfare Systems', *Journal of Social Policy*, vol.26 no.4, pp. 467-84.
Lee, E. (1998), *The Asian Financial Crisis: the Challenge For Social Policy*, ILO, Geneva.
Lee, H.K. (1999), 'Globalization and the Emerging Welfare State: The Experience of South Korea', *International Journal of Social Welfare*, vol.8, pp. 23-7.
Lee, J. (2000), *Stakeholder Housing, Social Development and Social Policy: Reflections on the Role of Public Housing in Hong Kong and Singapore*, paper presented at the Conference on Repositioning the State: Challenges and Experiences in the Asia Pacific, Centre For Social Policy Studies, Hong Kong Polytechnic University April 25-26, 2000, Hong Kong.
Lee, K.Y. (2000), *From Third World to First: The Singapore Story, 1965-2000*, Singapore Press Holdings, Singapore.
Lee, W. (2001), 'The Poor in Singapore: Issues and Options', *Journal of Contemporary Asia*, vol.31, no.1, pp. 57-70.
Midgley, J. (1984), *Social Security, Inequality and the Third World*, John Wiley and Sons, Chichester.
Midgley, J. (1992), 'Development Theory, the State and Social Development in Asia', *Social Development Issues*, vol.14, pp. 22-36.
Midgley, J. (1996), 'Towards a Developmental Model of Social Policy: Relevance of the Third World Experience', *Journal of Sociology and Social Welfare*, vol.23 no.1, pp. 59-74.
Midgley, J. (1997), *Social Welfare in Global Context*, Sage, Thousand Oaks.
Midgley, J. (1999), 'Growth, Redistribution and Welfare: Toward Social Investment', *Social Service Review*, vol.73 no.1, pp. 3-21.
Ministry of Community Development and Sports, Singapore (2001), *Press Release, Oct 18, 2001: More Help for Lower Income Families*, Singapore Government Press Release, Singapore.
Ministry of Human Resources, Malaysia (1999), *Labour Market Report, 1998*, Available at http://www.ksm.gov.my
Ministry of Labour and Social Welfare, Thailand (1998), *Labour Force Survey*, Ministry of Labour and Social Welfare, Bangkok.
Ministry of Labour and Social Welfare, Thailand (1999), *Labour Force Survey*, Ministry of Labour and Social Welfare, Bangkok.
Mokhtar, A. (1995), *Study on the Effectiveness of the EPF Retirement Schemes for the Retires*, report prepared for the Employees Provident Fund, October, 1995, Kuala Lumpur, mimeograph.
National Commission on Social Welfare (1999), *Social Development in Thailand: A National Report for the World Summit on Social Development*, 26-30 June, 2000, Geneva.
National Economic and Social Development Board (1998), *Eighth-Plan Mid-term Report, 1997-99*. National Economic and Social Development Board, Bangkok.
National Economic and Social Development Board (1999), 'Poverty and Inequality During

the Economic Crisis in Thailand', *Newsletter of the Indicators of Well-Being and Policy Analysis Project*, vol. 3 no.1, January 1999.
National Statistical Coordination Board, Malaysia (1999), *Movement of Food Commodities Prices*, various monthly reports, National Statistics Office, Kuala Lumpur.
National Statistical Office, Malaysia (1999), *Family and Expenditure Survey*, National Statistical Office, Kuala Lumpur.
Park, B.H. (1990), *The Development of Social Welfare Institution in East Asia: Case Studies of Japan, Korea and the People's Republic of China*, Ph.D. Dissertation, University of Pennsylvania, Pennsylvania.
Pasadilla, G.O. (2000), 'Social Impact of the Asian Crisis in the Philippines', in Thailand Development Research Institute (ed.), *Social Impact of the Asian Economic Crisis*, Thailand Development Research Institute, Bangkok.
Pillay, S.S. (2000), 'The Malaysian Model: Governance, Economic Management and the Future of the Development State', in F.J. Richter, (ed.), *The East Asian Development Model: Economic Growth, Institutional Failure and the Aftermath of the Crisis*, St. Martin's Press, New York.
Radelet, S.C. and Woo, W.T. (2000), 'Indonesia: A Troubled Beginning', in W.T. Woo, J.D. Sachs and K. Schwab (eds.), *The Asian Financial Crisis*, The MIT Press, Cambridge, MA.
Ramesh, M. (2000a), *Welfare Capitalism in Southeast Asia: Social Security, Health and Education Policies*, Macmillan, London.
Ramesh, M. (2000b), 'The State and Social Security in Indonesia and Thailand', *Journal of Contemporary Asia*, vol.30 no.4, pp. 534-46.
Reddy, S. (1998), *Social Funds in Developing Countries: Recent Experiences and Lessons*, UNICEF Staff Working Papers No.EPP-EVL-98-002, UNICEF, New York.
Social Security Administration (1999), *Social Security Programmes Throughout the World – 1999*, U.S. Government Printing Office, Washington D.C.
Statistical and Planning Office (2000), *Documents prepared for the Workshop on Economic Crisis Impacts on Social Culture and Health*, Statistical and Planning Office, Bangkok, mimeograph.
Tang, K.L. (2000), *Social Welfare Development in East Asia*, Palgrave, Hampshire.
Tang, K.L. and Ngan, R. (2001), 'China: Developmentalism and Social Security', *International Journal of Social Welfare*, vol.10, pp. 251-57.
Thailand Development Research Institute (2000), *Social Impacts of the Asian Economic Crisis in Thailand, Indonesia, Malaysia and the Philippines*, Thailand Development Research Institute, Bangkok.
UNESCAP (2001), *Economic and Social Survey of Asia and the Pacific, 2001*, UNESCAP, Bangkok.
UNSFIR (United Nation Support Facility for Indonesian Recovery) (1999), *The Social Implications of the Indonesian Economic Crisis: Perception and Policy*, UNSFIR, Geneva.
Vasuprasat, P. (1999), *The Social Protection in Thailand*, ILO, Bangkok.
White, G. and Goodman, R. (1998), 'Welfare Orientalism and the Search for an East Asian Welfare Model', in R. Goodman and H.J. Kwon (eds.), *The East Asian Welfare Model: Welfare Orientalism and the State*, Routledge, London, pp. 3-24.
Wong, D. (1998), *Social Consequences of the Economic Crisis*, paper presented at a seminar on The Economic Crisis in Malaysia and the Role of the Media, July 22, 1998, Asian Institute for Development Communication, Kuala Lumpur.
World Bank (1993), *The East Asian Miracle: Economic Growth and Public Policy*, Oxford University Press, New York.
World Bank (1994), *Thailand: Social Security System: Issues and Options*, World Bank, Washington D.C.
World Bank (1998a), *World Economic and Social Survey*, Oxford University Press, New

York.
World Bank (1998b), *World Development Indicators: 1998*, Oxford University Press, New York.
World Bank (1998c), *Addressing the Social Impact of the Crisis in Indonesia*, World Bank, Washington D.C., mimeograph.
World Bank (1999), *What are safety net programmes?*, retrieved in 11 November 1999 from the World Wide Web: http://www.worldbank.org/poverty/safety/index/htm
World Bank (2000), *East Asia: Recovery and Beyond*, World Bank, Washington D.C.

9 Educational Developments in Southeast Asia under the Global Impact of Marketisation

DAVID K K CHAN

Introduction

In recent decades, there has been considerable questioning of the state's ability to manage a monopoly of public services. In the West, some people have been arguing that the welfare state is in crisis (Habermas, 1976; Le Grand and Robinson, 1985). Realising the importance of productivity, performance and control, governments have begun to engage themselves in transforming the way that services are managed (Flynn, 1997). The traditional 'public administration' is now giving way to the 'new public management', the paradigm shift of which marks a move towards a more transparent and accountable public sector. There is a fundamental change in the philosophy of governance, shifting from the traditional paradigm of 'public administration' emphasizing the monopolistic role of the state in social provisions to the 'management-oriented' approach which centres around the notion of 'economic rationalism', which embodies a universal model of rationality in re-fashioning social policy, is the belief that economic factors are the most important ones that shape social and public policies and drive individual actions.

Central to the notion of 'new public management' is managerialism and marketisation of the public service. While the aim of managerialism is to introduce a more effective control of work practices, the marketisation of public services, on the other hand, is to develop market mechanisms and to adopt market criteria within the public sector (Hood, 1991). Given due importance to the 'free market' and 'individual choice', the role and function of the state should be reduced because 'marketisation' is seen as inherently more economically 'rational'. Adhering to a 'positivist' view in economics and perceiving 'economics' as a science, a new economistic rhetoric of individual rights, 'efficiency' and 'choice' has become more fashionable in public sector management. In practice, the notion of 'doing more with less' and 'working smarter with fewer staff and less resources' has unquestionably marginalised the noble goal of the 'social good', neglecting moral concerns about the quality of life for people in general.

This ideological commitment to 'economic rationalism', that is, 'the domination of social policy by the language and logic of economics' (Welch, 1996, p.4) has exerted a significant impact on education. Thus, by using the 'market principles' and introducing competition to the educational sector, people believe the delivery of educational services would become more efficient and thus a higher quality of education could be maintained. In this way, the school authorities in the United Kingdom, the United States of America, and Australia have tried to give more choices and options to students and their parents, and has thus adopted market principles and introduced 'competition' to the educational arena, so as to improve the quality of their educational provisions.

It is noteworthy that the economistic rhetoric of individual rights and ideologies of 'efficiency' is gaining momentum, not only in the developed countries, but also in the developing countries as well (Bray, 1996a; World Bank, 1988a). Levy (1986) reports that in Latin America, private schools are challenging the dominance of public schools. Other scholars have also noted that different countries, regardless of their levels of development, have a mixture of both public and private educational services (James, 1992; Tilak, 1991).

In fact, many empirical studies have revealed that the share of the private sector in providing educational services is becoming more significant than the public and state run education. Bray's work on the financing of education in East Asia also discovers that parents and local communities have played a more important role in the financing of education, while the state has gradually withdrawn from the frontier of educational provision. Similar experience is also reported in Mainland China, leading to a new definition of the state/society relationship and public/private boundaries (Cheng, 1995; Mok, 1997). In short, unlike the traditional notion of education which was dominated by the public sector, the emergence of 'internal markets' and the prominence of 'economic rationalism' in the educational sphere seems to be a feature of the globalisation agenda.

The Impact of Globalisation and the Changing Philosophy in Educational Governance

During the past decade or so, people have been focusing on the impact of globalisation on economic, political, societal and cultural fronts, and particularly so in the sphere of education (Castells, 1996; Carnoy, 2000; Currie, 1998, 1998a; Currie and Newson, 1998; Dale, 1999; Deem, 2001; Hirst and Thompson, 1995, 1999; Jones, 1998; Mok and Chan, 2002; Morrow and Torres, 2000; Robertson, 1992; Sklair, 1993, 1995; Spring, 1998; Tsang, 2001). However, globalisation is not a homogeneous process, nor are its effects homogeneous. It has been argued by some scholars that globalisation does constitute a new and distinct form of relationship between nation-states and the world's political economy, but that it takes many different forms. In general, the effects of globalisation have somewhat eroded both the individual states' capacities to control their own affairs, as well as their mutual arrangements for the collective management of their common interests (Dale, 1999).

One of the major impacts of the process of globalisation is related to the fundamental change in the philosophy of governance, and the way that the public sector is being managed. The considerable questioning of the state's ability to continue monopolising the provision of public services in the recent decades has led to the transformation of the states from being 'big government, small individual' to the trend of 'small government, big individual' (Flynn, 1997). As modern states are very much concerned with better performance in the public sector, fashionable jargons such as 'excellence', 'increasing competitiveness', 'efficiency', 'effectiveness' and 'accountability' have been introduced, and that different strategies such as management-by-objectives, internal audits, quality assurance, performance pledges have been adopted in trying to improve the efficiency and effectiveness of public services (Mok, 1999a).

In spite of the fact that different countries may have chosen various coping strategies in response to this global trend, it is quite evident that there are several ways that globalisation will have its impacts upon the public administration and management of individual countries. Politically speaking, the different states' reactions to the global changing circumstances may take two broad forms: individually, they may have taken on the form of a 'competition state' (Cerny, 1997); while collectively, they may have taken the route of setting up a framework of international organisations through which they try to establish their 'governance without government' (Rosenau, 1992). As one scholar points out, 'through the institutionalisation of the global economy; through imposition by the international organisations; by increasing interconnection, both formally and informally; by changing the values of both bureaucrats and policy makers; selection of management practices is shaped increasingly by globalisation; trans-nationalisation of the nation as apparatus' (Baltodano, 1997, pp.623-626).

In addition, globalisation has also altered the conventional relationship between the state and governance. Unlike the practices in the old days, the new vision of governance today conceives modern states as 'facilitators' instead of 'service providers', which is particularly true when the 'welfare state' is now turned into a 'competitive state'. Jones suggests that globalisation promotes a distinct 'New World Order' where 'much of the globalisation process came to be dependent on the adoption of reduced roles for government, not only as a regulator but also a provider of public services' (Jones, 1998, p.1). This 'New World Order' is characterised by governments which revamp the role of a government with a cutback in the scope of their work. At the same time, the notion of 'public goods' is replaced by the rhetoric of 'economic rationalism' whereby customers' choice and the three 'Es' (namely: economy, efficiency and effectiveness) are emphasized (Welch, 1996). Yet, there are limitations in terms of its convergence effects by the globalisation process (Unger, 1997).

Marketisation and Privatisation of the Educational Sector: A Global Trend

As discussed above, the impact of globalisation, crises of the state, the search for a post-Keynesian settlement, fragmentary impulses in society and the contradictions of identity politics have created immense pressures for the restructuring of the state. With increasing constraints on public expenditure, the public management today is much more concerned with how to reduce, or at least prevent cost from continuing to rise. Such concerns have inevitably changed the nature of government from service providers to regulators, thereby modern states are conscious about how to regulate the quality of public services. As Le Grand and Bartlett suggested, modern governments have become basically service purchasers, 'with state provision being systematically replaced by a system of independent providers competing with one another in internal or "quasi-markets"' (1993, p.125).

In short, the 'welfare crisis' that was led by economic globalisation has turned governments from a 'primarily hierarchical decommodifying agent' into a 'primarily market-based commodifying agent' (Cerny, 1997, p.256). Not surprisingly, the replacement of the welfare state by the 'competitive state' has also transformed the state from maximising its general welfare to maximising its returns on investment, and thus brought about greater managerialism among the public services. Nowadays, the public sector is not so much about the delivery of public values than about the management of scarce resources.

Under such a global tidal wave, modern states have begun to transform the ways they manage themselves. Notions such as 'entrepreneurial government' and 'reinventing government' (Osborne and Gaebler, 1992) have become far more fashionable and the concomitant consequence is the initiation of reforms in the public sector management. In order to improve the efficiency and effectiveness of public service delivery, new ways to maximise productivity and effectiveness comparable to that of the private sector are sought. With emphasis given to effectiveness, efficiency and economy in the delivery of public services, 'marketisation' and 'privatisation' are the two major strategies commonly adopted by governments in different countries in the running of public services (Walsh, 1995).

Despite the fact that there are different interpretations of these two 'terms', what are common to them is closely related to: (1) the belief in the ideological commitments of neo-liberalism, which holds the view that the state should not bear the primary responsibility to serve all public-good functions (Dale, 1997); and (2) the recognition of the state's severely limited capacity to act in certain policy areas (Offe, 1990). In this respect, 'privatisation' is closely associated with the reduction in state activities, especially in terms of the reduction in state provision, state subsidy and regulation (Le Grand and Robinson, 1985). Yet, 'some writers describe privatisation as another form of decentralisation. Certainly privatisation may be a form of decentralisation in which state authority over schools is reduced. However, it is not necessarily decentralising. Some forms of privatisation concentrate power in the hands of churches or large private corporations. In these cases, privatisation may centralise control, albeit in non-governmental bodies' (Bray, 1999, pp.208-209).

In essence, 'privatisation' is concerned with the transfer of responsibility originally shouldered by the state to the 'non-state' sector (Johnson, 1990), or that there is a change of the nature of the government involvement (Foster, 1992). It is under such a wider socio-ideological context that the demands of 'structural adjustment', that is the diminution of the public sector and the expansion of the private sector, have become increasingly keen in contemporary society. Turning into concrete policy terms, different ways and measures along the line of 'marketisation' and 'privatisation / decentralisation' have been introduced and implemented with the intention to lessen the financial burden of the state and to improve the performance of the public sector (Flynn, 1997; Hirst and Thompson,

1995; Hood, 1995; Prosser, 1995). Corporate management, devolution of power and authority, the role of the markets, and the popularity of the ideology of neo-liberalism are some of the key elements for the restructuring of the state in the public domain (Taylor et al, 1997; Welch, 1998).

Education, being one of the major public services, is not immune from this tidal wave of 'marketisation' and 'privatisation'. In the past two decades, the rhetoric of economic rationalism and the ideology of 'managerialism' have become very popular, creating a very strong force that has significantly affected the running of the public sector. Central to all these changes is a new concern with the principle of 'quality' in education. Schools, universities, and other learning institutions now encounter far more challenges, and are being subjected to an unprecedented level of public scrutiny. The growing concern for 'value for money' and 'public accountability' has also altered the way that people's value expectations have on education. All 'providers' of education today inhabit a more competitive world, where resources are becoming scarcer, yet at the same time, providers have to accommodate increasing demands from the local community as well as changing expectations from parents and employers – the 'customers'.

At the times of economic constraint and downturn, people begin to question the taken-for-granted belief that the government should control education. By 'control', here, we mean that education systems are state controlled and state-run (Dale, 1997). As Dale rightly highlights that the education system, similar to other state organisations, cannot avoid addressing the three central questions that the state in capitalist societies are now facing. They are as follows:

1. Supporting the capital accumulation process;
2. Guaranteeing a context for its continued expansion;
3. Legitimating the capitalist mode of accumulation, including the state's own part in it, especially in education' (Dale, 1997, p.274).

In the calling for 'cost-effectiveness' and 'value for money', new managerial doctrines are adopted and management-dominated type of decision-making has become common practices in the educational, and in particular the university, sector. In order to be more responsive to all those competing demands, emphases on 'quality assurance' have been introduced into both schools and universities, within an overarching paradigm of 'economic rationalism' in educational services.

Within such a policy context, various educational institutions have adopted market principles and introduced 'competition' to the educational realm. An entrepreneurial competitive culture has been emerging and becomes the new ethos, particularly in the university sector. In order to become more competitive, universities have changed the ways they manage themselves. As their research output and academic profile are increasingly determining the allocation of resources and funding for individual institutions, educational practitioners have become more 'cost-conscious'. Jargons of a 'new discourse' have emerged, such as mission statements, system outputs, appraisal, audit, strategic plans, cost centres, and public relations (Duke, 1992). In addition, the success of higher education reforms is merely measured by the lesser degree of state intervention, while increased management autonomy and market-oriented instruments are playing a far more significant role in such review exercises (World Bank, 1994).

Under the strong tide of managerialism, universities have become more managerialist and bureaucratic in nature. The global tide of managerialism has accelerated the movement of faculty and universities toward the market, which can clearly be reflected by the ideology of 'the market knows best', business practices, performance indicators, corporate managerialism and line management, commercialisation of research as well as commodification of knowledge (Currie, 1998, pp.4-5). Unlike the good old days in 'welfare state', universities nowadays experience pressures from governments, the main providers of higher education, to demonstrate maximum outputs from the financial inputs they are given. Instead, what has become increasingly popular in higher education governance is corporate models and market-oriented approach.

By 'corporate model', it is being referred to as turning universities into 'corporations' or 'entrepreneurial universities' (Clark, 1998), under which organisational structuring and functioning is altered in light of the popular belief that education should serve economic purposes (Slaughter and Leslie, 1997). Amidst the pressure for management efficiency in the face of widened access and reduced resources, the use of market or economic principles is seen as a disciplinary mechanism to make the higher education sector and its people work harder, more efficiently and effectively (Ball, 1990a, 1990b, 1999).

Such a new governance model has been supported and promulgated by certain supranational organisations like the World Bank and the Organisation for Economic Cooperation and Development (OECD, 1995; World Bank, 1994). Despite the fact that the World Bank has rethought the substantial import of the state's role in education in its most recent annual reports of 1997/98 and 1998/99, the impetus for change initiated by the Bank a few years ago undoubtedly has shaped the educational restructuring along the line of a managerial approach (World Bank, 1998, 1999). *In its* report, the OECD has projected the future development of higher education in the following way:

> Tertiary education is changing to address client and stakeholder expectations, to respond more actively to social and economic change, to provide for more flexible forms of teaching and learning, to focus more strongly on competence and skills across the curriculum (OECD, 1998, p.10).

It is against such a wider policy context that education has become a tool to accomplishing an 'integrated world system' along market lines as what scholars have suggested on the existence of the educational market place (Ball, 1998; Bridges and McLaughlin, 1994). Marketisation and privatisation in either parts, or whole, of the educational sector is often now considered as an instrument of economic and social policy, as in the case of a 'user-pays' principle in education, as in other social services as well.

Marketisation and privatisation of education has been underway in Britain since the 1980s in the belief that these processes would make the public sector more effective, efficient, more accountable to the public, and more responsive to the changing demands of the public (Walford, 1990). In recent years, the British government has implemented a scheme of Local Management of Schools (LMS), by decentralising budgets to schools it tends to either encourage or push schools to look for industrial and commercial sponsorships (Bridges and McLaughlin, 1994; Cooper, 1988). In addition, universities are also urged to make good the reductions in government funding by raising research money from trusts or from industry, and by securing sponsorships for particular activities, and so on (Morris, 1994; Roberts, 1994).

In order to assure 'quality control' in education, institutional auditing has emerged in the United Kingdom, with evaluations shifting from initially self-monitored, unthreatening and internal means to more formal and external controls (Craft, 1992, 1994). Similar developments are found in other European universities that are 'characterised by increased entrepreneurship, conflicting faculty and administrative values, especially around governance issues; and greater diversification of institutional funding' (Clark, cited in Slaughter and Leslie, 1997, p.2).

The domination of economic rationalism has not only affected United Kingdom's education, but has, in fact, shaped educational policies in the United States and Australia as well. By the introduction of competition to education, together with the adoption of a 'customer-oriented approach', different measures such as Total Quality Management, Statistical Processing Control, Employee Involvement, Process Re-engineering, and Just-in-Time Production have been adopted in both the private and public sectors to assure service quality in the USA (Brown, 1995). Breneman (1993) deploys financial data persuasively to present the case that State and Federal funding are diminishing as part of the resource mix in the US higher education; while other scholars suggest that the university sector in the USA has become increasingly market-driven and marketised (see Etzkowitz and Leydesdorff, 1997; Rhoades, 1997).

At the other end of the globe, Australian educational policy is also dictated by the 'logic' of economy and efficiency, thus encouraging competition and choice in the running of educational services. Given more weight to 'quality', to be measured by crude performance indicators such as research outputs and teaching performances, educational practitioners and academics in Australia feel very much demoralised and substantially de-professionalised (Currie, 1998a; Karmel, 1994; Welch, 1996). Both Smyth's edited volume *Academic Work* (1995) and Marginson's study (1995) suggest how Australia's education has been affected by strong market forces, thus it is not surprising to see market-like behaviors in which Australian institutions and faculty engage. Similar experiences are also found in Canadian universities such that state funding has been decreasing while the impacts of marketisation and globalisation have accelerated (Buchbinder and Newson, 1990; Buchbinder and Rajagopal, 1993, 1995; Levin, 1999).

It is particularly noteworthy that the economic rhetoric of individual rights and ideology of 'efficiency' are gaining momentum not only in the developed countries, but also in the developing countries as well (World Bank, 1998; Bray, 1996a). Bray's (1996b) work on the financing of education in East Asia also discovers that parents and local communities have played a more important role in the financing of education, while the state has gradually withdrawn from the frontier of educational provisions. In many societies, including socialist states such as Vietnam and China, there have been wider sets of changes, including encouragement for international investments, the scrutiny of public sector activities, with public sector wages to be held down (Chan, 2001; Do, 2001). At the same time, private economic activities are encouraged within a climate of increasing 'de-regulation', and the economy is re-shaped towards more export-oriented industries, and away from state responsibility for areas of social policy, such as health, housing and education, among others (Chan and Mok, 2001; Mok, 2000b; Yin and White, 1994). Similar experience is also reported in Mainland China, leading to a new definition of state / society relationship and public/private boundaries (Cheng, 1995; 1999; Mok and Wat, 1998).

It is quite evident that an educational reform agenda has been centred around such notions as 'excellence', enhanced 'international competitiveness', 'quality', 'increasing system effectiveness', and the like, among many nations of the Asia and Pacific region for the past decade. In the course of attempting to re-fashion education more directly to achieve national and international economic agendas, many countries have focused on aspects of education which are seen to impact most directly upon human resource management and development, such as the reform of higher education systems, or the modernisation of vocational education and training. Undoubtedly, higher educational institutions can have the ability to cope with the incentives to improve efficient use of human resources, such that 'quality, efficiency and accountability' have now become the 'yardsticks' in assessing the performance of the higher educational sector. All these developments have confirmed what Slaughter and Leslie (1997) call as 'academic capitalism'.

More importantly, the recent changes and transformations that are taking place in the educational sector of various countries seem to suggest that 'marketisation' of education has become a global trend, under the tidal wave of which educational financing, curriculum, governance and management should have been re-oriented / re-shaped by market-oriented approaches and practices (Chan, 2001; Currie and Newson, 1998; Spring, 1998; Taylor et al, 1997). This chapter is set against this wider global policy context discussed above to examine how educational developments have been influenced by strong market forces in Southeast Asia in general, and in Singapore and Thailand in particular.

The Marketisation and Decentralisation of Education in Singapore

Singapore's education system has been described as a 'highly centralised one' with 'no local education authorities and only a handful of private schools' (Lee, 1991, cited in Green, 1999; Tan, 1997). The Ministry of Education (MOE) has been responsible for determining the content of the national curriculum, prescribing the modes of assessment in schools, implementing strict quotas for enrolments to different types of institution, as well as in determining the rules for admissions to different schools. Realising the importance of human capital as the only resource in Singapore, the government has provided education in order to maximise the potential of its citizens in the furthering of its economic development under the impact of globalisation (Gopinathan, 1995, 2001).

Overall speaking, the Singaporean government is 'often credited with having an exceptionally tight fit between its education and external training systems and the needs of the economy' (Ashton and Sung, 1994, also cited in Green, 1999). As has been the same with many other East Asian countries, education and training in Singapore stresses on the dual goals of skills formation for economic development and citizen formation for nation-building. In this way, 'educational institutions have been typically centralised and standardised, placing strong emphasis on the acquisition of core skills and values by all' (Green, 1999, p.263).

While globalisation has been an important external factor in influencing the policy- and decision-making within a city-state like Singapore, the tension in centralisation and decentralisation is also another important factor which is internal to the city-state in question. The notions of centralisation and decentralisation denote processes, rather than static situations, and thus the national policies of the city-state of Singapore can fluctuate between these two poles in different periods of its national development, or that they can even co-exist together at the same period of time, depending upon the circumstances.

As far as the motives for centralisation and decentralisation are concerned, it might be either political, or administrative in nature, or a combination of both. For the former motive, the introduction of National Education and the formation of a national curriculum, which denotes centralisation, fosters the nation-building process as well as the civic consciousness within the city-state. As for the latter motive, both centralisation and decentralisation may be advocated in order to improve efficiency: the main argument on centralisation is that 'operations can be directed more efficiently by a small group of central planners', while that on decentralisation is that 'specialist parallel bodies are better able to focus on the needs of clients' (Bray, 1999, p.210).

With the fact that 'centralisation, in Singapore's experience, was empowerment of a state institution to unify and strengthen education; it enabled both the political and the educational challenges to be met' (Gopinathan, 2001, p.14), both the global and the local forces are affecting Singapore, in terms of intensified global economic competition in the world market, global pressures for economic liberalisation, the deregulation of the labour market, other demographic and social changes like growing demands for democratisation from the middle-class, and so on, such that it has become timely for the Singaporean Government to re-adjust its education system in order to meet the impending challenges ahead. Policy-makers in Singapore speak of encouraging '"managed creativity" which ... seeks the economic benefits of flexible thinking without the social and political costs of creative individualism.' (Green, 1999, p.276). With this, we witness the impetus for the recent education reforms.

The last decade has witnessed an increasing use of the language of market economics in the Singaporean education system after more than two decades of steady government centralisation of control over schools. Terms such as choice, competition and diversity are now commonplace. The Singaporean experience of marketisation and decentralisation differs quite substantially from that in most other countries in one important respect: while financial stringency is a key motivating force in many countries for educational reforms, the educational reform movement is taking place in Singapore against the backdrop of healthy budgetary surpluses and increased government expenditure of education, which is seen as a key role in enhancing its national economic competitiveness in the global knowledge economy.

The first major manifestation of the marketisation of education in Singapore is the increased school autonomy, since 1988, by allowing eight prestigious secondary schools to become 'independent schools' which enjoy increased autonomy in matters such as school management, finance, and teacher recruitment (Gopinathan, 2001; Tan, 1992). In response to public criticism of the elitist nature of the independent schools (Tan, 1993), the government has capped the number of independent schools and started a new category of schools. Since 1994, eighteen secondary schools have been designed as 'autonomous schools' which can also enjoy increased autonomy, but to a lesser degree than the independent schools. Further moves towards the delegation of operating autonomy include the formation of 'school clusters' in 1997. Under this scheme, clusters of schools are grouped together and placed under the charge of a senior principal. Apart from the pooling of resources, this arrangement is supposed to allow schools greater flexibility in having decision-making on financial and staffing matters, which can be considered as an indication of decentralisation policy.

The second feature of the growing marketisation of education in Singapore is the stress on competition among schools. Besides improving the quality of education, competition is supposed to provide parents and students with a wider range of choices and to improve accountability by forcing schools to improve their programmes of studies. Competition is fostered through the publication of inter-school league tables each year as well as other measures. In this way, as a result of competition, schools are increasingly resorting to marketing activities and to various strategies in order to improve their schools' standing in the league tables. The question arises as to whether fostering competition does improve the quality of education for all students and to promote greater choices and diversity for parents and students. At the same time, there are also concerns about a growing hierarchy of schools and social stratification (Tan, 1998).

It was in 1997 that the Prime Minister of Singapore, Mr. Goh Chok Tong, announced his famous speech on 'Thinking Schools, Learning Nation', commenting that 'We have to prepare ourselves for a bracing future – a future of intense competition and shifting competitive advantages, a future where technologies and concepts are replaced at an increasing pace and a future of changing values. Education and training are central to how nations will fare in this future.' (Goh, 1997, p.1), and thus he set the scene for a national movement on lifelong learning among the students and teachers. At the same time, universities are required to formulate their missions, goals, and strategic plans in order to help train future leaders of the city-state to meet the future challenges that are brought about by the strong tide of globalisation.

In a similar context, the Deputy Prime Minister, Mr. Lee Hsien Loong, also touched upon the importance of a 'Learning Nation' as follows:

> Our schools and tertiary institutions must become learning organizations, not teaching factories. Teachers and lecturers should continuously seek to improve, to pick up best practices elsewhere and to challenge students to find better solutions. These changes in our education system need to be supported by a national environment that promotes a learning mindset and a society which upholds the fundamental values of equal opportunity and meritocracy. This is the way to become a learning nation (Lee, 1997, as cited in Tan, 1999, p.125).

Furthermore, the Minister of Education, Mr. Teo Chee Hean, urged the Singaporeans to change their mindsets in order to face the new challenges ahead of them when he addressed the public on the Masterplan for IT in education:

> Mindset changes are necessary before we can break free of old ways of thinking and doing things and push beyond the boundaries of what is possible. Today information technology links us to the world in exciting new ways, but it requires a mindset change in our people – a mental revolution – before we can exploit IT's full potential. Those who do not make this mindset change will continue to live in their own little island. With IT, we are already connected with the rest of the world. The boundaries exist only in our minds (Teo, 1997, p.4).

With all these policy speeches well in place by mid-1997, the Singaporean Government started to initiate the recent educational reforms at all levels.

Another factor which contributes to recent reforms in the universities is the pressing need to ensure quality university education with the rapid expansion of higher education for the past years. There has been a seven-fold increase in degree places for student enrolments at the universities for the past thirty years from 1960 to 1990. A similar expansion in the student enrolments at the polytechnics has also occurred at the same period of time (Selvaratnam, 1994, as cited in Mok, 2000c). This turn from elitist to mass higher education has also triggered the growing concern for quality assurance in both university teaching and research.

As far as the higher education sector is concerned, it is far more autonomous than the primary and secondary sectors of education. All along, the relationship between the state and the universities and polytechnics in Singapore has been very 'co-operative', with the Ministry of Education being responsible for regulating the access conditions, curriculum, degree requirements, examinations, and appointment and remuneration of academic staff. However, the recent reforms have given greater autonomy to the universities in running their everyday affairs. A new private university, the Singapore Management University (SMU), has been established and admitted its first batch of student intake in the academic year of 2000 (Fieldwork, August 2, 2000). Furthermore, there have been talks by the government of establishing the fourth university and the fifth polytechnic in Singapore in order to meet the demands of the global marketplace in the future (Fieldwork, December 2, 2001).

Using Singapore as a case study to illustrate the processes of marketisation and decentralisation, it can be argued that both the two processes of centralisation and decentralisation have occurred in Singapore within its national constraints and circumstances. At the same time, while the so-called global trend in which user-pays principle, market competition, non-state provision, corporate governance, system-wide performance management have taken place in Singapore, this should not be construed as a reduced state role in educational provision and financing, nor does it suggest any kind of withdrawal from either state control or shaping by the state.

On the other hand, it can be argued that the Singaporean experience of marketisation and decentralisation in education is an attempt by the state to make use of market forces and new initiatives from the non-state sectors to enhance its national competitive edge in the regional and global markets, while retaining its state control in a more macro way of governance. A comparative study on the quality assurance systems in Hong Kong and Singapore has demonstrated that 'the state in Singapore seems to be a counter-proof on globalisation's contribution to the 'hollowing out' of the state. As Wilding suggested, the state of Singapore is able to shape the form and scope of globalisation' (Mok, 2000a). To this extent, the Singaporean Government has been very successful in dancing on the stage of globalisation according to its own tune, so to speak. In the conclusion of his study, Mok has pointed out that 'all in all, what really has happened to the university sector in Hong Kong and Singapore is a process of "re-regulation" instead of "de-regulation"' (Mok, 2000a).

The Decentralisation and Privatisation of Education in Thailand

The development of education in Thailand has a long history dating back almost 800 years. Figures have shown that Thailand has one of the highest literacy rates in Asia, with nearly 98 percent of school-age children nationwide completing at least six years of basic education (Bangkok Post, April 3, 1997). Here, in this chapter, we will mainly focus on its educational development since the mid-1990s to the present. It was during 1961-1966 that the First National Education Development Plan of Thailand was implemented. At present, we saw its educational development has just moved into the Ninth National Education Development Plan, aiming at preparing its people to cope with a rapidly changing in the 21st Century.

For the past few years, there has been a growing demand in Thailand for a new radical reform in education. It has been argued that one of the underlying factors in the cause of the economic and financial crisis that has hard hit the country in mid-1997 was Thailand's relatively weak basis for human resources. Many had highlighted the lack of independent thinking and analytical thought of Thai graduates that accounts for the country's economic downturn. To go back as early as on April 3, 1997, the then Deputy Prime Minister and Education Minister, Mr. Sukhavich Rangsitpol, had already called for Thailand's most important challenge – 'Education for Life' in which a radical, sustained and far-reaching reform of Thailand's national system of education was considered as the critical path to achieve the national priority goals of social equity and justice, of economic renewal for the new age of technology, and of political reform for the fulfillment of democratic principles (Rangsitpol, 1997).

Hence, the first successful attempt on education reform was the inclusion of various provisions relating to education in the new 1997 Constitution that was promulgated in October of 1997 (Office of Council of State, 1997). Among these provisions, two have had paramount impact on education in Thailand, namely: Equity for All in receiving at least 12 years of basic education; and the enactment of the National Education Act which is the first of its kind in the history of Thai education, and thus pave the way for a truly comprehensive reform of education to meet the challenges of the new century brought about by the forces of globalisation.

As the economic crisis in Thailand has directly affected the implementation of the Eighth National Education Development Plan (1997-2001), the National Education Act, which was promulgated on August 21, 1999, brought about changes and new initiatives in the management of education. The fact that the economic crisis has brought home the need for a thorough re-examination of the system for the development of the country's human resources, and thus set the stage for a comprehensive reform of Thai's educational system. With this, the National Education Act has called for drastic changes, with some of its essential features as follows (Office of the National Education Commission, 1999, pp.116-124):

1. Ensuring access to basic education for all;
2. Reform of curriculum and learning process;
3. Encouraging participation and partnership in education;
4. Restructuring of educational administrative structure;
5. Enhancing educational standards and quality assurance;
6. Reform of teachers, faculty staff and educational personnel;
7. Mobilisation of resources and investment for education;
8. Utilisation of technologies for education.

The Office of the National Education Commission, which is the main body responsible for the implementation of the National Education Act, has made various studies for effective strategies for educational reform through the concerted efforts of different committees. In this connection, an Education Reform Office was established to take up the responsibility of making the reform proposals of educational administration and management, in terms of general administration, budget, personnel and academic decentralisation (Rung, 1999).

On the one hand, as far back as mid-1996, both an academic and a former education minister had already called for the decentralisation of the management of education (Bangkok Post, August 21, 1996). The then Deputy Prime Minister and Education Minister, Mr. Sukhavich Rangsitpol, also claimed that the decentralisation of the national educational system was a critical component of the reforms (Bangkok Post, April 3, 1997). This move in itself posed a great challenge to the Thai society. This policy of decentralisation can be seen as a move by the central government to redeploy its resources, in terms of educational finance and investment for education. It called for the decentralisation of fiscal management to educational service areas and institutions, and the provision of incentives for the mobilisation of resources, particularly for the private sector, through tax rebate or tax exemption measures (National Education Commission, 1999, p.126; 2000a, p.102).

Historically, Thailand has had a very centralised approach to the education system. To make a shift to decentralisation will cause changes at all levels, national as well as regional and local levels, which will be very difficult for many people to embrace. Indeed, the administration and management of educational provisions will be administered by Local Administration Organisations (LAOs) (Office of National Education Commission, 2000, p.19). At the same time, the government called for the support from the private sector in providing educational services, especially in the higher education sector. At the same time, in early 1997, there has been a plan by the government to upgrade the standards of state schools, by putting them on a par with those of international schools, in allowing them the freedom to work independently (Bangkok Post, February 1, 1997), and even to become privatised. But, unfortunately, due to the economic crisis by the middle of the same year, this plan had to be put to a halt.

Yet, on the other hand, in terms of the restructuring of the educational administrative and management structure, there would be the downsizing of the central body, through the mergence of the original three bodies of the Ministry of Education, the Ministry of University Affairs and the Office of the National Education Commission, into one Ministry of Education, Religion and Culture, which is to be established by August 20, 2002, in accordance with the National Education Act 1999. This Ministry of Education, Religion and Culture will then decentralise its authority in educational administration and management directly to the different Committees and Offices of the educational service areas as well as the various educational institutions themselves (Office of National Education Commission, 2000a, p.19). To such an extent, this can be seen as another move of 'functional re-centralisation' (Bray, 1999) at the top management level, which is introduced in order to improve efficiency and effectiveness in the running of the educational administration and management across the country.

Another important trend of educational development has been the closer links between the industry and the higher education sector, more commonly known as university-industry linkages (UILs). Back in 1996, the previous Ministry of University Affairs had used the strategy of establishing 'centres of excellence', in which the state and private companies funded a central institute staffed by university academics and researchers. Such an institute would do applied research, introduce environmentally-friendly manufacturing methods or develop production technology for the private sectors. Among these projects, the electronics, auto and parts industries were fully explored, and the Burapha University in Chon Buri became the first university to adopt such a model of development (Bangkok Post, September 16, 1996; Ministry of University Affairs, 2000).

As a whole, the National Education Act has set the foundation for reform efforts in order to prepare its people for the new social requirements of the new knowledge-based global economy. It encouraged the Thai students to develop more critical, analytical and independent thinking in the long-run, so as to equip themselves with the abilities in finding solutions to problems that they will encounter in the new knowledge-based learning society of this globalised world. 'Education reform will bring Thai society to a new juncture crucial in improving the people's quality of life and prepare Thai citizens to be ready for any kind of competition in the coming millennium.' (The Nation, November 28, 1999).

In order to achieve the objectives as set out in the National Education Act 1999, major changes in the allocation of educational resources have to be made. Education in Thailand has been mainly financed through the 'supply-side', i.e., the government has always been the main provider of education. Now, the reform initiatives have proposed that the financing of education should be provided through the 'demand-side', i.e., by those who are in demand of the educational services – parents and students. With this change of mentality, accordingly, the government subsidies will then be provided to the learners instead of the educational institutions. In this respect, the government will provide 12 years of quality basic education, which is free of charge.

However, learners will be responsible for their own educational expenses in the higher education sector. 'A programme of phased increases in tuition fees will be introduced as a mechanism for cost recovery', while scholarships and loans will be provided to those who need financial assistance in either public or private institutions (Office of the National Education Commission, 2000a, pp.101-102). As recommended by the International Monetary Fund (IMF), more administrative autonomy should be given to public universities in Thailand. In this regard, twenty of the public universities will be given more administrative autonomy by the government within the next five years, resulting in their privatisation in terms of governance and finance. Among these twenty public universities, five of them have already been granted full autonomy such that they will have to find ways and means to finance themselves, while the government will no longer continue its financial support to them. This whole process can be considered as the transitional period for the change of educational governance for the Thai public universities (Ministry of University Affairs, 2000; Office of National Education Commission, 2000a; Yue, 1999).

Furthermore, in order to assure the 'quality control' of its education, the National Education Act 1999 requires that each educational institution will receive external quality evaluation at least once every five years, and the evaluation results will be submitted to the relevant agencies, and also to be made known to the general public. The Office of the National Education Standards has been established since November 4, 2000 to oversee this important mission. This kind of quality assurance mechanism will probably introduce some kind of league tables within the various educational sectors in the long-run, and will thus bring about intense competition among the different providers of educational services. The first round of this external quality evaluation of all educational institutions will be completed by August 20, 2005 (Office of the National Education Commission, 2000a, pp.110).

All in all, the Thai educational reforms, in terms of both decentralisation and privatisation, have indicated that the government is moving away from its role as the major provider of educational services with direct state control to one of service purchaser as well as a regulator in educational governance. This has mainly to do with the economic constraints that the central government faces, particularly after the economic crisis back in 1997.

Conclusion: The Changing State-Market-Education Relationship

In using Southeast Asia as the case study to illustrate the processes of decentralisation / privatisation, it has been argued that both the functional and territorial dimensions of these two processes have occurred in Thailand, mainly for the reason of financial stringency, but not so much for the case in Singapore. For the former case, it was the central government 'which realise that they do not have sufficient resources for adequate provision of services may choose to evade the problem by decentralising responsibility to lower tiers or to nongovernmental bodies... It has also been a major motive in various privatisation initiatives' (Bray, 1999, p.211).

What really happens in Southeast Asia is a transformation of the government's role as a sole provider of educational services to a regulator or a service purchaser. One point that deserves attention here is that, during the process of transformation, the state does not 'go away' in the Southeast Asian contexts. Rather, the nature of the work it does has differed, very broadly speaking, 'from carrying out most of the work of the coordination of education itself to determining where the work will be done and by whom' (Dale, 1997, p.274). Seen in this light, the policy of decentralisation and devolution does not necessarily mean that the state has reduced its control over the educational sphere. Instead of being merely a provider in education, whereby the state has to hold the primary responsibility in service provision, the shift from a direct state control to educational governance has caused fundamental changes to the state's role in education.

Realising the fact that modern states have to run their businesses with limited resources in the present socio-economic and political contexts, different modes of governance have emerged in the education sector. As for the Southeast Asian contexts, though the nature of the government does change in a very broad sense, what has actually changed is that the government has transformed its role from carrying out most of the work of education itself to determining where the work will be done and by whom. More specifically, the policy of decentralisation has not entirely 'de-regulated' the control of the government in education.

By the introduction of 'decentralisation' to allow individual educational institutions to have more autonomy in deciding their own development strategies, it does not necessarily mean that the state has genuinely reduced its control over the education sector. Instead, the government has used other measures in supervising the various educational institutions, and has thus empowered the government to re-assert its direct control over the educational sector and achieve the objectives of 'functional centralisation' (Bray, 1999). It is in this sense that the policy of decentralisation in education does not necessarily mean that the process of 'de-regulation' is evolving; on the contrary, it may mean that there is another process of 're-regulation', or 're-centralisation', that might be going on in the future (Currie and Newson, 1998; Mok, 2000a; Whitty, 1997; Whitty et al, 1998).

Clearly commercial aspects, user pays and a more expanding role for private provisions of education in Southeast Asia do suggest the reduced government role in educational provision and financing, but this process does not constitute a total withdrawal from governmental control and shaping. Despite the fact that the government has tried to 'roll back' from the direct provider role, it has taken different forms of state intervention. Moving from a direct control to different modes of educational governance, other agents and non-state sectors have emerged to involve in educational provisions.

As Dale puts it: 'as far as coordinating institutions are concerned in relation to different governance activities in education like funding, regulation, provision and delivery, the role of the state, market and community would normally be identified' (Dale, 1997, p.275). Here, we can see that the local government, the local community and the evolving market are coordinating with each other in order to provide for new ways of educational provisions, and this appears to be much more so in the case of Thailand than in Singapore.

However, as far as the processes of 'marketisation' and 'decentralisation' in Southeast Asia's education sectors are concerned, 'the state has never done all these things alone, the market and especially the community have been indispensable to the operation of the educational systems' (Dale, 1997, 1999). In other words, one should not analyse these processes of 'marketisation' and 'decentralisation' as simply a one-dimensional shift from the 'state' (as bureaucratic and non-market) to the 'market' (as corporate and non-state) (Mok, 2000b). The fact that the 'civil society', or local community for that matter, can play a more dominant role in between these two poles, means we believe this societal restructuring will have a strong bearing upon the various levels of governance in the future.

Society is more than a sum of its individuals, but creates the conditions within which such individuals live and develop. It is in this sense that decentralisation does not necessarily means 'de-regulation'. On the contrary, it is a process of 're-regulation' by the government to use its resources in a more efficient and effective manner in running educational services in the Southeast Asian contexts. To this extent, it is crucial that we would need to strike a delicate balance between the 'state' and the 'market' by empowering the often neglected function of a 'civil society' in bringing about a new vision of a society in which it is fit for humans to live with dignity and respect.

Whether or not Southeast Asia can rise to the challenges of globalisation and ride on the tide, so to speak, in order to make the best use of what it can offer will really have to depend upon the visions and missions that those policy-makers and decision-makers have for their respective societies, as well as on whether or not those national goals will be implemented according to their respective socio-economic, ideological and political conditions.

References

Ashton, D. and Sung, J. (1994), *The State, Economic Development and Skill Formation: A New East Asian Model?* University of Leicester Centre for Labour Market Studies, Leicester.
Ball, S. (1998), 'Big Policies / Small World: An Introduction to International Perspectives in Education Policy', *Comparative Education*, vol.34 no.2, pp. 119-30.
Ball, S.J. (1990a), *Politics and Policy Making in Education*, Routledge, London.
Ball, S.J. (1990b), *Markets, Morality and Equality in Education*, Hillcole Group Paper 5.
Ball, S.J. (1999) 'Labor, Learning and the Economy: A "Policy Sociology" Perspective', *Cambridge Journal of Education*, vol.29 no.2, pp. 195-206.
Baltodano, A. (1997), 'The Study of Public Administration in Times of Global Interpretation: A Historical Rationale for a Theoretical Model', *Journal of Public Administration Research and Theory*, issue 7 no.4, pp. 623-26.
Bangkok Post, 'Decentralisation Urged', August 21, 1996.
Bangkok Post, 'Making Better Use of Brainpower', September 16, 1996.
Bangkok Post, 'Plan to Upgrade School Standards', February 1, 1997.
Bangkok Post, 'Education for Life', April 3, 1997.
Bray, M. (1996a), *Privatization of Secondary Education: Issues and Policy Implications*, Division of Secondary Education, UNESCO, Paris.
Bray, M. (1996b), *Counting the Full Cost: Parental and Community Financing of Education in East Asia*, World Bank and United Nations Children Fund, Washington

D.C.

Bray, M. (1999), 'Control of Education: Issues and Tensions in Centralization and Decentralization', in R.F. Arnove and C.A. Torres (eds), *Comparative Education: The Dialectic of the Global and the Local*, Rowman and Littlefield, Lanham, MD, pp. 207-32.

Breneman, D. (1993), *Higher Education: On a Collision Course with New Realities*, Association of Governing Boards of Universities and Colleges, Washington D.C..

Bridges, D. and McLaughlin, T.H. (eds) (1994), *Education and the Market Place*, Falmer Press, London.

Brown, F. (1995), 'Privatization of Public Education: Theories and Concepts', *Education and Urban Society*, vol.27 no.2, pp. 114-26.

Buchbinder, H. and Newson, J. (1990), 'Corporate-university Linkages in Canada: Transforming a Public Institution', *Higher Education*, vol.20, pp. 355-79.

Buchbinder, H. and Rajagopal, P. (1993), 'Canadian Universities and the Politics of Funding', in P. Altbach and B. Johnstone (eds), *The Funding of Higher Education: International Perspectives*, Garland Publishing, New York.

Buchbinder, H. and Rajagopal, P. (1995), 'Canadian Universities and the Impact of Austerity on the Academic Work-place', in J. Smyth (ed.), *Academic Work: The Changing Labor Process in Higher Education*, Society for Research into Higher Education and Open University Press, London.

Castells, M. (1996) *The Rise of the Network Society*. Blackwell, Malden, MA.

Carnoy, M. (2000) 'Globalisation and Education Reform', in N.P. Stromquist and K. Monkman (eds), *Globalisation and Education: Integration and Contestation Across Cultures*, Rowman and Littlefield, London and Lanham, MD., pp. 43-62.

Cenry, P. (1997), 'Paradoxes of the Competition State: The Dynamic of Political Globalization', *Governance and Opposition*, vol.32 no.2, pp. 251-74.

Chan, D.K.K. (2001) 'Educational Developments in China Under the Tidal Wave of Marketization', in J. Muckle and W.J. Morgan (eds), *Post-School Education and the Transition from State Socialism*, University of Nottingham Continuing Education Press, Nottingham, pp. 92-114.

Chan, D. and Mok, K.H. (2001), 'Educational Reforms and Coping Strategies Under the Tidal Wave of Marketization: A Comparative Study of Hong Kong and the Mainland', *Comparative Education*, vol.37 no.1, pp. 21-41.

Cheng, K.M. (1995), 'Education: Decentralization and the Market,' in L. Wong and S. MacPherson (eds), *Social Change and Social Policy in Contemporary China*, Averbury, Aldershot.

Cheng, K.M. (1999), 'From Training to Education: Lifelong Learning in China', *Comparative Education*, vol.35 no.2, pp. 119-29.

Clark, B.R. (1998), *Creating Entrepreneurial Universities: Organizational Pathways of Transformation*, Elsevier, New York.

Cooper, B.S. (1988), 'School Reform in the 1980s: The New Right's Legacy', *Educational Administration Quarterly*, vol.24 no.3, pp. 282-98.

Craft, A. (ed.) (1992), *Quality Assurance in Higher Education*, Falmer Press, London.

Craft, A. (ed.) (1994), *International Developments in Assessing Quality in Higher Education*, Falmer Press, London.

Currie, J. (1998), 'Globalization as an Analytical Concept and Local Policy Responses', in J. Currie and J. Newson (eds), *Universities and Globalization: Critical Perspectives*, Sage, Thousand Oaks.

Currie, J. (1998a), *Impact of Globalization on Australian Universities: Competition, Fragmentation and Demoralization*, paper presented at the International Sociological Association's World Congress, 1998, Montreal.

Currie, J. and Newson, J. (eds) (1998), *Universities and Globalization: Critical*

Perspectives, Sage, Thousand Oaks.
Dale, R. (1997), 'The State and The Governance of Education: An Analysis of the Restructuring of the State's Education Relationship', in A.H. Halsey, L.P. Brown and A. S. Wells (eds), *Education: Culture, Economy and Society*, Oxford University Press, Oxford.
Dale, R. (1999), 'Specifying Globalization Effects on National Policy: A Focus on the Mechanisms', *Journal of Education Policy*, vol.14, no.1, pp. 1-17.
Deem, R. (2001), 'Globalisation, New Managerialism, Academic Capitalism and Entrepreneurialism in Universities: Is the Local Dimension Still Important?', *Comparative Education*, vol.37 no.1, pp. 7-20.
Do, Huy Thinh (2001) 'University Reform in Transition: the Emergence of Institutional Autonomy and Accountability in Vietnam', in J. Muckle and W.J. Morgan (eds), *Post-School Education and the Transition from State Socialism*, University of Nottingham Continuing Education Press, Nottingham, pp. 156-66.
Duke, C. (1992), *The Learning University: Towards a New Paradigm*, The Society for Research into Higher Education and Open University Press, Buckingham.
Etzkowitz, H. and Leydesdorff, L. (eds) (1997), *Universities in the Global Knowledge Economy: A Triple Helix of Academic-Industry-Government Relations*, Cassell, London.
Fieldwork Data on August 2, 2000. Interview with Mr. Tan Hang Cheong, who is responsible for the implementation of higher education in the Ministry of Education in Singapore.
Fieldwork Data on December 2, 2001. Interview with Associate Professor Low Guat Tin of the National Institute of Education, Nanyang Technological University of Singapore.
Flynn, N. (1997), *Public Sector Management*, Harvester Wheatsheaf, Hempstead.
Foster, C.D. (1992), *Privatization, Public Ownership and Natural Monopoly*, Blackwell, Oxford.
Goh, C.T. (1997), '*Shaping Our Future: Thinking Schools, Learning Nation*', speech delivered at the Opening of the 7th International Conference on Thinking, held at Suntec City Convention Centre, June 2, 1997, Singapore.
Gopinathan, S. (1995), 'Singapore', in P. Morris and A. Sweeting (eds), *Education and Development in East Asia*, Garland Publishing, New York.
Gopinathan, S. (2001), 'Globalisation, the State and Education Policy in Singapore', in J. Tan, S. Gopinathan and W.K. Ho (eds), *Challenges Facing the Singapore Education System Today*, Prentice-Hall, Singapore, pp.3-17.
Green, A. (1999), 'East Asian Skill Formation Systems and the Challenge of Globalisation', *Journal of Education and Work*, vol.12 no.3, pp. 253-79.
Habermas, J. (1976), *Legitimation Crisis*, Heinemann, London.
Hirst, P. and Thompson, G. (1995), 'Globalization and the Future of the Nation State', *Economy and Society*, vol.24 no.3, pp. 408-42.
Hirst, P. and Thompson, G. (1999), *Globalization in Question*, Polity Press, Cambridge.
Hood, C. (1991), 'A Public Management for all Seasons', *Public Administration*, vol.69, pp. 3-19.
Hood, C. (1995), 'The New Public Management in the 1980s: Variations on a Theme', *Accounting, Organizations and Society*, vol.20 nos.2-3, pp. 93-109.
James, E. (1992), 'Why Do Different Countries Choose a Different Public-Private Mix of Educational Services', *The Journal of Human Resources*, June, pp. 571-592.
Johnson, N. (1990), *Reconstructing The Welfare State*, Harvester Wheatsheaf, Hemel Hempstead.
Jones, P.W. (1998), 'Globalization and Internationalism: Democratic Prospects for World Education', *Comparative Education*, vol.34 no.2, pp. 143-55.
Karmel, P. (1994), 'Competition Must Not Tell Universities Short', *Australian*, no.9 (November), pp. 32-3.

Le Grand, J. and Bartlett, W. (eds) (1993), *Quasi-Markets and Social Policy*, Macmillan, London.
Le Grand, J. and Robinson, R. (1985), *Privatization and the Welfare State*, George Allen and Unwin, London.
Lee, H.L. (1997), 'National Education', speech delivered at the Launch of National Education, held at TCS TV Theatre, May 17, 1997, Ministry of Education, Singapore.
Lee, W.O. (1991), *Social Change and Educational Problems in Japan, Singapore and Hong Kong*, Macmillan, London.
Levin, J. (1999) 'Missions and Structures: Bringing Clarity to Perceptions About Globalization and Higher Education in Canada', *Higher Education*, vol.37, pp. 377-99.
Levy, D. (1986), *Higher Education and the State in Latin America: Private Challenges to Public Dominance*, University of Chicago Press, Chicago.
Marginson, S. (1995) 'Markets in Higher Education: Australia', in J. Smyth (ed.), *Academic Work: the Changing Labour Process in Higher Education*, Society for Research into Higher Education and Open University Press, Buckingham, pp. 17-39.
Ministry of University Affairs (2000), *Thai Higher Education in Brief*, Ministry of University Affairs, Kingdom of Thailand, Bangkok.
Mok, K.H. (1997), 'Privatization or Marketization: Educational Development in Post-Mao China', *International Review of Education*, vol.43 nos.5-6, pp. 547-67.
Mok, K.H. (1999), 'Education and the Market Place in Hong Kong and Mainland China', *Higher Education*, vol.37, pp. 133-58.
Mok, K.H. (2000a), 'The Impact of Globalization: A Study of Quality Assurance Systems of Higher Education in Hong Kong and Singapore', *Comparative Education Review*, vol.44 no.2, pp. 148-74.
Mok, K.H. (2000b), 'Marketizing Higher Education in Post-Mao China', *International Journal of Educational Development*, vol.20, pp. 109-126.
Mok, K.H. (2000c), 'Positioning Singapore for the 21st Century: "Thinking Schools, Learning Nation" Vision', *Chulalongkorn Educational Review*, vol.6 no.2, pp. 52-69.
Mok, J.K.H. and Chan, D.K.K. (eds) (2002) *Globalisation and Education: The Quest for Quality Education in Hong Kong*, University of Hong Kong Press, Hong Kong.
Mok, K.H. and Wat, K.Y. (1998), 'The Merging of the Public and Private Boundary: Education and the Market Place in China', *International Journal of Educational Development*, vol.18 no.3, pp. 255-67.
Morris, G. (1994), 'Local Education Authorities and the Market Place', in D. Bridges and T.H. McLaughlin (eds), *Education and the Market Place*, Falmer Press, London.
Morrow, R.A. and Torres, C.A. (2000) 'The State, Globalisation, and Education Policy', in N.C. Burbules and C.A. Torres (eds), *Globalisation and Education: Critical Perspectives*, Routledge, New York, pp. 27-56.
The Nation, 'Thailand's Education Reform: The National Education Act 1999 – Hope for a Better Thailand', November 28, 1999.
OECD (1995), *Governance in Transition: Public Management Reforms in OECD Countries*, OECD, Paris.
OECD (1998), *Rethinking Tertiary Education*, OECD, Paris.
Offe, C. (1990), 'Reflection on the Institutional Self-Transformation of Movement Politics: A Tentative Stage Model', in R.J. Dalton and M. Koehler (eds), *Challenging the Political Order: New Social and Political Movements in Western Democracies*, Oxford University Press, New York.
Office of the Council of State (1997), *Constitution of the Kingdom of Thailand, B.E. 2540 (1997)*, Foreign Law Division, Bangkok.
Office of the National Education Commission (1999), *Education in Thailand, 1999*, Amarin Printing and Publishing Public Company Limited, Bangkok.
Office of the National Education Commission (2000a), *Education in Thailand, 2000/2001*, ,

Office of Prime Minister, in cooperation with the Ministry of Education and Ministry of University Affairs, Kingdom of Thailand, Bangkok.

Office of the National Education Commission (2000b), *Guidelines for Higher Education Reform in Accordance with the 1999 National Education Act*, research paper prepared by ONEC for the Roundtable Meeting of Higher Education Reform in the U.S.: Guidelines for Thailand, Amarin Printing and Publishing Public Company Limited, Bangkok.

Osborne, D. and Gaebler, T. (1992), *Reinventing Government: How the Entrepreneurial Spirit is Transforming the Public Sector*, Addison Wesley, Reading.

Prosser, T. (1995), 'The State, Constitutions and Implementing Economic Policy: Privatization and Regulation in the UK, France and the USA', *Social and Legal Studies*, vol.4, pp. 507-16.

Rangsitpol, S. (1997), *Education for Life*, speech addressed at the Foreign Correspondences Club on April 3, 1997.

Rhoades, G. (1997), *Managed Professionals: Restructuring Academic Labor in Unionized Institutions*, State University of New York Press, Albany, New York.

Roberts, P. (1994), 'Business Sponsorship in Schools : A Changing Climate', in D. Bridges and T.H. McLaughli (eds), *Education and the Market Place*, Falmer Press, London.

Robertson, R. (1992), *Globalization: Social Theory and Global Culture*, Sage, London.

Rosenau, J. (ed.) (1992), *Governance Without Government: Order and Change in World Politics*, Cambridge University Press, Cambridge.

Rung, K. (1999), *Learning for the New Century*, address by the Secretary-General of the Office of the National Education Commission of Thailand to the Fifth UNESCO-ACEID International Conference, held on 16 December, 1999.

Selvaratnam, V. (1994), *Innovations in Higher Education: Singapore at the Competitive Edge*, World Bank, Washington D.C.

Sklair, L.A. (1993), 'Consumerism Drives the Global Mass Media System', *Media Development*, vol.11 no.2, pp. 30-45.

Sklair, L.A. (1995), *Sociology of the Global System*, John Hopkins University Press, Baltimore.

Slaughter, S. and Leslie, L. (1997), *Academic Capitalism: Politics, Policies and the Entrepreneurial University*, Johns Hopkins University Press, Baltimore.

Smyth, J. (ed.) (1995), *Academic Work: The Changing Labor Process in Higher Education*, Society for Research into Higher Education and Open University Press, Buckingham.

Spring, J. (1998), *Education and the Rise of the Global Economy*, Lawrence Erlbaum Associates Inc, Mahwah, N.J.

Tan, J. (1992), 'Independent Schools in Singapore: A Case of Organizational Decentralization of Educational Management', *Educational Journal*, vol.20 no.2, pp. 149-59.

Tan, J. (1993), 'Independent Schools in Singapore: Implications for Social and Educational Inequalities, *International Journal of Educational Development*, vol.13 no.3, pp. 239-51.

Tan, E.T.J. (1997), 'Singapore', in G.A. Postiglione and G.C.L. Mak (eds), *Asian Higher Education: An International Handbook and Reference Guide*, Greenwood, Westport, CT, pp. 285-309.

Tan, J. (1998), 'The Marketisation of Education in Singapore: Policies and Implications', *International Review of Education*, vol.44 no.1, pp. 47-63.

Tan, J. (1999), *Education in Singapore in the Early 21st Century: Challenges and Dilemmas*, paper presented at the Institute of Southeast Asian Studies Conference on Singapore in the New Millennium: Challenges Facing the City-State, August 25, 1999.

Taylor, S. et al (1997), *Educational Policy and the Politics of Change*, Routledge, London.

Teo, C.H. (1997), Speech by RADM Teo Chee Hean, Minister for Education and Second Minister for Defence at the Launch of the Masterplan for IT in Education on 28 April, 1997 at Suntec City at Opening Frontiers in Education with Information Technology,

Ministry of Education, Singapore.

Tilak, J. (1991), 'The Privatization of Higher Education', *Prospects*, vol.21 no.2, pp. 227-39.

Tsang, W.K. (2001) *'Hong Kong Education Reform in the Context of Globalisation'*, paper presented at the Hong Kong Sociological Association Third Annual Meeting, held on December 1, 2001 at the Chinese University of Hong Kong, Hong Kong.

Unger, B. (1997), 'Limits of Convergence and Globalization', in S.D. Gupta (ed.), *The Political Economy of Globalization*, Kluwer, Boston, pp. 99-127.

Walford, G. (1990), *Privatization and Privilege in Education*, Routledge, London.

Walsh, K. (1995), *Public Services and Market Mechanisms*, Macmillan, London.

Welch, A. (1996), *Australian Education: Reform or Crisis?* Allen and Unwin, Sydney.

Welch, A. (1998), 'The Cult of Efficiency on Education: Comparative Reflections on the Reality and the Rhetoric', *Comparative Education*, vol.34 no.2, pp. 157-75.

Whitty, G. (1997), 'Marketization, the State and the Re-formation of the Teaching Profession', in A.H. Halsey et al (eds), *Education, Culture, Economy and Society*, Oxford University Press, Oxford.

Whitty, G. et al (1998), *Devolution and Choice in Education: the School, the State and the Market*, Open University Press, Buckingham.

World Bank (1988), *Education in Sub-Saharn Africa: Policies for Adjustment, Revitalisation and Expansion*, World Bank, Washington D.C.

World Bank (1994), *Higher Education: The Lessons of Experience*, World Bank, Washington D.C.

World Bank (1998), *Annual Report 1997/98*, World Bank, Washington D.C.

World Bank (1999), *Annual Report 1998/99*, World Bank, Washington D.C.

Yin, Q. and White, G. (1994), 'The Marketization of Chinese Higher Education: A Critical Assessment', *Comparative Education*, vol.30 no.3, pp. 217-37.

Yue, M.P. (1999), 'The Success of Thai Institutes of Private Higher Education and Their Acceptance by Society and Government', in Z.Y. Zhang and J.Y. Li (eds), *Minban Jiaoyude Yanjiu yu Tansuo (Studies and Investigations on Minban Education)*, Beijing Normal University Press, Beijing, pp. 188-94.

10 Full Equality and Inclusion for People with a Disability: Strategies for the New Millennium in Southeast Asian Countries

JOSEPH K F KWOK

Who are People with a Disability?

The World Health Organization (WHO) defined the concept of disability when it introduced three independent classifications, namely impairment, disability and handicap in 1980 (WHO, 1980). According to the WHO 1980 classification, impairment refers to abnormalities of body structure and organ or system function resulting from any cause; disability refers to restrictions on functional performance and activity by an individual and handicap covers the disadvantages experienced by the individual in the course of interaction with the environment as a result of impairments and disabilities. This classification system has been adopted by most sectors in many communities. In the disability community, terms such as the crippled and handicapped people have been dropped as demeaning and stigmatic. The terms people with disability or disabled people are becoming the politically correct labeling and accepted by both the mainstream and the disability communities. Towards the end of 1990's, WHO's 1980 classifications for disability and handicap have become less popular. They are criticised as being too focused on the negative aspects and causing confusion in general use of the language rather than improving information dissemination. Responding to the criticisms, WHO published the International Classification of Impairments, Disabilities and Handicaps (ICIDH-2) final version (WHO, 1999) with a new title, 'International Classification of Functioning and Disabilities'. The revised classification tool uses functioning as an umbrella term for all body functions, activities and participation; and disability as an umbrella term for impairments, activity limitations or participation restrictions. These terms all have their specific meaning in the WHO classification system. The WHO Assembly approved the final version in May 2001 and gave it new acronym, ICF (WHO, 2001).

For the purpose of present discussion, a person with a disability is one who has activity limitations (e.g. seeing, hearing, talking, walking, lifting, carrying, activities of daily living) or participation restrictions (e.g. as a student and an income earner). Not all disabled people need assistance to perform basic activities. Those who should need assistance, such as assistive device, assistance from another person in order to perform one or more basic activities may be referred to as persons with a severe disability. The United Nations (UN) in its proclamation of the International Year of Disabled Persons (1981) estimated that one in ten of the population is person with such severe disability (UN, 1983). The UN estimate is confirmed by the USA 1997 Census, which reported that one in five of Americans has some kind of disability, and one in ten has some kind of severe disability (US Department of Commerce, Economics and Statistics Administration, Bureau of The Census, 1997).

Situation of Disabled People in Southeast Asia

Applying the same definition of people with disability and similar prevalence rate to the populations of Southeast Asia, there are about 32 million of people with some kind of severe disability, who are in need of assistance. Given the wide gap between USA and Southeast Asia in areas of medical and social support, the 32 million estimated numbers of disabled people should be on the low side (Statistics Division, UNESCAP, 1998). Moreover, because of war and civil unrests, some countries have even higher per capital rates of disability (e.g. Cambodia and Vietnam).

There are marked differences among countries of ASEAN (Cambodia, Indonesia, Lao People's Democratic Republic, Malaysia, Myanmar, Philippines, Thailand, and Vietnam) in areas of economic development, political, social and cultural dimensions. However, there are at least two common phenomena concerning people with disabilities frequently reported in ASEAN. First, majority of people with a disability in Southeast Asia live in rural areas isolated from major support groups, information, medical, rehabilitation and technical assistance. Second, they are discriminated and marginalised by the mainstream society.

Responding to these two major challenges, and building upon the United Nations International Year of Disabled Persons (1981) and UN

World Programme of Action 1983-1992, the ESCAP proclaimed the Asian and Pacific Decade of Disabled Persons 1993-2002 (ESCAP, 1993 and 1994). The United Nations Economic and Social Commission for Asia and the Pacific (UNESCAP) proclamation not only deals with disability prevention and rehabilitation, but also disabled people's full equality and participation in every sector of a society. During the decades of 1980s and 1990s, a strong regional non-governmental organisation (NGO) and governmental organisation (GO) network concerning disability has been evolved and supported by the movement of people with disability in the pursuit of the action targets of the Decade. Some marked improvements to disabled people's situations have been reported in some countries, but such improvements are relatively insignificant when compared to improvements seen in their respective mainstream societies.

This paper discusses key strategies that are considered of major significance to disabled people's full participation and equality in the society, namely: sectoral advocacy, multi-sectoral mainstreaming, human rights strategy, community based rehabilitation and self-help organisations. These strategies are interlinked in a dynamic manner dealing with policies at national and local levels, service delivery and leadership of disabled people at the grassroots level, including those in remote rural areas and islands, as well as focusing on key global issues that are seeking sound local solutions.

Sectoral Advocacy: Legislation and Policy Development through Regional Cooperation[1]

Since 1981, the main emphasis of disability advocacy and self-advocacy has been on sectoral advocacy. One important purpose of sectoral advocacy is to get the voice of disabled people heard at all levels of government, and to empower disabled people to take an active role in central government policy-making bodies. The UN has called upon its member governments to institute central high-level committees to oversee the development of national comprehensive policies and measures concerning disability (UN, 1983). Such committees are urged to have the representation of disabled advocates and disabled self-help organisations. International UN forums over the past two decades have indeed successfully encouraged governments to set up central level coordinating mechanisms with participation of disabled representatives.

In Southeast Asia, Philippines and Thailand are the two countries where the central governmental committees have been rather active in promoting legislative and policy developments in support of disabled people (ESCAP, 1997). In the Philippines, the National Council for the Welfare of Disabled People, a governmental organisation, comprises representatives from key governmental organisations and major NGOs of and for people with a disability. The first Executive Director of the Council was a disabled person, a popular singer as well as a prominent leader in the civic society. The disability sectoral representative to the Legislature appointed by former President Aquino based on the revised Constitution was a famous media celebrity, who also sat on the Council (Borjal, 1998). In Thailand, there is a high level committee in the Central Government dealing with disability issues, and one of its members in the formation years was a disabled leader (Patibatsarakich, 1998) who was elected into the legislature through a sectoral representation under the new constitution of Thailand. In both countries, fundamental laws for the protection of the rights of disabled people were enacted in the early 1990s after long years of debate and consultation. In the Philippines, the fundamental law, the Magna Carta for Disabled Persons of Republic Act 7,277 was enacted in 1992. In Thailand, the Rehabilitation of Disabled Persons Act B.E. 2534 and Ministerial Regulations B.E. 253 No. 1, 2 and 3, was enacted in 1991 for implementation in 1994. The Thai legislation provides for a high level committee consisting of Minister of Interior as Chairman, and the Permanent Secretaries to the Ministries of Defense, Interior, Education, Public Health, and the University Affairs, the Director of the Budget Bureau, the Director-Generals of the Departments of Medical Services, Public Welfare, General Education and not more than six other qualified persons appointed by the Minister, as members.

Among Southeast Asian countries, there are still marked differences in areas of legislation and policy, perhaps more as a reflection of the significant differences of these countries in economic, cultural and social conditions. The trend is, however, towards convergence, as a result of continued and persistent regional co-operation. Such a convergence is particularly obvious in legislation and policies concerning barrier free environment, quota employment and anti-disability discrimination.

Other countries in Southeast Asia without similar comprehensive legislation are still progressing significantly in a similar direction. Vietnam, for example, is moving ahead at fast speed. Barrier free legislation is already high in the agenda of their legislature, with barrier free laws going well into the drafting stage in 2000. Issues of employment of people with disabilities and community based rehabilitation are also gaining priority attention in the government's policy agenda. Such positive changes in Vietnam are partly due to the soft advocacy of their self-help organisations, as well as the increasingly intensive international cooperation. During the past decade, Vietnamese delegates have often been invited to intergovernmental forums and training courses/workshops initiated by UNESCAP as well as by international non-governmental organisations (INGOs). As the US-Vietnam inter-governmental relationship is coming out from frozen states, US leading bodies concerning disabilities such as its Presidents' Committee on Employment, and a number of NGOs are paying visits to Vietnam and sponsoring national forums and training concerning disabled people. UNESCAP with the funding support of Japan have conducted leadership training for people with disabilities in Vietnam, and such training has stimulated governmental initiatives to promote formal leadership and support of self-help organisations of people with disabilities. The most significant event would be Campaign 2001 for the Asian and Pacific Decade of Disabled Persons, 1993-2002, which is going to be held in Hanoi in December 2001, and hosted by the Ministry of Labour, Invalid and Social Affairs in collaboration with Vietnamese national NGOs concerning disabilities.

In terms of international cooperation in the Asia and Pacific Region, UNESCAP has been playing the pivotal role. The most important initiative has been the launching of the Asian and Pacific Decade of Disabled Persons, 1993-2002. This important UNESCAP resolution was sponsored by China and Japan, and adopted unanimously by all its governmental members. The action plans of the Decade are monitored through bi-annual intergovernmental monitoring forums and the accompanying INGO forum facilitated by UNESCAP. A number of important documents have been developed and adopted by UNESCAP forums, notably among which are the Decade's Action Agenda and its associated targets for implementation. At each intergovernmental forum, governments are asked to report progress in those identified targets. While most government representatives are keen to provide a positive image at such forums and making reports with rhetoric, still some significant improvements are seen in most countries. Such efforts have not been significantly dampened by the Asian crises. In fact an expanded list of targets for the implementation of the Agenda for Action for the Asian and Pacific Decade of Disabled Persons was endorsed by the 56th session of the Commission of UNESCAP in June 2000 (ESCAP, 2000). The lists now contain 107 Decade targets in 12 areas of concerns of the Agenda for Action for the Decade. These 12 policy areas and the newly identified associated critical issues are:

1. National coordination: national and sub-national coordinating bodies are still not well instituted in national policy to give an assurance of its effectiveness to go beyond the Decade.
2. Legislation: while progress has been witnessed in the enactment of basic laws concerning equalisation of opportunities for people with

disabilities, there is little or no progress in the review of substantive laws, such as those pertaining to marriage and inheritance, and criminal and civil procedure enactment.
3. Information: lack of and access to reliable and up-dated information concerning disability.
4. Public awareness: prevalence of negative perceptions and practices against disabled people continue to be major factors restricting the equal participation of people with disabilities.
5. Accessibility and communication: barrier free environment, communication and assistive devices continue to be major challenges.
6. Education: inclusive education has been recognised a major challenge for the Region for the years to address the educational needs of the vast majority of disabled children who are deprived of educational opportunities.
7. Training and employment: information technology has caused both new opportunities and restrictions to employment opportunities of people with disabilities. The major challenge is to open opportunities for disabled people in mainstream training centers leading to employable skills, and open up al sectors of the economy for disabled people.
8. Prevention of causes of disability: the major challenge is to set up comprehensive strategy to deal with all causes of disability, particularly those associated with lack of immunisation and malnutrition.
9. Rehabilitation: community based rehabilitation (CBR) continues to be recognised as the key strategy to address the needs for comprehensive rehabilitation services for people with disabilities in rural, slum, mountainous and island areas.
10. Assistive devices: The key challenges are to promote research and development of indigenous assistive devices that are culturally appropriate for and affordable by rural and urban disabled people, as well as promoting systems for their production and distribution.
11. Self-help organisations: The key challenges are for some governments to become more aware of the role of self-help organisations in national policy formulation concerning disability, and to develop national forums of self-help organisations as well as cross-disability groups to include other disabled groups, such as people with chronic illness, persons with psychosocial disabilities, users of psychiatric services, and HIV-positive persons.
12. Regional cooperation: to expand support, particularly funding for small countries in the Pacific and mountainous areas to pursue the achievement of the Targets.

Another significant development in Regional cooperation is witnessed by the formation of the Regional NGO Network for the Promotion of the Asian and Pacific Decade of Disabled Persons, 1993-2002 (RNN), which was formed in 1993 in Okinawa, Japan. RNN membership comprises major national NGOs and INGOs with activities in the Region, and sponsors annual campaigns on a rotational basis in each country for the promotion of the Decade. The campaigns together with the UNESCAP forums have formed strong alliance in advocating for actions at the national level in the 12 policy areas identified above. The unique characteristics of RNN are that it is a cross disability NGO forum with participation of GOs at their own choice. In fact, GOs are usually involved in supporting the RNN annual campaigns. RNN annual campaigns have a history of attracting a relatively large number of disabled delegations of various disabilities. Leaders with disability are taking prominent positions in these campaigns bringing positive impact at the national level to support self-help movement. Southeast Asian countries are among the most active participants in these campaigns, as Philippines, Indonesia, Korea, Hong Kong, Malaysia, Thailand and Vietnam are respective hosts for 1994, 1995, 1997, 1998, 1999, 2000 and 2001 Campaigns.[2]

However, the impact of sectoral advocacy on policy and legislation development at the national level seems to have lost steam after the Asian financial crises. After the crises, governments' attention shows an obvious shift to financial and economic targets, such as financial reforms and poverty eradication. Issues that are more politically sensitive are also getting higher priority in the government. For example, issues concerning old people and women, because they could draw major political concerns or attract more votes in popular election. In some countries priority is given to restore government credibility and civil security when civil unrests, and civil conflicts with racial and religious confrontation backgrounds have escalated to a serious level.

Against such a background of shrinking public attention, and towards the closing of the Asian and Pacific Decade of Disabled Persons 1993-2002, the Thematic Working Group on Disability-related Concerns (TWGDC) (formally known as Regional Interagency Committee for Asia and the Pacific) has been engaged in intensive deliberation to identify strategies to bring the disability movement forward. The TWGDC is facilitated by the Social Development Division of UNESCAP, and comprises major UN systems, INGOs and major NGOs concerning disability.[3] Members of TWGDC have identified the following key strategies: multi-sectoral mainstreaming, an international convention on the rights of people with disabilities, and community based rehabilitation.[4]

Multi-Sectoral Mainstreaming

The advocacy for integrated multi-sectoral policy has been taken up by UNESCAP as a major strategy towards the end of the Decade (ESCAP, 1999). This is a logical step as sectoral advocacy for representation in disability focused high-level government committees seems to have encountered major limitations in creating further social impact. The roles and functions of the high-level committee and ministry responsible for disability policies have been thoroughly debated and documented over the decade. This subject has received less and less controversies among government representatives to UN forums. It is therefore a logical step for the disability sector to seek alliance with non-disability focused government structures through integrated multi-sectoral mainstreaming approach.

The integrated multi-sectoral policy is to require all government institutions to ensure barrier free access of their policy provisions to disabled people. The relationship between the disability focused ministry and other ministries of a government should therefore require further strengthening. The ministry with primary responsibility for disability policies is expected to take on a resource person's role to educate other ministries and to provide technical support in achieving barrier free policy provisions. The support of NGOs for and of people with disabilities is also essential in supporting mainstream ministries to achieve such integrated policy targets.

In order to have an effective integrated multi-sectoral policy approach, there are at least two requirements to fulfill. First, there should be adequate technical officers on disability issues to be called upon by mainstream policy branches. A more effective arrangement is for each and every mainstream branch to have its own disability technical staff teams to review, improve and develop barrier free mainstream policies. Second, key information needs to be provided by mainstream technical departments so that integrated multi-sectoral policies are based on informed consideration. All technical support departments should be tasked with research and development roles concerning disability, notably among them would be the Census and Statistics Department.

It is worth noting Hong Kong's experiences in instituting multi-sectoral approaches to disability issues, as its disability policy responsibilities have a history of shifting between policy ministries sometimes on grounds of administration efficiency, while other times on integration considerations.

Hong Kong has now around 70 vehicles fitted with tail-lifts and other access facilities managed by an NGO and funded by government to provide special transport services to disabled people who for reasons of their disability cannot use public transport. In the beginning years in mid-1970s, a new service know as Rehabus, was monitored and funded by the Social Welfare Department. In those years, government considered special transport service for people with disabilities as a form of welfare assistance, and no reference was made to the failure of public transport services meeting special needs of the people with disabilities. In the late 1980s, as a result of intensive and persistent lobbying of the disability field, Rehabus policy has been shifted to the responsibility of the Commission for Rehabilitation, which is a senior government post dealing with all disability concerned policies, and within the Secretary of Health and Manpower. The monitoring of Rehabus operation has since been placed under the Transport Department, which is within the Secretary for Transport. The policy change has brought major improvements to Rehabus service, which is immediately placed on par with regular public transport service in terms of service and safety standards. As a result, maintenance of Rehabus including depot requirements, safety, vehicle technical considerations, as well drivers training on motor driving skills and handling of disability issues all receive review and monitoring by transport professional, and the whole service has moved far away from welfare services notion. A second and no less important advantage as result of the change is that the Transport Department has become more aware of disability issues and the importance of adopting the principle of barrier free transport for people with disability. In monitoring land transport franchises, the Transport Department now requires operators to provide buses with special access facilities. The next stage in the development of comprehensive transport policy hopefully is to have an integrated service between Rehabus and all other forms of public transport, so as to achieve seamless passenger transfer from barrier free public transport to Rehabus with the aim to widely broaden the mobility of people with disabilities all over the territories.[5]

The second example of integrated multi-sectoral approach in Hong Kong comes from the Census and Statistics Department (CSD). Over the years, the CSD had great hesitation to provide statistical support and research in this area and claimed that respondents may not be able or reluctant to give correct answers concerning disability enumeration. After years of resistance, the CSD has finally conceited to carry out an exercise to enumerate selected disability statistics in its general household survey. Since early 2000, the general household survey, which is a standard monthly random survey to collect vital economic and other data of the city, has incorporated a section on disability related demographic questions and other major service related questions. The survey lasted for most months of the year 2000 so as to collect enough respondents to ensure adequate sampling reliability' the findings were reported in late 2001. The survey estimated the total number and prevalence rate of disability as 269,500 and 4%. The survey covered their demographic and household profile, impacts of disability on day-to-day living, carers profile, and transportation arrangements. The survey also included sections on people living in institutions and people who were mentally handicapped. The outcome of the general household provides useful data for mainstream ministries, as well as technical references for similar technical departments in the region.[6]

It is quite obvious that the successful implementation of a multi-sectoral strategy faces not only challenges on technical grounds, but also political challenges. The handling of disability related political issues should require firm commitment of decision makers at very senior government levels. The political will of the legislature will also have a major bearing, as it provides the political importance and priority of the strategy, as well as the legislation framework to make it work.

The integrated multi-sectoral approach builds on two fundamental principles. First, the principle of inclusion, which requires that disabled people are taken into account in all mainstream sectoral policies, programmes and systems. Second, a rational coordination of all the sectoral services concerned disabled people.

United Nations systems are strong supporters of the multi-sectoral inclusive approach. The International Labour Organization (ILO), as an example, has moved beyond the conceptual limitations of the mandate given in the Convention 159 and Recommendation 168 on the vocational rehabilitation and employment of disabled persons adopted by the ILO Conference in 1983. Currently, ILO strategies give priority to the integration of disabled youth and adults into the ordinary structures of vocational training and salaried employment or of micro- and small enterprise creation (ESCAP, 1999, p.129). Such an approach is radically distinguished from the segregative approaches of the past, e.g. the support for sheltered workshops. ILO is now launching new initiatives to support governments in the region to develop strategies for the effective integration of disabled persons into ordinary vocational training and employment programmes.

Community Based Rehabilitation (CBR) and the Role of Self-help Organisations

CBR was first initiated by WHO and joined by ILO as an alternative strategy to institutional rehabilitation to meet the service needs of the vast majority of disabled people in rural, mountainous, and urban slum areas. Institutional rehabilitation are centre-based, with high concentration of professionals and equipment and facilities, and are all relatively very costly. Yet the number of disabled people they can serve is very limited, and they are also out of reach to most disabled people who live far away from such centres. WHO pilot tested CBR in rural areas beginning from the late 1970s with a complete set of training manuals for groups of disabled people with most commonly found disabilities (Helander, et al, 1989). The training manuals cover all key areas of identification, rehabilitation exercises, use of low cost appropriate assistive devices, and making referrals. The manuals also give guidelines in mobilising local authority and community leadership in supporting CBR activities. The training manuals aim to assist local trainers for disabled people, who may be family members or neighbourhood carers. Those training local trainers are called CBR supervisors who are given more intensive training in the development and monitoring of CBR programmes.

In 1984, the Philippine Department of Social Welfare and Development, assisted by ILO, embarked a pilot CBR vocational programme to serve people in either isolated rural or metropolitan slum area. The CBR method developed in the Philippines has been tested in remote rural communities, semi-urban settings, depressed areas of metropolitan Manila and has been found to be acceptable to both Christian and Islamic communities (Tugwell, 1989). In 1990s, CBR is reaffirmed by the Philippines government as an effective approach in mobilising indigenous contribution as well as the collaboration of all efforts in the society. Philippines government has since been promoting CBR on a national scale covering remote rural areas and islands (Capadocia, 1998).

In the early years of CBR practice, CBR was promoted more as a simplified and popularised version of professional practice, so as to provide some kind of service to disabled people who otherwise would never be able to get access to professional or institution based services. The success of CBR practice, as well as its popularity among developing countries, has prompted UN systems to enlarge its mission and service coverage. Since 1990's, CBR is considered as an important measure to protect the dignity and human rights of disabled people through community development approach and empowerment of disabled people's organisations. The service coverage of CBR is also extended through multi-sectoral approach (Helander, 1992; ESCAP, 1998). To emphasis on the multi-sectoral approach, UN systems involved in promoting CBR issued a joint statement in 1994, which defines CBR as follows (ILO et al, 1994):

> Community-based rehabilitation (CBR) is a strategy within community development for the rehabilitation, equalization of opportunities and social integration of all people with disabilities. CBR is implemented through the combined efforts of disabled people themselves, their families and communities, and the appropriate health, education, vocational and social services.

People with a disability have been given a more prominent role in CBR strategy. A key characteristic of CBR is the involvement of disabled self-help groups in its development, monitoring as well as serving as trainers and role models. To be CBR supervisor or trainer, formal qualification is not a pre-condition, but relevant experiences and on the job training. Disabled people naturally have more experiences than non-disabled people in dealing with challenges associated with disability, and are better equipped to take on trainers' roles, and to become role models to demonstrate the kind of contributions they can make to the community and society. Leaders of self-help groups are also effective self-advocates in such CBR programmes, showing to the local leadership they voice should be counted in local policy and national policies.

Philippines give a useful example on the parallel development of self-help organisations of people with disabilities and CBR programme. About the same time when CBR was promoted on a nation-wide scale, a federation of people with disabilities was formed, which is KAMPI. It started with only around 20 people with disabilities who attended a leadership training workshop organised by Disabled People's International and ESCAP in the early 1980s. Now KAMPI has over 120 chapters across the country. KAMPI is formally accredited by the National Council on the Welfare of Disabled Persons to be a partner in providing leadership training to disabled people and CBR programmes (KAMPI, 1997-98).

Self-help movement of people with disabilities has made significant development in the Region since the UN International Year of Disabled Persons (1981), with the founding of a cross-disability international non-governmental organisation of people with disabilities, the Disabled People's International (DPI). Although relatively young in history, DPI has received major funding support from some governments and recognised by UN with consultative NGO status (Dredger, 1989). DPI has since been very active in the region in developing cross-disability self-help organisations of people with disabilities (SHOPs) at the national level in collaboration with UNESCAP and with funding support primarily from Japan. An expert with disability from Japan has been seconded to UNESCAP as a special project officer to assist in leadership training seminars for SHOP leaders at the national level. During this period several major cross disability national SHOP were founded, the notable of which are the DPI Japan, DPI Thailand, and DPI Philippines (Takamine, 1998). The leaders of these SHOPs have succeeded in gaining political and civic recognition, with some even assuming leadership roles in local and central government. These cross-disability national SHOPs in turn organise community level SHOPs. As a result, some national NGOs have witnessed phenomenal expansion in their local level branches and membership. Such a development has not been affected by Asian crises, as the leadership training and local branches are mainly people based community development and mobilisation work, requiring very little infrastructure investment. Experiences in the Region have therefore shown that SHOPs is an important partner in CBR strategy, and in turn they have also gained strength from such partnership activities.

The Human Rights Strategy

To protect and promote human rights of people with disabilities has always been a major concern for international and national bodies dealing with disability issues. International NGOs are among the strongest advocates for an international convention on the rights of people with disabilities. UN, on the other hand, have already made two important declarations concerning the rights of disabled persons, namely: UN Declaration on the Rights of the Mentally Retarded Persons (UN, 1971), and UN Declaration on the Rights of Disabled Persons (UN, 1975). The UN systems are also not unfamiliar with the recommendations for a convention on the rights of persons with disabilities. In fact, in 1988 and 1989, the Italian and the Swedish Governments made unsuccessful attempts respectively to the UN General Assembly. The Swedish Government's proposal received committee stage consideration by the UN governing bodies, but failed to go through the committee discussion stage.

Upon conclusion of the UN World Programme of Action Concerning Disabled Persons (UN, 1983), the UN resolved on the Standard Rules on the Equalization of Opportunities for Persons with Disabilities (UN, 1994), and assigned a Special Rapportuer to monitor its implementation by member states. However, member states of UN are not under mandatory sanctioning to report on the progress on the implementation of the Standard Rules in their respective countries. Since its proclamation, the Standard Rules has received relatively low publicity within UN networks, not to mention individual countries and the international community. Furthermore, the Standard Rules is criticised as being less than comprehensive in promoting the rights of disabled people. There is now a general feeling and consensus around the world that the UN Standard Rules could not possibility live up to the expectations of the international disability movement in dealing with challenges of the new Millennium. Something more powerful within the United Nations systems is needed. Bengt Lindqvist, UN Special Rapportuer on Disability, in a consultation paper for his expert panel members and selected INGOs, recognised one definite advantage with a special convention; that is it would come with a monitoring mechanism on a regular basis. He is however uncertain how to involve existing UN bodies responsible for the monitoring of the general conventions, in order to get their support for the special convention (Lindqvist, March 1999; Division for Social Policy and Development, UN Secretariat, 2001).

The uncertainty within UN systems, however, does not dampen the INGO sector's will to advocate for an international convention on the rights of disabled persons in the beginning of the new Millennium. Rehabilitation International (RI) is among the first international NGOs to launch a worldwide appeal for such a special convention. In welcoming the arrival of the New Millennium, RI invited its senior leaders as well as world leaders concerned with the disability movement to revisit its Charter for the 80's (Rehabilitation International, 1980). As a result, RI published the RI Charter for the New Millennium (Rehabilitation International, 1999), and commits itself to campaign for an international convention on the rights of disabled persons. RI's initiative has received a strong echo from countries in the Asia and Pacific Region.

The Beijing Declaration for the New Millennium, March 2000

Countries in the Region have a wide divergence in culture and politics as well as marked differences in legal and monitoring practices dealing with disability discrimination. In spite of such discrepancies, there is a strong political consensus among countries in protecting the rights of disabled people, as shown by the unanimous consensus in supporting the Asian and Pacific Decade of Disabled Persons, 1993-2002. Therefore building on the prevailing strong political will and rich experiences of all the countries in the region, the call for UN to proclaim an international convention on the rights of all people with disabilities is considered long overdue by the disability communities in the region.

For the first time in the history of world disability movement, five major international non-governmental organisations as well as several national non-governmental organisations convened the World NGO Summit on Disability from March 10 to 12, 2000 in Beijing, China and concluded with a joint declaration, the Beijing Declaration on the Rights of People with Disabilities in the New Century (CDPF, 2000). These five INGOs are: DPI, Inclusion International, RI, the World Blind Union and the World Federation of the Deaf. Together in one voice, they call on all concerned with equality and human dignity to ensure the adoption of an international convention on the rights of all people with disabilities. Together they commit themselves to strive for the legally binding convention. It should be noted that leaders of these INGOs from Asia-

Pacific played a leading role in the Summit, including those from China, Hong Kong, India, Japan, New Zealand, and Thailand.[7]

Immediately following the Beijing World NGO Summit 2000, all INGOs, GOs and NGOs in the Region attending the Campaign 2000 for the Asian and Pacific Decade of Disabled Persons, 1993-2002, held in Bangkok, Thailand in December 2000, reaffirmed their commitment to strive for the international convention (RNN, 2000).

The purpose of the Convention is to provide a common reference against which human rights standards can be assessed, and member states, upon ratifying the Convention, will be obliged to bring their legislation, policy and practice in line with the rights standards. The human rights standards will also provide common references and barrier-free standards to multi-national and bilateral projects, which may concern the quality of life of disabled people. The proposed convention should have at least the following characteristics: (a) comprehensive, covering civil, political, economic, social and cultural rights; (b) universal and applying to all people with disabilities in all situation in the entire world; (c) unconditional and calling on all governments, including those with scarce resources to take action; and (d) holistic in that all rights are essential, indivisible, interdependent and equal.

If the UN is to proclaim the Convention, it will have to create a high office, e.g. a commission on the rights of people with disabilities to monitor progress and review government reports. Such a Commission will have to be formed by international experts selected by member states. The Commission together with current and future governmental, statutory and NGO disability rights monitoring bodies will become very useful and influential global networks. The Convention and this new global network will become the centrefold of disability movement in both national and global levels in the new Millennium, and is expected to create new and strong momentum to move the disability movement forward.

Future of the Disability Movement in Southeast Asia

What can we tell from the decades of experiences of disability movement and what would be its future in the Southeast Asia. Over the past decades, we have certainly witnessed significant changes in the field of disability and rehabilitation in Southeast Asia. As expected, changes in some countries are more significant than others. These changes are witnessed in legislation, in efforts to reach out to the unreachable disabled population, in leadership and self-advocacy, and in forging the human rights strategy in mainstream development. Such a trend could be explained as outcomes of deliberations and campaigns of UN specialist bodies and some intergovernmental forums, as well as the lobbying of INGOs. Moreover, contents of UN documents enshrining principles, values, goals and objectives concerning disability measures are being incorporated in similar forms in national policies and legislation of increasing number of countries. However, in practice, national governments are still having a high degree of discretion in their implementation. Even legislation on barrier free environment in Philippines and Thailand as well as other Asian countries face great difficulty in its enforcement.

If we analysis further the actual situations of disabled people, the changes are not so significant when compared to the mainstream population. For example, unemployment rates of disabled population remain far higher than the corresponding mainstream unemployment rates; disabled children having school education are still far less than mainstream children; and disabled women continue to face discrimination and suffer much more than the mainstream population. Furthermore old people with disabilities are growing in large numbers and their needs are often ignored. Disabled people continue to be marginalised, and maybe relatively even more so than decades ago.

How are we going to explain such a contradicting phenomenon, which is happening across the countries in Southeast Asia? It seems that a hollow process of globalisation is occurring. The disability-concerned sector within a country, itself alone, is less powerful in dealing with discrimination and negative actions of the mainstream society. The disability-concerned sectors, joining hands, across the region would have a much greater power and resources in dealing with acute situations of discrimination in any one mainstream society. Regional cooperation in its present format as developed over the past decades has already served its purpose, and would not be able to further empower the disability-concerned sectors in the region in any significant degree as compared to the past decade. The regional disability movement has to look forward to a substantive sense of globalisation of disability issues through the UN forum, including the adoption of a special convention on the rights of disabled persons, to be backed by mandatory monitoring systems that shall be observed by all members. The Special Convention would serve the very purpose of putting UN bodies and UN member governments on the proper focus and same high level of awareness as other human rights convention.

The future of the disability movement in the Asia and Pacific Region, in particular Southeast Asian countries, is getting more and more dependent on the globalisation process of disability issues. The key action agenda in the coming years of most IGNOs concerning disability, and the several lead governments (including China and Japan) would be working inside and outside all relevant UN systems and forums in order to bring forward the proposal on the special convention to UN governing bodies. The groundwork has been firmly laid down, and the hope for a success is bright. But the process is definitely very challenging and would take years to complete.

Notes

1 Some of the information given in this section was from the author's interviews with key informants during his field trips to the countries concerned between 1998 and 2001.
2 The author is a founder member of RNN, and has participated in all its annual campaigns.
3 See World Wide Web: http://www.dinf.ne.jp/doc/twg/eng/index_e.html
4 The author is a member of the TWGDC.
5 The author is a member of the Rehabus Management Committee since 1985.
6 The author was consulted by CSD in 2000 in the development of the disability section of the general household survey.
7 The author had been involved in the preparation of the Summit.

References

Borjal, A (1998), 'Disability and the Media: The Philippine Experience', in J. Kwok, A. Mak, S. Purves and P. Yuen (eds), *Proceedings of 11th Rehabilitation International Asia and the Pacific Regional Conference cum Campaign '98 for the Asian and Pacific Decade of Disabled Persons 1993-2002*, Joint Council for the Physically and Mentally Disabled/The Hong Kong Council of Social Service, Hong Kong, pp. 152-53.

Capadocia, M. (1998), 'Community Participation in Community-based Rehabilitation', in J. Kwok, A. Mak, S. Purves and P. Yuen (eds), *Proceedings of 11th Rehabilitation International Asia and the Pacific Regional Conference cum Campaign '98 for the Asian and Pacific Decade of Disabled Persons 1993-2002*, Joint Council for the Physically and Mentally Disabled/The Hong Kong Council of Social Service, Hong Kong, pp. 153-55.

China Disabled Persons' Federation (CDPF) (2000), *Beijing Declaration on the Rights of People with Disabilities in the New Century, adopted on 12 March 2000 at the World NGO Summit on Disability held in Beijing, China*, CDPF, Beijing.

Division for Social Policy and Development, United Nations Secretariat (2001), *Report of Informal Consultative Meeting on International Norms and Standards for Persons with Disabilities held in United Nations, New York, 9 February 2001*, United Nations, New York.

Dredger, D. (1989), *The Last Civil Rights Movement. Disabled People's International*, Hirst and Company, London.

ESCAP (1993), *Asian and Pacific Decade of Disabled Persons, 1993-2002: The starting point*, United Nations, New York.

ESCAP (1994), *Asian and Pacific Decade of Disabled Persons, 1993-2002: Mandates for Action*, United Nations, New York.

ESCAP (1997), *Legislation on Equal Opportunities and Full Participation in Development for Disabled Persons: Examples from the ESCAP Region*, United Nations, New York.

ESCAP (1998), *Understanding community based rehabilitation*, United Nations, New York.
ESCAP (1999), *Asian and Pacific Decade of Disabled Persons: mid-point – regional perspectives on multisectoral collaboration and national coordination*, United Nations, New York.
ESCAP (2000), *107 Targets for Action for the Full Implementation of the Asian and Pacific Decade of Disabled Persons, 1993-2002*, retrieved from World Wide Web: http://www.dinf.ne.jp/doc/twg/eng/pagnd1sc_e.html.
Helander, E. (1992), *Prejudice and dignity: An introduction to community-based rehabilitation*, United Nations Development Programme, New York.
Helander, E., Mendis, P., Nelson, G. and Goerdt, A. (1989), *Training in the community for people with disabilities*, World Health Organisation, Geneva.
ILO, UNESCO and WHO (1994), *Community-Based Rehabilitation for and with People with Disabilities, 1994 Joint Position Paper*, ILO, Geneva.
KAMPI (Katipunan Ng, Maykapansanan, sa Philipinas, Inc.) (1997-98), *1997-98 Accomplishment Report*, KAMPI, Manila.
Lindqvist, B. (1999), *Promotion of Disability Policy Within the UN System After the Year 2000*, Stockholm.
Patibatsarakich, N. (1998), 'Legisalation for People with Disabilities in the Asia Pacific Region' in J. Kwok, A. Mak, S. Purves and P. Yuen (eds), *Proceedings of 11th Rehabilitation International Asia and the Pacific Regional Conference cum Campaign '98 for the Asian and Pacific Decade of Disabled Persons 1993-2002*, Joint Council for the Physically and Mentally Disabled/The Hong Kong Council of Social Service, Hong Kong, pp. 386-90.
Rehabilitation International (1980), *RI Charter for the 80s*, Rehabilitation International, New York.
Rehabilitation International (1998), *Community Based Rehabilitation: Worldwide Applications, Visions and Resources for the 21st Century*, United Nations Development Organizations through the United Nations Voluntary Fund on Disability 1998, New York.
Rehabilitation International (1999), *Rehabilitation International Millennium Charter*, Rehabilitation International, New York.
RNN (2000), *Bangkok Millennium Declaration on the Promotion of the Rights of People with Disabilities in the Asian and Pacific Region, Campaign 2000 for the Asian and Pacific Decade of Disabled Persons*, December 11-15, 2000, Bangkok.
Statistics Division, ESCAP (1998), *Asia and the Pacific in Figures 1998*, retrieved from World Wide Web: http://www.unescap.org/stat/statdata/apinfig.htm
Takamine, Y. (1998), 'Self-help Movements of People with Disabilities in Asia and the Pacific' in J. Kwok, A. Mak, S. Purves and P. Yuen (eds), *Proceedings of 11th Rehabilitation International Asia and the Pacific Regional Conference cum Campaign '98 for the Asian and Pacific Decade of Disabled Persons 1993-2002*, Joint Council for the Physically and Mentally Disabled/The Hong Kong Council of Social Service, Hong Kong, pp. 245-48.
Tugwell, I.F. (1989), 'An Asian Approach To Vocational Rehabilitation Of Disabled People Through Community Based Methods', in *Proceedings of 16th World Congress of Rehabilitation International, Japan 1998*, The Organizing Committee of 16th World Congress of Rehabilitation International, Tokyo.
United Nations (1971), *Declaration on the Rights of the Mentally Retarded Persons -- General Assembly Resolution 2856 (XXVI) Adopted 20 December 1971*, United Nations, New York.
United Nations (1975), *Declaration on the Rights of Disabled Persons -- General Assembly Resolution 3447 (xxx) Adopted 9 December 1975*, United Nations, New York.
United Nations (1983), *The World Programme of Action Concerning Disabled Persons -- General Assembly at its 37th regular session on 3 December 1982, Adopted Resolution*

37/52, United Nations, New York.
United Nations (1994), *United Nations Standard Rules on the Equalization of Opportunities of Persons with Disabilities*, United Nations, New York.
US Department of Commerce, Economics and Statistics Administration, Bureau of The Census (1997), *Census Brief, December 1997*, retrieved from World Wide Web: http://www.census.gov/prod/3/97pubs/cenbr975.pdf
WHO (1980), *International Classification of Impairments, Disabilities and Handicaps: A Manual of Classification Relating to the Consequences of Disease*, WHO, Geneva.
WHO (1999), *ICIDH-2: International Classification of Functioning and Disability Beta-2 Draft*, WHO, Geneva.
WHO (2001), *Outcome of the Fifty-Fourth World Health Assembly (May 22, 2001)*, WHO, Geneva.

PART 4
REVIEW AND PROSPECT

11 Globalisation, Inequality and Governance

KEVIN HEWISON

The spectre haunting Southeast Asia is no longer communism. It is globalisation. The Asian economic crisis has shown that the progress of globalisation is no longer – if it ever was – unproblematic. The papers in this collection indicate this. If there is a theme that holds them together, it is a notion of globalisation as both threat and opportunity.

Globalisation means many things to many people. It has aroused passionate debate. There are those who extol its virtues, arguing that the imminent 'borderless world' is a pinnacle of progress. These 'globalisers', led by neo-liberal economists, have been keen to promote corporate capitalism, the advantages of liberalisation and the operation of the market (see Ohmae, 1990). Those not so enamoured by this prospect portray globalisation as far more problematic and, like imperialism, a product of Western desire to subject and exploit the developing world (see Chossudovsky, 1998). But, as Higgott and Reich (1998, p.1) have pointed out, 'globalisation' is also a 'most overused and under-specified' term.

Much of the recent academic discussion appears to agree that 'globalisation' catches the essence of a historical movement, a triumph of a neoliberal and characteristically Anglo-American ideology, a more intense stage of capitalism, a confluence of events and technologies, or some combination of these. While it is acknowledged that there was an earlier phase of globalisation, it is generally agreed that there is something novel about the contemporary process, which is bringing rapid change for business, government and, indeed, ordinary people (Woods, 1998). However, this debate produces competing perspectives regarding the nature of these processes, how recent they are, the impact they will have on the state, and especially on the power of the nation-state (Gill, 1995; Evans, 1997; Hirst, 1997; Weiss, 1997).

This chapter does not attempt to engage arguments concerning the nature and meaning of globalisation. Whether this current phase of globalisation is renewed or new, the processes and ideologies identified with globalisation are indeed having real impacts. Rather, this paper seeks to examine an aspect of the debate that has arisen since the Asian economic crisis that began with the devaluation of Thailand's baht in July 1997. Specifically, the paper seeks to develop an argument that suggests that the proponents of globalisation – political and economic liberals – have something to gain from an examination of the anti-globalisation position. This argument is made, not to support the liberal position, but rather to critique it.

Some readers will not see my argument as a critique of neo-liberal globalisation at all. Rather, they will view it as providing a reformist agenda. This is not my intention. My underlying assumption is that the anti-globalisation movement, while offering trenchant criticism of neo-liberal globalisation, is not showing a way forward or an alternative to neo-liberal globalisation. Thus, by arguing with liberals, and suggesting the need for reform – for good liberal reasons – I hope that I am also offering an insight into how the anti-globalisation movement may well be 'defeated' through reformism. There is an urgent need for anti-globalists to move towards a radical internationalism that truly challenges neo-liberal globalisation (see Radice, 2000). Having said this, I must admit a significant failing; I am not contributing much to that goal. Nonetheless, I believe that this debate with liberals is a potentially useful exercise.

Before the Asian financial and economic downturn in mid-1997, globalisation was not the controversial force it is now. When many Southeast Asian economies were experiencing booms, globalisation seemed to promise further opportunities for growth. There were some who opposed the political liberalism that adhered to globalisation; an example was seen in the Asian Values debate (see Rodan and Hewison, 1996). There were others who saw the liberal values associated with globalisation as potentially liberating, and especially from authoritarian politics (see Chai-Anan, 1997). But globalisation could not – and should not – be taken for granted.

Since the economic crisis first struck in 1997, the global mood and that in Southeast Asia has changed significantly.[1] It was in Seattle in late 1999 that 'anti-globalisation' became a force to be reckoned with. Anti-globalisation has since been highly visible at almost all major meetings of global institutions and rich country organisations since. So potent, in fact, that business groups, The Economist and the BBC, amongst others, have devoted considerable attention to it. It is no coincidence that a range of organisations and the media have been concerned to address the rise of anti-globalisation, even if to oppose it.

Liberals may not feel any great affinity with the street protesters of Seattle, Genoa, Melbourne, and Prague – after all, some are anarchists and others are portrayed as a part of a resurgent Left (Epstein, 2001). However, I want to suggest that liberals should be concerned about at least some of the same issues that motivate anti-globalisation activists. This is not to say that liberals and anti-globalists will speak the same language when discussing such issues. However, some of the issues that form the core of anti-globalism have a resonance in liberalism. Of these issues, I suggest that liberals should be thinking about inequality and global governance. Before turning to these, it is appropriate to outline some of the positions of the anti-globalisation movement.

Anti-Globalisation

Anti-globalisation is not an entirely accurate depiction of the diverse groups brought together by their opposition to liberalisation and globalisation. It has been suggested that a number of these groups are not 'anti' at all, but more interested in transforming the economic policies that have dominated the recent phase of globalisation. This is why many opponents target the neo-liberal elements of globalisation or what has been labelled 'corporate globalisation' (Epstein, 2001, pp.9-13). In the discussion that follows I will focus on Southeast Asian opponents of globalisation. While the thrust of their opposition will be clear, this 'group' is certainly not homogenous. It includes a range of political positions from the conservatism of localists in Thailand, and the illiberalism of Malaysia's Prime Minister Dr Mohamed Mahathir, to vaguely Leftist elements associated with some advocacy NGOs. Even so, there are enough common elements in this discourse to consider it broadly representative of the anti-globalist position in Southeast Asia.[2]

Nationalism

Anti-globalists are notable for their nationalism. Their nationalism is considered a corollary of globalisation, as well as a reaction and opposition to it. In the furnace of the Asian economic crisis, calls for the 'nation' to be saved from the vagaries of international capitalism and the predations of foreign investors were heard. Such sentiments are common in the post-crisis populist politics that emerged in the region, sometimes resulting in calls for self-reliance and self-sufficiency. This approach is sometimes modified to also include a 'cultural nationalism', where the 'nation' includes certain features deemed threatened by the power of homogenising Westernisation.

A more powerful approach is seen in the economic nationalism of groups such as the Southeast Asian-based advocacy groups, Focus on the Global South, the Third World Network and a number of like-minded Southeast Asian NGOs and union organisations. They support a return to more nationally based economic policies, viewing import substitution industrialisation (ISI) as protective of national economies and workers.

Dependency

The emphasis anti-globalists place on ISI is deliberately nationalist. National development is seen as the antithesis of globalisation. It also avoids dependency, exploitation by foreign capital and any 'new colonialism' by the West in Southeast Asia. Anti-globalists argue that the modern capitalist system entrenches privilege and power. This kind of analysis posits a fundamental exploitation in the relationships between the rich North and the poor South, and means that the emphasis of their proposals for an alternative world is on breaking the links that maintain exploitation. Most importantly, this involves the control of finance capital, transnational corporations and the international economic institutions such as the World Trade Organisation (WTO), World Bank and the International Monetary Fund (IMF).

In explaining this dependent relationship, anti-globalists argue that exploitation results from the pernicious impact of the factors that liberal economists usually consider critical for growth – foreign investment, the free flow of finance, international loans and international trade regimes. The Asian crisis was seen to challenge this liberal orthodoxy (see Surin, 1998). Most Southeast Asian economies had favoured this liberal orthodoxy and the decade-long boom of 1986-96 was identified as having grown out of enhanced liberalisation. The crisis suggested that these factors had made some of these economies vulnerable to capital flight and the machinations of hedge funds and other money traders. The crisis also reinforced ideas that there was a conspiracy of Western countries and agencies at work. The affected economies faced demands from Western business and governments and from international financial institutions seen as doing no more than entrenching Anglo-American values, institutions and ways of doing business.

The State and Industrialisation

Some anti-globalists reject industrialisation as exploitative and environmentally and culturally destructive. The self-reliance movement falls into the category, and is, at the same time, wary of the state and its officials. This movement is thus loathe to promote further industrialisation, and favours agriculture and sustainable development.

Other anti-globalists, however, call for a revised approach to industry. This group accepts that industrialisation can have national benefits. To achieve this, it is argued that the state is critical. The state must maintain controls on foreign investment and capital flows, and support local industry and national capitalism. In this, anti-globalists could identify with Keynes' 1931 argument on national self-sufficiency: 'Let goods be homespun whenever it is reasonably and conveniently possible; and, above all, let finance be primarily national' (cited in James, 1999, p.3).

Liberalisation

Anti-globalists consider that liberalisation has failed. Indeed, the Asian economic crisis was seen to be evidence of this failure. Liberalisation, involving deregulation, free trade, export orientation and privatisation, is identified as the critical element of contemporary globalisation. Anti-globalists assert that rapid and unfettered liberalisation causes great damage to weak economies. Their remedies involve either abandoning liberalisation or accepting it, but as a process that is somehow controlled at the national level, allowing each nation and its government to determine the pace of liberalisation. Not only is the South seen to be unprepared for liberalisation, but it lacks bargaining and negotiating strength in international fora that promote such reform. The North, however, has great strength in these fora, and uses this for its benefit (Khor, 2000, p.9). Such liberalising processes are seen to result in increased inequality and the marginalisation of the majority of the world's population.

The perceived failures of the IMF's interventions in the initial stages of the Asian crisis suggested to anti-globalists that countries should develop their own policies and ignore the orthodox advice of the IMF and the World Bank. Further, many argue for a new international financial architecture that is more 'progressive', under 'democratic' control or, more radically, that the IMF, World Bank and WTO be abolished, to be replaced by more democratic, regional, national and local organisations.

Global Governance

Anti-globalists fear that the existing institutions of global governance are anti-South and anti-poor. The obverse of this position is that these institutions are pro-Western and dominated by the US. As mentioned, the IMF, World Bank and WTO are seen as part of the problem. In this area, conservatives and radicals appear to agree. Not only did the Meltzer report to the US Congress call for limits on these international agencies. Meanwhile, some in the anti-globalisation movement find that UN agencies offer developing countries an enhanced voice because they are more likely to deal with nation-states without heeding financial contributions or perceived power. But this is seen as a weak trend that needs to be supported and strengthened.

Should Liberals be Interested in the Anti-Globalist Critique?

As already noted, liberals are not the natural allies of those in the anti-globalisation movement. Indeed, political liberals have generally been content to adopt the positions of those the anti-globalists most vehemently oppose, the liberal or orthodox economists. Liberals see that freedom is critical for markets and individuals. In this sense, it could be said that globalisation represents the supranational nexus of political and economic liberalism. It is for this reason that liberals would like to agree with The Economist (Crook, 2001, p.4) when it points out that liberalism provides the strongest theoretical case for globalisation:

> International economic integration, on the liberal view, is what happens when technology allows people to pursue their own goals and they are given the liberty to do so.... People choose what serves their own self-interest, each of them making that judgement for himself. The result is that society as a whole prospers and advances – spontaneously, not by design of any person or government.

It is not surprising, then, that the Asian economic crisis has been seen as heralding the end of statist 'Asian capitalism', and a victory for liberalisation and, indeed, globalisation (Fukuyama, 1999).

So why should liberals be interested in the anti-globalisation critique? As noted above, when answering this question it is worth considering the coincidences between the anti-globalist and liberal positions. Liberals have a long-standing concern for social justice (Rawls, 1971), and the anti-globalists also worry about justice when they attack inequality in the globalised world. They may conceive of justice in quite different ways, but the concern remains. Liberals also have a theoretical and practical interest in government and democracy. Anti-globalists place much emphasis on these issues, especially when they examine global economic governance. It would therefore seem important for liberals to give more attention to both inequality and global governance. While the significant ideological differences between liberals and those in the anti-globalisation movement remain, this should not prevent liberals from examining the issues raised by the opponents of globalisation.

In the remainder of this paper I wish to concentrate on just two aspects of the anti-globalisation discourse which should also be of some interest to liberals. As just suggested, these are inequality and global governance.

Inequality

It is only recently that inequality has re-emerged as a significant concern. The anti-globalisation movement has done much to focus attention on global inequality in the contemporary period. This is not to say that the concern for inequality is in any sense new. Rather, it is to acknowledge that, from the time of US President Ronald Reagan and British Prime Minister Margaret Thatcher, liberal economic orthodoxy has held that the best way to overcome poverty is to emphasise markets and growth. Hence inequality has taken a policy back seat, behind the emphasis on growth. In fact, where growth was rapid and sustained – especially in East Asia – the World Bank (1993) argued that growth was achieved with equity. In reality, this was something of an exaggeration. For example, in parts of Southeast Asia, while poverty was indeed reduced with rapid growth, inequality also increased. As I will show, this uncomfortable Southeast Asian result has not been incongruent with other studies of inequality.

Is inequality of a scale that should concern liberals? The short answer seems to be affirmative. This is illustrated in a number of recent studies that have shown increasing inequality to be a global trend, in both developed and developing countries.

In many developed countries, despite significant and sustained economic growth, studies are indicating greater inequality than ever before (see Slaughter, 1999). This trend is also evident in developing countries. In a provocative study, Robert Wade (2001) examines the impact of globalisation on world income distribution. Wade (2001, p.2) ponders this question in the belief that a more equal world income structure would provide powerful supporting evidence for liberal economic growth theory. More generally, such evidence would support the view that globalisation delivers benefits to the great majority of the world's population. If contrary evidence was to be found, Wade believes that this would represent a dramatic challenge for growth theory and liberal globalisation.

Wade begins by noting that world income doubled between 1960 and the late 1980s. He then turns to data for the past quarter century. Using a range of accepted methodologies for measuring inequality, Wade (2001, p.10) concludes that the data produce results on inequality ranging from 'very much more unequal' incomes to 'little change'. This is disturbing enough, but using better quality World Bank data for the much shorter period of 1988 to 1993, he concludes that there has been a sharp increase in inequality. Summarising, Wade (2001, p.15) states that the inescapable conclusion is that world inequality is indeed increasing. His data are supported by UNDP figures indicating that the share of global income received by the poorest fifth of the world's population has declined from a paltry 2.3 percent in the 1960s to just 1.1 percent in 1994. The ratio of the top fifth's income to that of the poorest fifth over the same period has gone from 30 to 1 to 78 to 1 (cited in Ramphal, n.d., p.2).

As a footnote, my own survey of data for Thailand shows that, despite significant poverty declines, inequality worsened during the economic boom. Worryingly, during the economic crisis, there has also been a transfer of wealth from the poor to the already rich (Hewison, 2001b).

Should liberals worry about rising inequality? Again, the answer must be affirmative.

A particular issue that needs to be addressed when considering inequality is justice. Many liberals would agree that if the poor have restricted opportunities or if power is abused, and the result is increased inequality, then this should be a concern. In many parts of Southeast Asia these situations continue to prevail. For example, in much of the region, high quality, open-access education systems remain the exception rather than the rule. Likewise, one does not need to look very far to find abuses of power that restrict opportunities. There have been many examples of great, often corruptly obtained, wealth flowing to those with political power. Marcos and Suharto are but two recent examples.

As I have noted, the most usual liberal response on questions of inequality, and especially from economists, is to argue that it is poverty that matters, not distribution. For example, the World Bank has consistently suggested that even if there is rising inequality, this is not necessarily negative (see Wade, 2001, p.27). In line with de Tocqueville's observations of early 19th Century America, these liberals argue that inequality can offer valuable incentives for individuals. Of course, de Tocqueville was also aware that inequality could be a cause for rebellion.

Liberals often assert that growth is good for the poor, being obviously better than the no growth alternative, where poverty is maintained and deepens with population growth. Indeed, we can find recent data to support this position (see Crook, 2001, p.12). Some also assert that growth will eventually lead to a convergence of incomes across the globe, as suggested by a recent World Economic Forum report (cited in Murphy, 1999, p.293). The problem is that this does not appear to be happening. The secretary-general of UNCTAD, reflecting on growing inequality between and within nations, has drawn attention to the 'dismal' record on growth in the 1990s for developing countries (Ricupero, 1999, p.21).

Liberal economists will often respond to such claims by suggesting that growth has simply not taken hold or gone far enough. This point has not been lost on Marxists either. Some Marxists assert that the problem for developing countries is not capitalist exploitation, but the fact that capitalism does not exploit these countries enough. In the words of Arghiri Emmanual, 'if capitalism is hell, there exists a still more frightful hell: that of less developed capitalism...' (cited in Kiely, 1998, p.19). For these Marxists, capitalism is progressive, a position that distinguishes them from anti-globalists.

Of course, liberals can readily agree that the market and capitalism are progressive and empowering, but should they link with Marxist arguments by seeing the market and capitalism as potentially exploitative as well? Is it good enough to suspend notions of justice for so long as it takes for a trickle-down of the benefits of capitalism and globalisation to reach the poor and less well off? In other words, can liberals afford to wait for this trickle-down and enhanced distribution and risk an even more serious backlash against globalisation and its progressive and empowering elements? Despite significant 'trickle-down' in Southeast Asia, there is a backlash against liberalisation and globalisation. This suggests that relying on trickle-down may be poor public policy.

Of course, there is another liberal response that argues that the problems of exploitation and inequality result not from the market and capitalism, but from the actions of governments in poor countries. This response calls for the role of government to be reduced to allow for the freer operation of the market, thus resisting any urge for collective action to rectify such problems (Henderson, 2000, p.30 and 37).

Not all liberals are so vehemently anti-collectivist however. Many recognise that the market has limits, especially as businesses are ultimately interested in profits (Crook, 2001, p.4). Indeed, the benefits of growth that flowed to the populations of Western Europe, the US and Japan after World War Two grew out of a system that John Ruggie (1982) has called 'embedded liberalism'. In essence, this arrangement permitted relatively free markets to operate in international trade, while different domestic welfare mechanisms were permitted. This approach, while excluding colonies and newly-independent countries, produced significant benefits for developed country populations.

Some analysts argue that liberalism was increasingly disembedded from the late 1970s. They target an ideologically driven neo-liberalism and globalisation as the culprits in this. They suggest a need to radically rethink globalisation in a way that sees a move from an overly individualistic conception of capitalism to one that is 'profoundly social' (based on comments in Lacher, 1999, p.345). In other words, can the market be socially re-embedded? Some liberals would argue that social welfare, safety nets or social insurance play a significant role in legitimising the market and maintaining social cohesion (Dani Rodrik cited in Rajan, 2001, p.7). Hence, as well as tackling the issue of economic injustice, re-embedding can have important extra-economic consequences.

The Asian crisis provided an opportunity for some economic liberals to reassert their orthodoxy – that the market, and not the state, was important. The challenge of statist 'Asian capitalism' to the Anglo-American model was seen to have failed. But it is clear that liberal economists were concerned that rapid market deregulation could also have negative consequences. Thus, for example, the World Bank expanded its interest in the political dimensions of markets and the kinds of institutions and state capacities necessary to support and enhance deregulation. Interestingly, as the crisis deepened, the World Bank began to take a revised position on regulation, the state and social welfare (see Rodan, Hewison and Robison, 2001, p.19). The Bank began to use participatory language, urging the development of civil society, as well as a concern for social capital, social safety nets and community organisation. It was argued that these were necessary elements in economic recovery, supporting markets and sustainable growth (see World Bank, 1998). In essence, a muted call for a social re-embedding of the market.

The Economist goes further. Usually anti-collectivist, it has issued a call for more serious effort to re-embed the market. It points out that, due to 'the fact that corporate interests exercise undue influence on government policy', the trade rules of rich countries and their subsidies 'discriminate unfairly against the developing world'. It suggests that '...capitalism as it exists in the West, with safety-nets, public services and moderate redistribution bolted on' is a way to have capitalism while not hurting the poor too much. More radically, The Economist argues that if anti-globalists could accept this 'mixed-economy' alternative, then this would allow for a more generalised attack on the power that rich-countries exercise over trade (Crook, 2001, p.28 and 30). For much of Southeast Asia this approach has had limited impact; worse, in many countries, the idea of redistribution has barely been considered.

This raises questions regarding global governance, to which I now turn.

Global Governance

Globalisation not only involves a 'growth of connections between people across the planet', but also implies a certain 'deterritorialisation'. This suggests that globalisation is creating a 'social space' that, at least in part, 'transcends the confines of territorial place, ...distance and ...borders' (Scholte, 2001, p.7). This space requires some form of governance.

Anti-globalisers have repeatedly argued that the leading organisations of global governance – the WTO, World Bank and IMF – are biased against the poor and the South. They also assert that these agencies are hopelessly skewed towards the interests of the West, and especially those of the US. They believe that, unilaterally and through these institutions, the US is asserting its national and corporate interests as if they were global interests. Even some conservatives agree on this. For example, worrying about a world of a single superpower, the noted political scientist Samuel Huntington (1999, p.38) states:

> ...the United States has, amongst other things, attempted or been perceived as attempting ... unilaterally to ...; pressure other countries to adopt American values and practices regarding human rights and democracy; ... enforce American law extraterritorially...; apply sanctions against countries that do not meet American standards...; promote American corporate interests under slogans of free trade and open markets; shape World Bank and International Monetary Fund policies to serve those same corporate interests; [and] bludgeon other countries to adopt economic policies and social policies that will benefit American economic interests....

As noted above, even The Economist is prepared to concede a bias against poor countries in trade policies. Some Southeast Asian leaders have complained of the rampant materialism and cultural blandness of globalisation (Abdurahman Wahid cited in Reyes, 2000, p.42). And, Dr Mahathir (1999) has attacked globalisation as an instrument of control and a conspiracy of Western capitalists, international financial and regulatory institutions, governments, and international NGOs.

As many analysts have shown, the globalisation of the last part of the 20th Century is not the first time that there has been such a movement. Towards the end of the 19th Century there was considerable internationalisation, often associated with imperialism and colonialism. However, as Singapore Trade Minister George Yeo (2000, p.8) has observed, the new phase of globalisation is taking place in an era where empire has passed. He also notices that the revolution in information technology is 'undermining the established structures of global governance...'. This perspective has certainly strengthened since the Asian economic crisis.

Global institutions and global governance matter. States remain critical to governance, but it can be acknowledged that global institutions, including those beyond the state, have been expanding. These include transnational corporations, global NGOs, international ratings agencies and regional organisations (O'Brien et al, 2000, pp.7-8). Scholte (2001, p.10) estimates that there are now over 250 suprastate institutions operating. States no longer have the same level of monopoly on political, economic and social space they once had. But, as markets become increasingly global and complex, it is clear that the major global institutions remain inter-governmental and relatively undeveloped. The impact of the Asian and other economic crises has demonstrated the problems faced by such institutions.

As mentioned, the Asian economic crisis saw anti-globalists arguing that the principal global economic institutions actively worked against the interests of developing countries. Liberals need not agree with this proposition in order to see that the major global institutions have lost some of their legitimacy. There are many reasons for failing legitimacy. It is not unrelated to the previous discussion of inequality. Both World Bank President James Wolfensohn and former IMF Managing Director Michel Camdessus belatedly discovered or rediscovered poverty following the Asian crisis. The initial failure of IMF efforts when the Asian economic crisis struck sapped confidence. The apparent lack of consultation and transparency in many of the international economic institutions was also identified as a reason for declining public support.

Liberals have long been interested in democracy, participation and representation at the level of the nation-state. It seems reasonable and logical for liberals to expect and promote these characteristics at the global level and in international institutions. The legitimacy problems already mentioned should ring alarm bells for liberals. That the loss of legitimacy has also coincided with a rise of national and international civil society should also be a concern. The alarm bells might suggest that global governance requires different conceptions of democracy, participation and representation than have operated at the level of the nation or in the existing inter-governmental global institutions. Certainly, liberals should not assume that democratisation at the national level will automatically be translated or summed to mean increased democratisation in the international sphere. Indeed, liberals might consider how global governance might go beyond states and governments, while enhancing participation and the rule of law.

States have not been especially consultative with their citizens when dealing with global institutions. At the same time, global institutions are often unrepresentative of people and states. A number of analysts have suggested that the democratic deficits of global governance might be reduced if the role of international civil society could be enhanced. International civil society has expanded rapidly in recent years. Whereas there were only about 200 international NGOs at the beginning of the 20th

Century, there were more than 30,000 by the end of it (Ramphal, 1999, p.3).

Scholte (2001, pp.15-17) suggests five reasons for taking international civil society more seriously. These are:

1. civil society groups can have a direct impact on democracy, participation and contribute to an enhanced understanding of global governance by direct education and promotion, creating a better informed global citizenry;
2. civil society can give voice to stakeholders;
3. international civil society may generate debate about global governance, encouraging new voices to be heard and promoting uninhibited discussion;
4. the mobilisation of people and groups can increase the pressure for transparency in global governance; and
5. civic groups can greatly increase the public accountability of global institutions.

It should not be imagined that this entity we call civil society is inherently good and just. Indeed, civil society organisation is not naturally democratic. Civil society will inevitably include a range of groups that are not particularly noble or oriented to the greater good of society. Even so, for the reasons Scholte suggests, greater transparency and consultation can enhance democracy in global institutions, and this can increase the legitimacy of these institutions. Improved global governance will not mean an end to injustice and inequalities, but as Ramphal (1999, p.7) argues, '...improved global governance can make the world system more hospitable to the efforts of the poor to achieve human development.'

Of course, various liberals will have cause to question this approach. For example, some will assert that NGOs are hopelessly anti-capitalist and essentially anti-liberal (see Henderson, 2000, p.25). This may be so for some NGOs, but the disposition of social groups has not usually been a central element of liberalism's approach to representation.

The point is that liberals should be interested in enhancing democracy. At the global level this should include the provision of opportunities for the strengths of international civil society to emerge, and for greater representation of civic groups within the institutions of global governance. At the same time, these institutions themselves must also be subject to greater democratisation, including enhanced transparency.

Concluding Remarks

The variety of globalisation seen in recent decades has been driven by neo-liberalism. As this paper has indicated, this kind of globalisation is not without its negative consequences. The economic crisis that began in Southeast Asia has been critical for drawing attention to some of these consequences. At the same time, it was a critical event in the formation of the anti-globalisation movement.

Globalisation is not inevitable. History shows that the pace of globalisation can be slowed or reversed. Globalisation is, at least in part, about liberal values and liberalisation. Therefore, I have suggested that it makes sense for liberals to be interested in defending globalisation. However, this support should not blind liberal defenders to the arguments of the anti-globalisation movement. That globalisation may have increased inequality should raise issues of injustice. That the institutions of global governance often seem unrepresentative, undemocratic and lack transparency should also be a cause for concern and, hopefully, a call to innovation in establishing global governance that goes beyond governments and states.

If liberals believe, with The Economist (Crook, 2001, p.4), that the strongest case for globalisation and economic integration is the liberal one, then inequality and global governance need to be addressed in a serious manner. These matters are highly significant for the future direction of Southeast Asian development.

Notes

1. For detailed discussions of the impact of the crisis in Southeast Asia, and the role of globalisation, see the various essays in the two collections by Robison, Beeson, Jayasuriya and Kim (2000) and Rodan, Hewison and Robison (eds) (2001).
2. This section draws on Hewison (2001a).

References

Bishop, M. (2001), 'The New Wealth of Nations: A Survey of the New Rich', *The Economist*, 16 June 2001, pp. 1-22.

Chai-Anan, S. (1997), 'Old Soldiers Never Die, They Are Just Bypassed: The Military, Bureaucracy and Globalisation', in K. Hewison (ed.), *Political Change in Thailand: Democracy and Participation*, Routledge, London, pp. 42-57.

Chossudovsky, M. (1998), '"Financial Warfare" Triggers Global Economic Crisis', *Third World Network*, retrieved on 23 September 2002, from World Wide Web: http://www.southside.org.sg/souths/twn/title/trig-cn.htm

Crook, C. (2001), 'Globalisation and Its Critics. A Survey of Globalisation', *The Economist*, 29 September 2001, pp. 1-30.
Epstein, B. (2001), 'Anarchism and the Anti-Globalization Movement', *Monthly Review*, vol.53 no.4, pp. 1-14.
Evans, P. (1997), 'The Eclipse of the State? Reflections on Stateness in the Era of Globalization', *World Politics,* vol.50 no.1, pp. 62-87.
Fukuyama, F. (1999), 'Second Thoughts: The End of History 10 Years Later', *New Perspectives Quarterly*, vol.16 no.4.
Gill, S. (1995), 'Globalisation, Market Civilisation, and Disciplinary Neoliberalism', *Millenium,* vol.24 no.3, pp. 399-423.
Henderson, D. (2000), *Anti-Liberalism 2000*, Wincott Lecture, The Institute of Economic Affairs (UK), 12 October, retrieved on 12 December 2000 from World Wide Web: http://www.iea.org.uk/
Hewison, K. (2001a), *Nationalism, Populism, Dependency: Old Ideas for a New Southeast Asia?*, Southeast Asia Research Centre Working Papers Series No. 4, City University of Hong Kong, Hong Kong.
Hewison, K. (2001b), *Thailand: Class Matters*, Southeast Asia Research Centre Working Papers Series No. 8, City University of Hong Kong, Hong Kong.
Higgott, R. and Reich, S. (1998), *Globalisation and Sites of Conflict: Towards Definition and Taxonomy*, Centre for the Study of Globalisation and Regionalisation, Working Paper No. 1/98, Warwick University, Coventry.
Hirst, P. (1997), 'The Global Economy – Myths and Realities', *International Affairs,* vol.73 no.3, pp. 409-25.
Huntington, S.P. (1999), 'The Lonely Superpower', *Foreign Affairs*, vol.78 no.2, pp. 35-49.
James, H. (1999), 'Is Liberalization Reversible?', *Finance and Development*, December, pp. 11-4.
Khor, M. (2000), *Globalization and the South: Some Critical Issues*, United Nations Conference on Trade and Development, Discussion Paper No. 147. Geneva.
Kiely, R. (1998), *Industrialisation and Development*, UCL Press, London.
Lacher, H. (1999), 'Embedded Liberalism, Disembedded Markets: Reconceptualising the Pax Americana', *New Political Economy*, vol.4 no.3, pp. 343-59.
Mahathir, M. (1999), 'Globalisation Not Suitable for All', *Bangkok Post*, 18 July 1999.
Murphy, C.N. (1999), 'Inequality, Turmoil and Democracy: Global Political-economic Visions at the End of the Century', *New Political Economy*, vol.4 no.2, pp. 289-304.
O'Brien, R., Goetz, A.M., Scholte, J.A. and Williams, M. (2000), *Contesting Global Governance. Multilateral Economic Institutions and Global Social Movements*, Cambridge University Press, Cambridge.
Ohmae, K. (1990), *The Borderless World : Power and Strategy in the Interlinked Economy*, Collins, London.
Radice, H. (2000), 'Responses to Globalisation: A Critique of Progressive Nationalism', *New Political Economy*, vol.5 no.1, pp. 5-19.
Rajan, R.S. (2001), 'Economic Globalization and Asia. Trade, Finance, and Taxation', *ASEAN Economic Bulletin*, vol.18 no.1, pp. 1-11.
Ramphal, S. (n.d.), *Globalisation: A Political Perspective'*, The Commission on Global Governance, retrieved on 10 October 2001, from World Wide Web: http://www.cgg.ch/globo.htm
Ramphal, S. (1999), *Governance and Democracy. Empowerment for the New Millennium*, Speech to the Olof Palme International Foundation Seminar on 'Governance at the End of the Millennium', February 26, 1999, Barcelona, retrieved on 10 October 2001, from World Wide Web: http://www.cgg.ch/barcelon.htm
Rawls, J. (1971), *A Theory of Justice*, Harvard Press, Cambridge.
Reyes, A. (2000), 'Asia's New Agenda', *World Link*, Mar/April, pp. 42-5.

Ricupero, R. (1999), 'The Final and Optimal Crisis of the Century', *The UNESCO Courier*, March, pp. 20-2.

Robison, R., Beeson, M., Jayasuriya, K. and Kim, H.R. (eds) (2000), *Politics and Markets in the Wake of the Asian Crisis*, Routledge, London.

Rodan, G. and Hewison, K. (1996), 'A "Clash of Cultures" or the Convergence of Political Ideology?', in R. Robison (ed.), *Pathways to Asia: The Politics of Engagement*, Allen and Unwin, Sydney, pp. 29-55.

Rodan, G., Hewison, K. and Robison, R. (2001), 'Theorising South-East Asia's Boom, Bust, and Recovery', in G. Rodan, K. Hewison and R. Robison (eds), *The Political Economy of South-East Asia. Conflicts, Crises, and Change*, Oxford University Press, Melbourne, pp. 1-41.

Ruggie, J. (1982), 'International Regimes, Transactions, and Change: Embedded Liberalism in the Postwar Economic Order', *International Organisation*, vol.36 no.2, pp. 379-416.

Scholte, J.A. (2001), *Civil Society and Democracy in Global Governance*, Centre for the Study of Globalisation and Regionalisation Working Paper No. 65/01, University of Warwick, Coventry.

Slaughter, M.J. (1999), 'Globalisation and Wages: A Tale of Two Perspectives', *World Economy*, vol.22 no.5, pp. 609-29.

Surin, K. (1998), 'Dependency Theory's Reanimation in the Era of Financial Capital', *Cultural Logic*, vol.1 no.2, retrieved on 23 January 2001, from World Wide Web: http://www.eserver.org/clogic/1-2/surin.html

Thomas, C. (2001), 'Global Governance, Development and Human Security: Exploring the Links', *Third World Quarterly*, vol.22 no.2, pp. 159-75.

Wade, R.H. (2001), *Is Globalization Making World Income Distribution More Equal?* Development Studies Institute Working Papers Series, No. 01-01, London School of Economics and Political Science, London.

Weiss, L. (1997), 'Globalization and the Myth of the Powerless State', *New Left Review*, no. 225, pp. 3-27.

Woods, N. (1998), 'Editorial Introduction. Globalization: Definitions, Debates and Implications', *Oxford Development Studies*, vol.26 no.1, pp. 5-13.

World Bank (1993), *The East Asian Miracle. Economic Growth and Public Policy*, New York: Oxford University Press.

World Bank (1998), *East Asia: The Road to Recovery*, World Bank, Washington D.C..

Yeo, G. (2000), 'Devolution and World Order', *New Perspectives Quarterly*, vol.17 no.2, p. 8.

Index

Page numbers in *italics* refer to tables, *n* indicates a note

Acciaioli, G. 76
accountability 107, 193
Acharya, A. 5, 12-13*n*, 14*n*
Alawiyah, T. 67
Alexander, P. 60, 62
anti-globalisation movement 242-6
  liberal perspective 242-3, 246-54
anti-government activists, Malaysia 31-2
Ashton, D. and Sung, J. 202
Asia-Pacific Economic Cooperation (APEC) forum 6, 8, 78-9*n*
  Women Leaders Network 67
Association of Southeast Asian Nations (ASEAN)
  ASEAN-4 86, 88, 90
  Bangkok Declaration 5, 12*n*
  Confederation of Women's Organisations 67
  consensus politics 4-6
  formation 4-5
  Free Trade Area 6, 95-6
  Great Power politics 6-10
  Regional Forum (ARF) 4, 6-8, 9, 10, 13n
  subregionalization and regionalization 4-6, 8-10, 14*n*
Athukorala, P. 96
Australia 8-9, 98, 201
authoritarian–democratic regimes 18, 20-1

Baltodano, A. 195-6
Bangkok Declaration 5, 12*n*

Beijing Declaration 232-3
Benaria, L. 61, 63, 64
Booth, A. 69
Bray, M. 197, 203, 211, 212
Brunei 9, 134

Cambodia 7, *125*
capitalism 249-50
  see also globalization; marketization
Carino, T. 42, 43, 46
Castells, M. 37, 38
CBMs *see* Confidence Building Measures
CBR *see* community-based rehabilitation
Census and Statistics Department (CSD), Hong Kong 227-8
Central Provident Fund (CPF) 138, 140, 141, 142, *168*, 169, 186, 187
Chew, S.B. 22, 23, 25, 26-7
China (PRC)
  'China Threat' 4
  economic reform 38, 39-42
  Great Power politics 6-8, 9-10
  investment by Chinese overseas 39-47
  South China Sea dispute 5, 9-10, 12*n*, 14*n*
  Special Economic Zones (SEZs) (Xiamen/Fujian) 38, 39, 40, 41, 43, 51
Chinese overseas ('China Circle') 37-8

economic policy 39-42
ethnic associations 41
ethnic tensions 42-7
from culturalist explanation to orientalism 47-50
and globalisation 50-2
re-sinification 43-4, 45-7
civil society 17-18, 156
international 253
suppression of 20-1
see also democratisation
Cohen, E. 70, 71
collective bargaining 121-2
Collier, R.B. 20
community welfare role 151-3, 155-6
family and 132, 133, 143, 144, 146, 153
community-based rehabilitation (CBR) 224, 228-30
Confederation of Women's Organisations, ASEAN 67
Confidence Building Measures (CBMs) 7, 13n
conflict avoidance/resolution 5-6
Connors, M.K. 76
consensus politics 4-6
CPF *see* Central Provident Fund
craft sector 70-2
Crook, C. 250, 254
current account deficits 91, *92*

Dale, R. 198, 211, 212
'decent work' concept 109
decentralization 197, 212-13
Thai education system 207-11
see also marketization
Declaration on Fundamental Principles and Rights at Work (ILO) 108-9
Declaration on the South China Sea 5, 12*n*
Declaration on the Zone of Peace, Freedom, and Neutrality (ZOPFAN) 5, 12*n*
democratisation 33n

economic benefits 107-8
of the family 117-18
labour activism 19-20
pro-democracy movements 17
Deng Xiaoping 39, 40, 41-2
dependency issue, anti-globalist critique 244
disability/disabled people
Beijing Declaration 232-3
community-based rehabilitation (CBR) 224, 228-30
coordination of services 223, 224, 225, 228
future of movement 233-5
human rights strategy 231-2
multi-sectoral mainstreaming 226-8
sectoral advocacy 221-5
self-help groups 224, 230-1
situation of 220-1
social security programmes *166*
WHO definition 219-20
Disabled People's International (DPI) 230
divorce rates 154-5
Dixon, C. and Drakakis-Smith, D. 86, 88, 94

East Asian welfare model 132, 133
economic cooperation 5, 6
economic crisis *see* financial crisis
economic growth 85-9
ASEAN-4 86, 88, 90
and inequality 113-18
inflation 88-9, *90*, *151*
projections 109-10, *111*, 156-7
rates 18-19, 87-8
significance of women 60-5
structural change 89-92
unemployment 89, *90*
see also globalisation; gross domestic product (GDP)
economic indicators 100
'economic rationalism' in education 194, 196, 198, 200-1
economic reform, China 38, 39-42

education 137
  higher/university 137, 199-200, 205-6, 207, 209-10
  impact of financial crisis 151, 207-8, 209
  impact of globalization 195-202
  inclusive of disabled people 224
  league tables 204, 210-11
  private 137, *138*
  reforms 196-202, 211-13
  school dropouts 59, 74
  secondary 114, 137
  women's 114, 116, 117, 117-18
  see also specific countries
elderly
  care of 155
  retirement pensions 142, 167, *168*, 173, 174, 179
  social security programmes *166*
Emmanual, A. 249
Employees Provident Funds (EPF) 140, 141, 142, *168*, 182
employment *see* labour force participation; unemployment
entrepreneurs
  Chinese overseas 50-2
  craft sector 70, 71
ethnicity
  Chinese overseas 41, 42-7
  constraints on labour activism 32
export sector 95, 97-8, 99, 100, 101-2
  electronics 60, 110
  see also manufacturing sector

family
  -based welfare systems 132, 133, 143, 144, 146, 153
  changing trends 153-5
  'living democracy' within 117-18
  role in economic success 47-8
  stress and domestic violence 59
Federation of the Filipino-Chinese Chamber of Commerce and Industry Inc. (FFCCCII) 44, 46
fertility rates 154, 155

financial crisis 6, 18, 107, 131
  challenges in 21st century 97-102
  government responses 152-3, 172-6, 181-3, 184-5, 186-7
  as 'growth crisis' 76
  impact on education 151, 207-8, 209
  impact on labour market 109-13
  impact on women 57-60, 65-77, 166
  social impacts 149-53, 163-6, 170-87
flexibility of female labour 60-2
'flexible citizenship' 45-6
Flynn, N. 195
Food and Agriculture Organisation (FAO) 69
foreign direct investment (FDI) 92-3, 94, *95*, 96, 98-9, 100, *101*
  Chinese overseas 39-47
  and trade unionism 118-19
freedom of association 108, 118, 119
  constraints 120-3
  improvements 123, *125-6*
  see also trade unionism
freedom from discrimination 108

GDP *see* gross domestic product
gender development index (GDI) 116, *117*
gender empowerment index 115, 126n
gender inequalities
  empirical evidence 115-18
  indicators 116, *117*, *149*
  labour market 111-13, 114-18
  secondary school enrolment 114
  wage gap 112-13
  see also women
Gill, T.A. 75
global governance, anti-globalist critique 245-6, 250-3
globalisation 85-7, 92-7, 241
  Chinese overseas 50-2
  future impact 97-102
    disability movement 234-5

impact on education 195-202
    see also anti-globalisation
    movement
Goh Chok Tong 204-5
Government Official Pension Act
    (GOPA) 174
Government Service Insurance
    System (GSIS), Philippines 184,
    185
Great Power politics 6-10
Greater China see 'China Circle'
Green, A. 202, 203
gross domestic product (GDP)
    changes in sectoral shares 89-92
    sex sector contribution 73
    and social expenditure 135, *136*,
        168, *169*
    see also economic growth

HDI see human development index
health 140-1
    insurance 141
    malnutrition 59
    regional inequalities 146-7
Heller, P. 69
Hewison, K. 77
higher education/universities 137,
    199-200, 205-6, 207, 209-10
Hodder, R. 47, 48, 49
Hong Kong 226-8
housing 138-40
human development index (HDI)
    115, *116*, 133-4, *135*, 146, *148*
human rights standards 120, *125*,
    127n
    disability movement strategy 231-
        2
Huntington, S. 49, 251

ILO see International Labour
    Organization
IMF see International Monetary
    Fund
inclusion principle 228
    education 224
income 18-19

    inequalities 112-13, 144-5, 150
        see also regional inequalities
    post-crisis 149-50
    and social security 144-6
India 7, 8
Indonesia 8-9
    'customary societies' 76
    'dualist economic structures' 98-9
    education 137, 151
    family stress and domestic
        violence 59
    health 141, 151
    housing 139
    illegal labour migration 58
    informal sector 64
    labour standards *125*
    malnutrition 59
    post-crisis GNP 57
    poverty 59, 146-7, 150, 176-7
    rural sector 69
    school dropouts 59
    sex workers 73
    social expenditure 135, *136*
    social impact of financial crisis
        149-50, 151, 152, 153, 176-80
    social security/safety nets 142,
        167, *168*, 177-80
    unemployment 58, 67, 68, 150
    women's issues 58, 59, 66-7, 73
Industrial Relations Act, Malaysia
    30-1
industrialisation
    anti-globalist critique 244-5
    see also export sector;
        manufacturing sector
inequalities
    anti-globalist critique 247-50
    income 112-13, 144-5, 150
    social security/safety nets 165-6,
        169-70, 176, 179-80, 182-3
    see also gender inequalities;
        regional inequalities
inflation 88-9, *90*, *151*
informal sector 64-5
Internal Security Act (ISA),
    Malaysia 31-2

International Federation of Agricultural Producers 70
International Labour Organization (ILO)
  Convention on Freedom of Association 120, *121*, *125*
  Declaration on Fundamental Principles and Rights at Work 108-9
  disability rights 228, 229
  human rights standards 120, *125*
  Minimum Standards on Social Security (1952) 164
  sex workers 72-3
  social security issues 164, 175
  unemployment 58
International Monetary Fund (IMF) 69, 175, 177, 244, 245, 252
  relief packages 177, 178-9
International Year of Disabled Persons 220-1
ISA *see* Internal Security Act, Malaysia

Japan 7, 8, 9, 94, 132
job-creation schemes 66-7, 175-6
Joekes, S. 63
Jones, S. 69

Keynes, J.M. 245

labour activism *see* freedom of association; International Labour Organization (ILO); trade unionism
labour cost reduction schemes, Singapore 186
labour force participation
  disabled people 224, 228
  Thailand, post-crisis 171-2
  women 60-5, 111-12, 118
labour lay-offs 58, 173, 174
labour market
  inequality and growth 113-18
  post-crisis 109-13
  social dialogue and economic outcomes 118-20
labour migration 96
  illegal 58
  return to rural sector 68-9, 150
  women 74, 155
labour rights
  to bargain 121-2
  to organise 120-1
  to strike 25, 31, 122-3
Laos 7, 72
Le Grand, J. and Bartlett, W. 196
Lee Hsien Loong 205
Lee, W. 166-7
Lee, W.O. 202
Legget, C. 26, 27, 28
liberal perspective, on anti-globalisation movement 242-3, 246-54
liberalisation, anti-globalist critique 245
linguistics, and ethnicity 46
localism 76-7, 156

McCloud, D. 6
Malaysia 9
  constraints on labour activism 28-32, 121, 122
  economic growth rates 18-19, 91
  education 137
  female labour force 60
  health 141, 151
  housing 140
  income levels 18-19
  post-crisis GNP 57
  poverty rate 147
  as 'pseudo-democracy' 18, 28
  sex workers 72
  social expenditure *136*
  social impact of financial crisis 149-50, 152, 153, 180-3
  social security/safety nets 142, *168*, 181-3
  social services 144
malnutrition 59
managerialism
  in education 198, 199-200

in public sector 193-4
manufacturing sector 91
  gender wage gap *113*
  labour lay-offs 58
  women's employment 58, 60-5, 115
marketization
  of education 196-206
  of public sector 193-4
  see also decentralization
Marxist perspective on globalisation 249
Mason, K.O. 155
migration *see* ethnicity; labour migration
'miracle economies' 60-5, 86, 103*n*
Mok, K.H. 206
Muller-Hofstede, C. 97
multinational firms 64
Myanmar 7

National Education Act (1999), Thailand 207-8, 209-10
National Trade Union Congress (NTUC), Singapore 21, 22
  membership and objectives 22-3
  and PAP 23, 24-8
nationalism, anti-globalist critique 243-4
non-governmental organizations (NGOs)
  disability 226-7, 230-3
    international 231-3, 234-5
    networks 221, 222, 223, 225
  increased number of 252-3
  Malaysia social services 144
  rural craft sector 71-2
Nonini, D.M. and Ong, A. 50, 51

Ong, A. 45-6, 49-50, 50, 51
Organization for Economic Cooperation and Development (OECD) 199-200

PD *see* Preventative Diplomacy
pension schemes 142, 167, *168*, 173, 174, 179
  see also provident funds
People's Action Party (PAP), Singapore 20-1
  anti-welfare ideology 166-7, 186
  and NTUC 23, 24-8
personal social services 143-4
Philippines 9
  Chinese-Filipinos 39-40, 41, 42-6, 51
  collective bargaining 121-2
  disabled people 221-2, 229-30, 234
  education 137
  GDP 87
  housing 139-40
  informal sector 64
  labour export 74
  labour rights/standards 120, 121-2, *126*
  malnutrition 59
  poverty 59, 147, 150
  sex workers 72-3
  social expenditure 135, *136*
  social impact of financial crisis 149-50, 183-4
  social security/safety nets 142, *168*, 184-5
  social services 144
  unemployment 58, 150
poverty 59, 146-7, 150, 170-1, 176-7
  see also financial crisis; income, inequalities
Praparpun, Y. 64
PRC *see* China
Preventative Diplomacy (PD) 7, 13-14*n*
private sector
  education 137, *138*
  health expenditure 141
  housing 140
  welfare services 146
pro-democracy movements 17
provident funds 167, 170, 179
  central (CPF) 138, 140, 141, 142, *168*, 169, 186, 187
  employees (EPF) 140, 141, 142,

168, 182
public sector
  health expenditure 141
  managerialism 193-4
  privatization *see* decentralization;
  marketization

quality assurance, in education 200-1, 210-11

Radelet, S.C. and Woo, W.T. 176
Rangsitpol, S. 207, 208
re-sinification 43-4, 45-7
regional diversity 3-4, 86-7, 103-4n
regional inequalities
  between nations 97-102
  within nations 146-7
regional interdependence *94*, 95-6
regional security 6-8
regionalization 8-10, 14*n*
Rehabilitation International (RI) 232
Rehabus 226-7
retirement protection programmes
  see pension schemes
Rhampal, S. 253
rights *see* labour rights
Rosa, L. 24, 25
rural sector 69-70
  crafts 70-2
  return to 68-9, 77
rural–urban disparities 146-7
Russia *see* Soviet Union

safety nets *see* social security/safety
  nets
Said, E. 47, 48, 49
savings programmes 142, 167
  see also pension schemes;
  provident funds
Scholte, J.A. 250-1, 252, 253
Seagraves, S. 47, 48-9
security community 5-6, 12*n*
Seguino, S. 115
self-help groups, disabled people 224, 230-1
self-orientalisation 49-50

self-reliance
  individual 143, 146, 153, 156, 157
  national 244-5
Sen, A. 107-8
severance payments 173, 176
sex workers 72-4, 77
Shambaugh, D. 37
Singapore
  'authoritarian-democratic regime' 18, 20-1
  collective bargaining 122
  constraints on labour activism 20-8, 122
  economic growth rates 18-19
  education 137, 202-6
  family values 143
  health 141
  housing 138
  income levels 18-19
  social dialogue 119-20
  social expenditure *136*
  social impact of financial crisis 152, 153, 185-7
  social security/safety nets 142, 143, 152, *168*, 186-7
Singh, D. 7
Sklair, L. 52
Slaughter, S. and Leslie, L. 200, 202
slum resettlement programmes 138-40
small and medium enterprises (SMEs) 64, 78*n*
Smith, N. and White, M. 70
social benefits of capitalism 249-50
social dialogue, labour market 118-20
social expenditure 135, *136*
social impacts of financial crisis 149-53, 163-6, 170-87
social indicators 146, *148*, *149*
social insurance 140-1, 142, 167, *168*, 184-5
social security 142, *143*, 144-5
  inequalities 165-6, 169-70, 176, 179-80, 182-3
  types of programmes *166*, 167-8

Social Security Act (SSA), Thailand 173-4
Social Security System (SSS), Philippines 184-5
social security/safety nets
    importance of 187-9
    inequalities 165-6, 169-70, 176, 179-80, 182-3
    underdevelopment of programmes 166-70
    UNESCAP recommendations 188-9
    see also financial crisis; *specific countries*
social services, personal 143-4
social trends, impact on welfare systems 153-7
socialism, China 38, 39
South China Sea dispute 5, 9-10, 12n, 14n
Soviet Union 6, 8
SSA *see* Social Security Act, Thailand
SSS *see* Social Security System, Philippines
Standing, G. 61-2, 64-5
states, anti-globalist critique 244-5, 251-3
subregional politics 4-6
    and regionalization 8-10, 14n
supply-side economics 65, 79n

Tarling, N. 7
Teo Chee Hean 205
Thailand
    collective bargaining 122
    'community culture' 76
    craft sector 70, 71
    disabled people 221-2, 234
    education 137, 207-11
    family stress and domestic violence 59
    health 141
    housing 139
    labour rights/standards 120, 122, 125

malnutrition 59
post-crisis GNP 57
poverty 59, 147, 150, 170-1
rural sector 69
sex workers 73, 77
small and medium enterprises (SMEs) 64
social care responsibilities 143
social expenditure *136*
social impact of financial crisis 149-50, 151-2, 153, 170-6
social security/safety nets 142, *168*, 172-6
unemployment 58, 68-9, 112, 150, 172
women's issues 58, 59, 73, 77
trade unionism
    constraints on rights 120-3
        Malaysia 28-32, 121, 122
        Singapore 20-8
    democratisation and 19-20
    and foreign investment 118-19
    see also freedom of association
Trade Unions Acts
    Malaysia 29-30
    Singapore 24-6
transnationalism *vs* globalism 52
transparency 107, 193
transport, for disabled people 226-7
Treaty on Amity and Cooperation (TAC) 5
Treaty on the Southeast Asia Nuclear Weapon Free Zone (SEANWFZ) 5, 12n
tuition fees 210

unemployment
    insurance 163-5, 170, 174, 187, 188
    post-crisis 58, 67, 68-9, 110, *111*, 112, 150, *151*, 172
    pre-crisis 89, *90*
United Nations (UN)
    Development Programme (UNDP) 114, 115, 116
    disability issues 220-1, 225, 226,

230, 231-2, 233-5
Economic and Social Commission for Asia and the Pacific (UNESCAP) 163, 188-9, 225, 226, 230, 233-5
Food and Agriculture Organisation (FAO) 69
International Year of Disabled Persons 220-1
UNIFEM 72, 73, 75
World Programme of Action 220-1
United States (US) 8, 10, 94, 98, 200-1, 251
  Department of State 26
  terrorist attacks 10, 107, 110, *111*
universities/higher education 137, 199-200, 209
university-industry linkages (UILs) 209
unpaid family workers 71, 76-7

Valenzuela, S. 20
Vietnam 7, 9, 75, 118
  disability 222-3
  labour rights 120, 122-3

Wade, R.H. 247-8
Wang, G. 49
Weidenbaum, M. and Hughes, S. 47, 49
welfare system
  achievements and problems 144-9
  characteristics 133-49
  current threats *158*
  development 133-44
  impact of changing social trends 153-7
  models 132-3

sustainability 157-8
WHO *see* World Health Organization
Wickberg, E. 43, 44
women
  education 114, 116, 117, 117-18
  labour force participation 60-5, 111-12, 118
  labour migration 74, 155
  post-crisis impacts and strategies 57-60, 65-77, 166
  see also entries beginning gender
Women Leaders Network, APEC 67
Women's Solidarity for Human Rights 58
World Bank 18, 86, 87, 156, 185
  economic recovery programme 66-7
  family-solidarity based welfare system 132
  globalisation debate 244, 245, 247-8, 250, 252
  job creation schemes 175
World Health Organization (WHO)
  community-based rehabilitation 228-9
  definition of disability 219-20
World Programme of Action, UN 220-1
World Trade Organisation (WTO) 50

Yeo, G. 251

Zhu Rhongji 41, 44
Zone of Peace, Freedom, and Neutrality (ZOPFAN), Declaration 5, 12*n*